Personnel computer systems

Personnel computer systems

Tony Ive

McGRAW-HILL Book Company (UK) Limited

London · New York · St Louis · San Francisco · Auckland · Bogotá
Guatemala · Hamburg · Johannesburg · Lisbon · Madrid · Mexico
Montreal · New Delhi · Panama · Paris · San Juan · São Paulo
Singapore · Sydney · Tokyo · Toronto

Published by

McGRAW-HILL Book Company (UK) Limited

MAIDENHEAD · BERKSHIRE · ENGLAND

British Library Cataloguing in Publication Data

Ive, Tony
  Personnel computer systems.
  1. Personnel management—Data processing
  I. Title
  658.3'0028'54   HF5549

  ISBN 0-07-084572-7

Library of Congress Cataloging in Publication Data

Ive, Tony.
  Personnel computer systems.

  Includes index.
  1. Personnel management—Data processing.
  I. Title.
  HF5549.I89   658.3'0028'54   81-1185
  ISBN 0-07-084572-7   AACR2

12345 MCL 85432

Printed and bound in Great Britain by Mackays of Chatham Ltd

To the members of the Personnel Department
Foster Wheeler Reading

Contents

Preface

This is a practical book about the design and implementation of personnel computer systems. It has been written in the belief that too much attention has been devoted in the past to developing sophisticated manpower systems, and not enough to basic personnel administration. The problems of personnel administration are more complex than is generally realized, and it is not possible to resolve them successfully without the aid of a fully integrated personnel computer system, that is, one which replaces all the manual records and performs such basic administrative tasks as writing letters to individuals. Recent developments in computer technology have revolutionized the possibilities in this area, and have presented personnel managers with the opportunity to take a major step forwards. Defining the requirements of a personnel computer system is, therefore, inseparable from questions about the role of the personnel department.

The greatest obstacle to exploiting this opportunity as far as personnel managers are concerned is that there are already so many people trying to exploit it from a commercial point of view. A number of organizations are marketing systems for which they make extravagant claims. Are these claims realistic? Most personnel managers have insufficient experience of computer systems to answer this question confidently. The purpose of this book is to provide them with the information that they need in order to do so.

The book takes the view that a package should be purchased, because the dangers and expense of development work are too great. It then addresses the central question: what should the package do? This question is dealt with in detail, chapter by chapter. Apart from the conventional areas of concern— personnel records, remuneration, and redundancy calculations—particular emphasis is placed on two aspects: the need for a recruitment system, and the need for integrated letter writing, that is, a system whereby updating a person's record automatically produces the appropriate letter. Flexibility is regarded as a key requisite, but the need for a package to supply substance as well as flexibility is stressed. The book considers, for example, not only what report generating facilities should be provided with a package, but also which reports should already have been written when it is supplied.

These requirements are summarized in a series of questions, which, it is suggested, the personnel manager should raise with suppliers when evaluating a package. Finally, advice is given on implementation. What are the problem areas? These are discussed in turn, and the point is made that a package should be selected not only on the basis of what it does, but also on the basis of the willingness and ability of the organization supplying it to provide adequate support and training during implementation.

The book caters for two types of readers: those who require a general appreciation of the subject, and those with responsibility for the practical details of implementing a system. The former should find it sufficient to read Chapters 1 and 2, the first half of Chapter 9, and Chapter 10. The latter will find Chapters 3 to 8 invaluable. The most difficult decision for a personnel manager to make is which package to buy, and advice on this can only be given by means of detailed discussion of the facilities which should be provided.

I should like to thank Valerie Harrison for the immense contribution she has made to the development of the ideas and practical details contained in this book over a period of five years, during which we were both involved in the development of a personnel computer system, and for the help she gave with the planning of the book in its early stages. I should also like to acknowledge the extent to which I have drawn on work done by Polly Dickinson, particularly in the sections dealing with letter writing facilities and the generation of statistical reports. Thanks are due to Nicholas Hall for commenting on some of the technical sections, and to Glenis Waggott for typing the manuscript. Finally, I should like to thank Carolyn Sefton for her support with the writing of the book.

Tony Ive

1. The scope of a personnel computer system

The credibility problem

There seems to be a problem with personnel management: nobody takes it seriously, at least not as seriously as personnel managers would like it to be taken. For years the Institute of Personnel Management has been preoccupied with setting standards of practice in the hope that personnel management will one day acquire the status of accountancy or the legal profession. But despite this, despite the stringent examination requirements, and despite the sophisticated material that has been written on many aspects of the subject, there is no evidence of any progress. Of course, this is not the view gained from reading the professional journals, but it is the view gained from talking to personnel managers. Once the formalities are dispensed with, and more detailed plans are discussed, most personnel managers will eventually confess that they have a problem, which, as the details gradually emerge, may perhaps best be described as a credibility problem. Naturally, they add, this is only expected to be a temporary state of affairs; it derives from the attitude of the current managing director, who is not very sympathetic towards personnel or, rather, does not understand what it is all about; he should be retiring soon, and then things may be expected to be different. But the strange thing is that they never are different. At some point a question must be asked, 'Why, do so many personnel managers just happen, for reasons entirely outside their control, to be prevented from doing what they would like to do?' In short, why has personnel management got a credibility problem?

The first step towards answering this question is to admit that the problem exists. It is a relatively simple matter to go on elaborating manpower planning systems. But it is more relevant, even if less palatable, to ask whether anyone is really going to take any notice of them when it comes to key policy decisions. An organization can always feed its key policy decisions back through line management. It does not have to use the personnel function. The fact that organizations take important decisions on personnel matters does not mean that their personnel managers are playing an important role. They may have had no part in the decision, or they may have been overruled. Personnel managers can easily inflate their status outside the company by alluding to the personnel-orientated decisions which have to be taken. Inside the company they are more likely to be asked, for example, why Mr Lambert has not arrived for interview. There are discrepancies between what they think they should be doing and what their managing directors think they should be doing. To get closer to the problem we need to examine the kind of attitude which personnel managers frequently find themselves up against with their managing directors.

How can you expect me to take your ideas on manpower planning seriously when you cannot even produce a reliable set of figures on the number of people we employ?

How can we discuss recruitment policy if you cannot produce a consistent set of reports on the level of activity over the past six months?

If the standard of input from other companies on this salary survey is anything like it appears to be from this company, I do not see how it can possibly have any relevance.

You want to discuss fringe benefits, and you cannot even produce an accurate list of people with company cars.

Before we discuss succession planning, I think we ought to have a report on all relevant personnel showing their qualifications and training, and a brief summary of their history with the company—which departments they have worked in, job functions, if they have been abroad, and salary progression.

What is the use of a personnel department if a man gets one salary quoted on his letter of increase and another one stored in the personnel records?

These types of remark are very irritating. Nevertheless, they are characteristic, and they lie at the heart of the personnel manager's credibility problem. The curious thing is that, despite the frequency with which such sentiments are expressed, personnel managers very rarely ask themselves what the answer really is. They tend to take the view, on each successive occasion, that they have been caught out by an unfortunate set of circumstances, and that the criticism is essentially unjust. For example, in the case of the statistical discrepancy it may well be that the managing director has been comparing two sets of figures which are not strictly comparable. It might be possible to reconcile them, but this would involve recompiling both sets—an unacceptably lengthy operation. In the case of the recruitment reports, the company may recently have been through an intensive recruitment drive. The recruitment team was probably fully employed processing the required number of applicants, and the personnel manager had to choose between interviewing applicants and producing reports. Choosing the former ensured that the recruitment effort was maximized. There was a limit to what could be done and the managing director does not understand this. In the case of the salary survey, perhaps it had been necessary to redo the input at the last minute, when discussion with the other participants indicated that the job title groupings used required adjustment. In the case of the fringe benefits, someone was probably given the job of maintaining a list of people with company cars, and they did not think to check who had left on a weekly basis with the personnel records officer, and cross them off. In the case of succession planning, it is unlikely that the manpower would have been available to compile the information requested. Compiling career summaries would probably involve searching back through the personal files, and the training records may well be held in a different place. In the final case—the salary discrepancy—an error has occurred, but surely a perfectly understandable one. A salary increase letter was typed, and a record card was updated. These are separate operations and, occasionally, through human error, the results will conflict.

In any one of these cases personnel managers could regard themselves as the victims of an unfortunate set of circumstances. Fundamentally, they have things under control, but their managing director has caught them out, and now refuses to take them seriously. Most personnel managers choose to view the situation in these terms. But there is another way of looking at it. Why, if things are basically under control, do they go wrong so often? The answer is straightforward. In these areas of operation there are always unfortunate and confusing circumstances. The basic administrative requirements of a personnel department may be basic, but they are certainly not simple. To provide an efficient basic administration system is a highly complex task. But without it, the personnel manager can do nothing. The managing director is right; there really is no point in the personnel manager offering advice until the administration system has been sorted out. It is not just a case of learning to walk before you run. It is a simple case of logical priority. You cannot run a manpower planning system unless your information about people is accurate and flexible. This last point will be certain to meet with widespread agreement. But what is not so widely appreciated is how difficult it is to achieve. Books on practical manpower planning frequently devote a section to the importance of sorting out the information system. But the reader is left with the impression that this is a straightforward task. In fact, it is much more complicated than the manpower planning which presupposes it. The trouble with personnel management is that too much time has been devoted to developing sophisticated tools and not enough to establishing basic systems.

'Solutions' that only make it worse

How should this problem be tackled? The key to establishing a satisfactory basic administration system is to get a correct measure of the problems with which it will have to cope. Many personnel managers devote considerable amounts of time and money to improving their systems, but never have much to show for it. The reason for this is that they have begun to look for solutions before fully identifying the problems. This may sound absurd, but it is a common occurrence, and examples are given below. They have a vague idea of the whole administrative process being transformed by advanced technology, but no concrete ideas as to what this is likely to entail. Equipment manufacturers play an important role here by creating an impression that the technology is so advanced that it is, firstly, impossible for a layman to understand and, secondly, bound to revolutionize anything to which it is applied. Both these suppositions are wrong. Personnel managers must define their requirements in sufficient detail for them to be tested out on a prospective system. Chapter 9 is devoted to describing how this can be done. Unless this approach is adopted, the manufacturer will demonstrate the equipment performing a task to which it is ideally adapted, and this is certain to be impressive. Personnel managers who are desperately searching for a solution to a vague set of problems are likely to overestimate the contribution that such a piece of equipment could make in their particular environment. Only when it is too late do they realize that its contribution in their own case is peripheral. A sophisticated tool has been acquired, but the desired transformation has not occurred.

Such occurrences are sufficiently common for it to be worth considering some of the 'solutions' that are adopted and subsequently fall short of expectations. They fall into five main categories.

1. Enhancing the manual system.
2. Card shuffling.
3. Adding on to the payroll system.
4. Word processing.
5. Manpower systems.

Enhancing the manual system is not normally considered seriously. Most personnel managers feel that they have extensive experience in this area, and do not need to be told about the drawbacks. There are five principal drawbacks.

1. The system does not produce reports. It only records things.
2. Answering statistical enquiries is very laborious.
3. The production of letters is a totally separate operation, involving duplication of effort and leading to discrepancies.
4. The accuracy of the system is entirely dependent on the competence of the person running it.
5. In order to provide information readily in the form required for different purposes, many items have to be recorded in several places, leading to further duplication of effort and discrepancies.

There is normally scope for improving a manual system, for example, putting flags on the cards so that essential information is available at a glance, but no amount of effort will remove the fundamental problems.

Card shuffling systems were developed to provide a basic enquiry system. The idea is that employees' record cards have holes punched in them in specified positions to indicate, for example, sex or possession of a car. When an enquiry is made, rods are passed through the appropriate holes and, after some shuffling, the cards of employees with the specified characteristics are retrieved. These systems cause more problems than they solve. First of all, their range is extremely limited. An employee can only either have a characteristic or not have it. But most of the characteristics which are of interest to personnel managers involve ranges: age, salary, length of service, job title, department, location. Everybody has these things, but they vary from person to person. Thus the typical enquiry, 'How many engineers do we have with over five years experience, earning between £8000 and £9000, aged between 35 and 45 and working in head office?' is totally beyond the scope of a card shuffling system. This in itself destroys their usefulness. But there are further difficulties. The cards often get stuck, and so fail to answer a question accurately. A hole cannot be removed if the status of a characteristic changes. And above all, this system, which is relatively complicated to maintain, does not replace the main body of the manual system, which is still required in its old form for normal personnel record keeping purposes.

Adding on to the payroll system was a popular solution at one time (this assumes that the payroll is already computerized). The popularity has subsided now that many people have tried it and found that not much was achieved. An immediate objection to this approach is that the extent to which data is shared by the two systems is by no means as great as is often supposed. Only about 15 per cent of the data stored in a normal personnel records system is also stored in the payroll system (such things as employment history, qualifications, training, and medical records are irrelevant to payroll). But more important than this, the whole philosophy is wrong. Adding personnel requirements on to the payroll system assumes that personnel is an adjunct to payroll. It is not. The problems of personnel management are infinitely more complex, and require an intricately designed and purpose-built system. This partly explains why the number of computerized payroll systems in existence is so much greater than the number of computerized personnel systems. The only thing likely to be achieved by adding on to the payroll system is the production of some basic reports, in particular salary reports. These will certainly not fulfil all the reporting requirements—a payroll system would not store enough information to do that—but they may be a useful adjunct to the manual system, provided there are not too many discrepancies. What is unfortunate is that this 'useful' adjunct is often mistaken before implementation for a total 'solution'.

What about word processing? This is a very popular 'solution' at present. The term requires some explanation. It was originally used to describe a form of typewriter equipped with a memory for storing standard texts, and a simple means of editing the text. So, for example, standard recruitment letters could be stored under a code, and when the operator called one of them up, the word processor would type out the text, pausing wherever it came to a variable, so that the operator could insert the relevant particulars, such as name, address, or interview details. Another function would enable the operator to alter the standard text. As these systems developed, more functions became available. The means of editing was improved, and the storage capacities were increased. Systems emerged which had more in common with a mini computer than a typewriter. Standard texts were stored on discs, the operator sat at a visual display unit, and the whole system was controlled by a central processor. The visual display unit would have a facility for displaying a whole page of text at one time, and the operator could roll pages up and down as required. Once word processors had reached this degree of sophistication, it was natural to move to large systems which could support many visual display units at once, several disc drives, and even linked processors. These were effectively mini computers designed for the specific application of handling standard texts, and this was reflected both in their price and in the complexity of their operation. Finally, special software packages have been written to enable word processing to be done on mini computers which are primarily dedicated to other tasks.

To carry out a review of the whole field of word processing would be a lengthy operation. But it would also be an unnecessary one, for all word processing alternatives have basic drawbacks when regarded as a 'solution' to a personnel department's administrative problems. First of all, the supposed increase in the speed of letter production, which is always held up as their great virtue, rests on a misapprehension. It is true that they type much faster than a human typist. But they can only do this for standard letters. If the letters are standard, then a personnel manager with any sense would already have had a supply of them printed off, so that typists could simply fill in the blanks. Although a word processor types fast, it will still be slower than the simple act of putting a sheet of pre-printed text into a typewriter. A typist operating a word processor will have to sit and wait for the standard parts of the text to be typed, so that she can fill in the blanks. Furthermore, the majority of standard letters in use in a personnel department are very short. A substantial part of the work involved in letter production is the filling in of variables. This takes exactly the same amount of time on a word processor as on a typewriter. Consequently, letter production will be slower rather than faster, although it is true that an improvement in appearance will be achieved.

The second drawback is that word processing does not do anything to alleviate the problems identified earlier as the failings of a manual system. It does not produce reports (at least not reports with the required range and flexibility). It does not answer statistical enquiries, or provide a link between the production of letters and the data stored in the personnel records. Clearly, it cannot do anything to improve the accuracy of the personnel records, or to remove the need for items of information to be stored in several places. In short, it does nothing which affects the administration system in any area except letters, and here its only effect is to slow down the process in return for an improvement in appearance. On top of this it is necessary to consider the third drawback: the equipment is expensive, and operating it is a complex business which requires specialized training. This amounts to a total condemnation of word processing, and leads to consideration of the fifth alternative—manpower systems.

The term 'manpower systems' is used here to denote a wide range of software packages developed by personnel departments to assist them in specialist areas. Typically, they are connected either with manpower planning or with enquiries of the kind, 'How many engineers do we have with over five years experience aged between 35 and 45?' There is nothing wrong with these systems *per se*, but it is important to note two things:

1. They can only be of use if the fundamental problems of record keeping have already been resolved.
2. They are in no way a solution to the problems of basic administration, but an adjunct to it.

The packages connected with manpower planning would be designed to assist with such matters as wastage analysis and succession planning. Those connected with *ad hoc* enquiries normally involve a data base of essential information and an English language enquiry system to enable it to be accessed with complete flexibility. The fundamental criticism here is one that has already been made: too much time spent on the development of sophisticated tools and not enough on establishing basic systems. A manpower system extends the service a personnel department can provide, but only at the expense of a substantial amount of additional effort. It will not replace the existing record system or do anything to assist the production functions of the department, for example, the processing of standard letters.

The underlying problem with all the 'solutions' considered so far, quite apart from their specific drawbacks, is that they require information to be fed into them to perform a specialized function. No system can be entirely satisfactory—or begin to save work rather than creating it—until it stores all the information that is required for every purpose. Establishing an effective basic administration system entails directing all the processing and administration functions within the department through a single channel. Only in this way can consistency be ensured and duplication of effort eliminated. These 'solutions' reflect an inadequate appreciation of the scope of the problem, and bring us back to the original point that the problems must be identified before a solution is sought. It will become clear during the analysis of the problems that the only way in which a genuine solution can be provided is through a purpose-built and fully integrated personnel computer system. The first task, then, is to consider the administrative problems with which a personnel department is faced.

Analysis of the problems

A curious feature of many personnel computer systems is that they completely ignore recruitment. Recruitment is a major activity of any personnel department, and it requires separate consideration, because the data with which it is concerned are separate from that with which the other personnel functions are concerned. There are overlaps—company statistics will compare recruitment activity with forecast manpower requirements and there will be a need to compare applicant information with personnel requirements—but the basic fact remains that the information and functions are different.

To assess the extent of a company's difficulties in the area of recruitment it is necessary to examine two factors: the level of activity and the extent of the fluctuations. The relevance of level of activity is obvious. If it takes one person to recruit one hundred people in a year, it will presumably take two people to recruit two hundred. But the difficulties arise because the process of recruitment is not one that generates a constant workload. First of all, although some companies are in a position to spread their recruitment evenly throughout the year, many are not. A contractor, for example, is bound to find that the pressure falls on recruitment when a contract is awarded or when a critical stage of a project is reached. Manufacturers operate in a less explosive environment, but here too an unexpected demand for a product will result in an increased pressure on recruitment. Secondly, even if the level of build-up is spread evenly throughout the year, the process of recruitment is necessarily one which proceeds in waves. An advertisement is placed in the paper, and people telephone over a period of days to request an application form. This generates a substantial amount of correspondence, which tails off rapidly through the stages of interview and offer until confirmation is received that the required number of people are ready to start. The number of letters required on different days of the exercise varies by a factor of about ten.

The initial problem generated by a high level of activity is that a large number of people are required to deal with it. The significance of fluctuations is that they necessitate the extensive use of temporary staff. Most personnel managers will not need to be persuaded that this is undesirable. Temporaries are expensive; somewhere has to be found for them to sit; and they require close supervision, partly because they are unfamiliar with the work and partly because they are often not at all concerned about the standard to which they perform. These are not the only problems associated with letter production in a recruitment campaign. Inevitably, when the volume of work increases dramatically, mistakes occur. Under a manual system the letters have to be preprinted, and so do not convey a good image of the company to outsiders. And when all these problems have been dealt with, there remains a monotonous burden of filing, which falls increasingly behind because of the general disinclination of all concerned to do it. Overall, the basic task of processing recruitment letters is a much bigger burden than the casual observer might suspect, and the methods by which it is generally tackled are primitive in the extreme.

All these difficulties apply with equal force to the production of recruitment reports. (The term 'reports' is being used here to cover a wide range of information on recruitment at various levels of detail.) First of all, it is essential to maintain a record on each applicant, so that the current status of their application is always to hand. This will be used mainly for dealing with individual enquiries, either from managers or from the applicants themselves. Secondly, the recruiter will need a detailed report on the status of each vacancy for which he is recruiting, showing the progress of every applicant within it. Thirdly, the manager will want a brief summary of progress on vacancies within his department: applications, interviews, offers, starts. Finally, at the most general level, reports will be required on the overall recruitment picture, indicating whether or not the recruitment effort is on target. To produce information at all these levels of detail under a manual system is virtually impossible. At least as many people would have to be employed generating reports as producing letters before it could even be attempted. All the problems mentioned in connection with the production of letters—fluctuations in activity, the need to employ temporaries, expense, space, the supervision problem, and the inevitable mistakes—recur here with the problem of coordination added in. And with report generation, coordination is undoubtedly the most serious problem. It is never possible to be certain that if the applicant had been sent a particular letter it would have been logged on the records. Every operation has to be duplicated, and there is endless opportunity for discrepancies. Letter production is bound to take priority over record keeping and report maintenance, with the result that when the pressure builds up, record and report maintenance will suffer. Too often a recruitment team is faced with a choice between producing letters or producing reports; naturally, they produce the letters. Consequently, the records and reports are always inaccurate and incomplete; the detailed reports are useless, and the ones on overall level of activity largely mythical. It is not practical to produce accurate recruitment reports at every level required under a manual system.

The problems connected with a manual personnel records system have already been alluded to. The points made are repeated here with further elaboration. Basically, they amount to saying that the system is very cumbersome, and has considerable potential for inaccuracy.

1. The system does not produce reports. It only records things. Most personnel departments require reports on such things as starters, leavers, transfers, assignments, salary increases, holidays, medicals, service awards, company cars, and staff listings. All of these involve substantial typing exercises.
2. Answering statistical enquiries is very laborious. The volume of statistics that personnel departments have to handle is constantly increasing. The Government and the Training Boards require statistics. The company will require figures for reviewing its own manpower. Depending on the nature of the business, clients may require statistics. The requirements are often complex and diverse, and although the task of sorting through all the records and extracting the relevant information is basically a clerical job, it needs to be done by a senior member of the department because of the amount of interpretation involved. Salary surveys fall into this category. Somebody has to sort through the records identifying the relevant categories and extracting the information required. If discussion with other companies indicates that the interpretation of the categories should be modified, the whole exercise has to be repeated.
3. The production of letters is a totally separate operation involving duplication of effort and leading to discrepancies. When the records officer is under pressure, letter production will take precedence over record maintenance. Therefore, the records are never entirely reliable.
4. The accuracy of the system is entirely dependent on the competence of the person running it. A manual system has no means of validating the information fed into it, and checking to see that procedures are followed.
5. In order to provide information readily in the form required for different purposes, many items have to be recorded in several places, leading to further duplication of effort and discrepancies.

In summary, a manual personnel records system is cumbersome, involves duplication of effort, is prone to inaccuracy, and is seriously inadequate for the production of reports and statistics.

The next problem area to consider is remuneration. A substantial amount of the work that falls within this general term is covered elsewhere. The production of salary reports and the handling of salary surveys fall within the sections on personnel records and the enquiry system. But there is a substantial problem area within remuneration which stands all on its own: the annual salary review. For many personnel departments the annual salary review is a nightmare. It begins with the requirement to supply senior management with a considerable body of information on individuals' salary progress and current status. During this phase, questions of the sort dealt with under the enquiry system below are likely to be asked. 'What would be the effect of giving an extra two per cent to everyone with over two years service?'. The information sheets will then be marked up by managers. Undoubtedly, there will be complaints at this stage that people are missing from the reports, or that employees who have transferred to another department have appeared, or that various people's salary histories are wrong. Amidst a general atmosphere of abuse, the personnel department has to begin to type the required number of salary review letters. This will normally be done by the use of preprinted letters which require only the blanks to be filled in. Copies will be required for the employee himself, his manager, the personnel department, payroll, and pensions. This process is guaranteed to produce inaccuracies. Occasionally, the typist makes a mistake which is not picked up during the checking process. More frequently, the last couple of carbon copies are so faint that they are misread by payroll or pensions. Or again, a mistake is made first time round and the typist corrects it, but somehow half of the incorrect letters get sent out together with half the correct ones.

When this time-consuming and frustrating exercise is well advanced, the board of directors will probably decide to make some further modifications to the basis of the review, and the exercise has to be started again from the beginning. It is not unusual for a personnel department to end up retyping all the letters four times in succession to accommodate changes of mind by the board. This, of course, increases the potential for error enormously. When the letters have been produced the personnel records still have to be updated, and this major operation may continue for a considerable amount of time after the review has become effective. The whole operation from the original issuing of salary information to completion of updating the personnel records is likely to extend over several months, leading to further problems. People are constantly starting, leaving, transferring departments, going on assignments, and having salary increases unrelated to the annual review. The longer the process takes the more inaccurate the original information supplied by the personnel department becomes, and the more complicated it is to complete the exercise satisfactorily. These are the problems associated with an annual review. Not all companies have annual reviews. Some operate a rolling review system, with salary adjustments related to performance appraisals or anniversary of start. The essential problems remain the same, except that a rolling review is more complicated to operate. Although the volume of work is smaller, the problems recur on a monthly basis throughout the year, and there are the additional difficulties of trying to identify the employees due for review each month and attempting to relate the monthly reviews to an overall budget.

The final problem area to be considered may be referred to as the enquiry system. This is particularly concerned with the things which the department is requested to do on a one-off rather than a regular basis. For example, if a salary policy which involves giving an extra two per cent to anyone who has more than five years service with the company is under consideration, a report will be required, sorted alphabetically within department, of everyone who qualifies according to these criteria, giving employee number, name, department, job title, and salary. Under a manual system, requirements such as these will always involve time-consuming individual exercises, and they will constantly have to be performed again as the policy is modified. A normal personnel department cannot cope with many such exercises. But they are always expected to do so. The feeling is that, if the personnel department stores the information, it should be able to produce it in whatever form is required. Failure to do so results in a failure of credibility. It is important that a personnel department should arrange its records in such a way as to make the maximum possible contribution to these requests, and so to key policy decisions. This cannot be done with a manual system.

A related problem is the one-off question of the type: 'How many engineers do we have aged between 35 and 45, with at least five years experience with the company, earning between £7000 and £12 000, and currently based in the head office?'. The only way to supply an answer with a manual system is to work laboriously through all the record cards. And when, at the end, the question is modified to include a wider age band or fewer years experience with the company, the whole exercise has to be repeated. Dealing with such questions as these, though vital for a personnel department, is not really feasible with a manual system. Of course, it is not only personnel records which give rise to such require-ments. They arise in recruitment as well. When a particular vacancy arises, it is a basic requirement to be able to search the existing bank of applicants rapidly for someone with the required attributes. Similarly, managers will often ask for one-off reports which do not conform to the regular format, or for statistics that would not normally be produced. Monitoring the various functions of the personnel department necessar-ily gives rise to specific questions from time to time—questions which are not answered by the information generally available—and a means of answering them quickly and accurately is a fundamental requirement of an efficient personnel department.

Summary of the solutions

The administrative problems with which a personnel department is faced have been discussed. At first sight it looks like an overwhelming mul-titude of problems, but on analysis it can be seen that the same themes are recurring in each area in slightly disguised form. In fact, there are only three main problems, and these problems recur in each area, so that the solutions to them must be regarded as the three main principles on which a successful system should be built.

1. Store everything in one place.

2. Combine the process of updating records with the production of letters.
3. Design the system around a fully flexible report generator.

These principles are interlinked. It is only feasible to store everything in one place, for example, if a fully flexible report generator is available; information is duplicated under a manual system in order to facilitate the production of specialized reports. Other facilities will also be required (these are dealt with in full in Chapters 3 to 8) but the three basic principles outlined are those on which the system should be designed. Each of the problem areas will therefore be considered in the light of these principles.

The major problem in the area of recruitment was fluctuations in the level of activity, necessitating the employment of temporaries and so leading to expense and inaccuracies. If the process of producing letters is combined with the updating of records, duplication of effort is immediately removed. Furthermore, there is no possibility of the records not reflecting an accurate picture of the applicant's progress to date. Again, if the information is all stored in one place, nothing will be required to update an applicant's record and send a letter other than the applicant number and the standard letter number. The applicant's name and address, the letter reference, the description of the vacancy, and the name and job title of the appropriate recruiter can be added by the system. Obviously, if the letter is inviting the applicant to an interview or making an offer of employment, the operator will have to supply the relevant details. In practice this method of producing letters works out ten times as fast as the use of preprinted letters, and so irons out the effect of fluctuations in the level of recruitment activity. It also eliminates the need for a separate operation of record keeping, and ensures that there can never be any discrepancies between the letters and the records. It was mentioned above that to produce adequate reports required as many people as the production of letters. If a flexible report generator is available, all reports are produced as an automatic spin-off of the information stored, which has been created in the process of letter production. The time savings are therefore substantial, the possibility of inaccuracy is removed, and the range and flexibility of reports available is greatly increased. Finally, the process of searching the data base for a suitable applicant when a new vacancy arises is a straightforward feature of the enquiry system. Overall an enormous amount of duplication of effort is removed and the possibility of discrepancies is eliminated. The whole process is streamlined to the extent that a small permanent staff can cope confidently with substantial fluctuations in workload, where once an army of temporaries would have been required even to perform the most basic tasks.

How do these principles help with personnel records? In the first place, it was mentioned that a considerable amount of information often has to be stored in several places so that it is readily accessible for reporting purposes. Storing everything in one place and having a flexible report generator removes the need for this. It also removes the possiblity of discrepancies between different sources of information, and does away with a substantial burden of typing to produce standard reports. Combining the process of updating the records with the production of letters removes duplication of effort and also the possibility of discrepancies. Most important changes to the personnel records (job title, location, salary) involve the production of a letter, so this is a substantial saving. Statistical enquiries should be handled readily by a good report generator and enquiry system. There is one point which does not come within the scope of these principles; one of the problems with a manual system was said to be that the accuracy of the system depended entirely on the competence of the person running it. This problem is dealt with during computerization by building validation into the system. The system is told to expect the input for specified fields to come in a given form (for example, dates can be checked to see that they are valid, and the system can also check that start date is earlier than date of promotion to senior staff, etc.). Such things as job titles or locations can be checked against a dictionary to see that they are valid. There are many ways in which a computer system can provide checks which are outside the scope of a manual system, and it is part of the detailed design of a system to make the maximum use of this.

The third problem area considered was remuneration. The first difficulty here was to extract the required information for carrying out the review. If the information is all stored in one place, and a mechanism for generating reports exists, this problem disappears. A further difficulty was the production of letters and updating of the data base. The principle of combining these saves time and eliminates discrepancies between what appears on the letter to the person concerned, what is stored on the personnel records, and what appears on any subsequent reports. However, more detail is required about the mechanism for doing this (see Chapter 6) for, as with recruitment, it is possible to so design the system that each letter takes only a couple of seconds to produce. If a review is conducted entirely, or predominantly, according to agreed principles about the increases appropriate to various categories of staff, the whole exercise can be performed in a matter of minutes. There is also a requirement here for something which lies outside the three main principles, that is, a system for experimenting with various kinds of salary adjustment and examining the results, prior to making the final policy decision. The advantages of such a system for carrying out calculations during pay negotiations should be immediately apparent.

Finally, the enquiry system requires consideration. This will be dealt with entirely by the principle of designing the system around a fully flexible report generator. A report generator is a means of retrieving any item of stored information and reporting it in whatever format is required, with appropriate heading lines, sort order, totals, and some degree of editing for the sake of appearance, for example, suppressing leading zeros, inserting slashes between dates, skipping lines at specified places, and grouping items together. Such systems are available for use by the layman, who, with a little practice, should be able to sit down at a terminal and produce his own purpose-built report in a couple of minutes without any programming knowledge. Further information about the nature and potentialities of such systems is given in Chapter 7. However, to make the fullest possible use of them it is first necessary to store all information in one place and to be confident of its accuracy.

The three basic principles around which a personnel computer system should be designed are outlined as follows.

1. Store everything in one place.
2. Combine the process of updating records with the production of letters.
3. Design the system around a fully flexible report generator.

They are not, of course, the only points to be borne in mind when developing a system: Chapters 3 to 8 are concerned with other vital considerations. It is important to make realistic estimates of the response times required, the volume of work to be handled, quantity of data to be stored, necessity to communicate between locations, and security restrictions. But they are the basic design considerations without which the system is unlikely to justify the amount of time it will demand.

Benefits of a personnel computer system

This chapter has analysed some of the basic problems by which personnel departments are commonly faced: problems so basic that their existence can be extremely damaging. It has been suggested that the solutions popularly put forward only have the effect of making the problems worse, and that what is really required is a purpose-built computer system. The rest of this book examines in detail the design and implementation of such a system. What should be clear by this stage is that computerization is very far from being a simple business. If anything significant is to be achieved, a major project has to be undertaken. Almost certainly it will be the most demanding project that the personnel department has ever undertaken, and as such it involves major costs, problems, and benefits. A successful computer project will revolutionize the administrative processes of a personnel department, increasing its effectiveness, and boosting its credibility within the company. It is difficult to see how any personnel department can play a major role within a company until it has sorted out its own basic administration; and that, given the complexities of personnel administration, demands a personnel computer system.

What of the costs? It is impossible to give guidelines in the abstract. The cost of introducing a computer system into a company employing 100 000 people will obviously be different from the cost in a company employing 1000 people. To give an indication of costs, it is first necessary to state the size of the project under consideration. The hardware cost in 1981 for a company employing under 3000 people and with a labour turnover of 20 per cent per annum should be around £50 000. The software cost, assuming that a package were bought, would be around £30 000. The cost of implementation is the hardest figure to estimate without any concrete facts, but it would probably be in the region of £20 000. The total cost would therefore be around £100 000.

The difficulty with justifying this cost is that it raises basic questions about the role of the personnel department. How much manpower will the computer save? The answer is that if all the tasks to be performed by the computer were to be performed manually instead, the personnel department would probably have to employ over a hundred people. In this sense the cost of the computer system will be recovered many times over in its first year of operation. But, in practice, personnel departments muddle along without employing all these people, and simply fail to provide the service which they should. It follows, ironically, that a well-organized department stands to save more manpower by computerizing than a badly organized one. The badly organized one is simply not providing an adequate service.

These points are worth making to highlight the fact that the justification for computerization hinges more on arguments about the role of the personnel department than on arguments about manpower savings. Nevertheless, it would be extraordinary if a company employing 1000 people were unable to justify the purchase and installation of a personnel computer system on strict economic grounds alone. The problem would be not so much the identification of these savings as the highly emotive issue of how they were to be realized.

The overriding benefit of a personnel computer system is the change it brings about in the department's image—an increase in credibility. Instead of the department that can never get anything right, it becomes the department that handles administration fast and efficiently, despite fluctuations, and responds instantly to *ad hoc* enquiries and requests for one-off reports. What is the size of company at which a personnel computer system becomes viable? The answer is that any company with a serious need for a personnel function has a serious need for a personnel computer system, and should be able to justify it. A personnel computer system supplies a department with the tools and the credibility that it needs to get on with the rest of its work.

Mention has been made of the costs and the benefits. What of the problems? Implementing a successful system depends on the choice of hardware and software, the standard of project management, the quality

16

of data preparation and coding, the thoroughness of the training provided, the adequacy of system testing, the way in which system development is carried out, and the amount of thought given to establishing procedures for running the system. Although each of these is important, there is one point which is more important than all of them taken together. This single most important point is to decide with absolute clarity, and in the greatest possible detail, exactly what the system is to do. It is possible, despite the best project management, data preparation, and training, for the system to fail because of uncertainty or misunderstandings as to what it is supposed to do. If the objectives are not specified clearly, they certainly will not be achieved. But if they are specified, and specified in detail, the other points have a certain amount of 'give' in them.

It is not possible to give a general statement of requirements. The finished product always appears disappointing, or even disastrous. Every tiny detail of operation—volumes, speeds, number of key depressions—must be specified. All other considerations are secondary to this. Equally well, it should be recognized that this is much the most difficult task of the project, and places a heavy burden on the person who undertakes it. Chapters 3 to 8 are devoted to an exposition of the design features which are required in a personnel computer system, if it is to provide a solution to the problems examined in this chapter. Chapter 9 explains in detail how a system can be screened and tested. But before embarking on the details, it is necessary to consider the field of computing in general, in order to gain an adequate appreciation of the background against which such a project must be undertaken.

2. The revolution in computing

Many personnel managers who decide to investigate computerization know nothing at all about computers. This is only to be expected. Computing is still not regarded as one of the fundamentals of business awareness, in the way that accounting is, for example. People who have a scientific or technical background will generally acquire some knowledge of computers. But nontechnical people remain completely in the dark. Ignorance about computers is a major problem in industry today. A full appreciation of them is rare amongst managers, and almost unknown at board level. Consequently, a personnel manager who decides to investigate the contribution that computers could make to the running of his department is faced by two problems: firstly, he feels a very natural unease about taking decisions concerning a subject about which he has no knowledge or experience; secondly, when he does try to probe a little further into the darkness, he finds himself up against a wall of mystique, erected and maintained by the computer specialist.

Surely, no branch of technology has suffered so badly from the stultifying effects of jargon as computing. It seems equally clear that computer specialists are fighting a determined rearguard action against the increasing simplicity of computer operations. As the systems become simpler, so the jargon becomes ever more dense, and all but the boldest are kept at bay.

This chapter introduces some basic computer terms, which a personnel manager with a serious interest in the subject will need to understand. The explanations assume a starting-point of complete ignorance, and readers who already have some familiarity with the subject will therefore need to be patient. The chapter is not pitched entirely at this level. Apart from explaining some basic terms, its objective is to highlight the revolutionary nature of recent developments in computing, to draw attention to the possibilities arising from them, and to argue in favour of a narrowing of the gap which has grown up in the past between users and specialists.

The first stage in understanding computers is to become familiar with some basic concepts. Computing consists of three parts: input, processing, and output. Something is put into the system; it is processed; and something comes out. In the case of a mathematical calculation, the input would be the calculation to be performed, the processing would be the performance of the calculation, and the output would be the answer. In the case of an information system, the input might be the employment details of everyone working for a particular company, the processing might be the retrieval and sorting of certain items, and the output might be an alphabetical list of people working for the company.

Input and output have something in common which distinguishes them from processing: they require the performance of a mechanical operation. To feed information into the system it is necessary to do something like typing on a keyboard. Similarly, output involves something like printing out on a piece of paper. Processing, on the other hand, is entirely electronic, and so is very much faster. Input and output are directly related to the human element; processing is not. For this reason, and for many others, all of which in a sense stem from this basic point, input and output are generally referred to together as input/output, or more commonly I/O.

These two concepts, processing and I/O, are fundamental to computing; they crop up again and again in different contexts, with a slightly different angle on them. The main parts of a computer are known as the central processing unit (CPU) and the peripherals. Computer peripherals are devices for I/O. Most computers have parts that do not fall into either of these categories, but these are the key parts. If it has peripherals and a CPU, a computer will be able to do something, because it has processing power and a means of handling I/O. It is able to complete the basic cycle.

Input → Processing → Output

This analysis began by introducing these three terms as basic concepts which define the function of a computer. It went on to see how they are reflected in a basic division of computer equipment into CPU and peripherals. The same concepts are reflected again in the disciplines that are followed in the design of a computer system. The basic questions asked are 'What do you want to store?' (Input) and 'What do you want to get out?' (Output). Designing a system entails designing the processes by which the one will be converted into the other. Systems which meet this objective may differ in the speed at which they can perform these processes.

The reason for emphasizing these seemingly abstract concepts at the outset is that they put computing in perspective. The basic questions which need to be asked when a computer system is designed are:

1. What will it be required to store?
2. What will it be required to produce?
3. How will the data be put in?
4. How will the data be extracted?
5. What are the time constraints?

Questions 1–4 concern I/O. Question 5 is concerned with processing. So many questions are asked during the design phase of a system that it is easy to lose track of what is critical and what is not. It is useful to bear in mind that these are the underlying questions.

Input, output, and processing are the three basic concepts in which computing subsists. Having said this, it is necessary to introduce a fundamental distinction which arises immediately any computer system is analysed: the distinction between hardware and software. Hardware is the machine itself. Software is the sets of instructions which it carries out. Hardware is made in a factory; it stands in the office; it can be picked up; it goes wrong. Software is written by a programmer; it is fed into the computer; you cannot see it; it does not wear out with the passage of time.

Examples of hardware would be the devices for performing I/O—a keyboard or a printer—and the CPU itself. An example of software would be a program for producing a specified report. The distinction between hardware and software cuts across the conceptual division into input, output, and processing. Both of these depend upon a combination of hardware and software. The hardware aspect of input, output, and processing is the physical devices required to perform them, for example, keyboard, printer, and CPU. The software aspect is a series of instructions stored within the computer which enable it to accept the input from a peripheral, use the CPU to process it in a specified way, and direct the output to another peripheral.

The history of computing is to a considerable extent the history of the development of hardware and software. There is another aspect to it, which may be referred to as systems philosophy, that is, the accepted views on how to design and implement a computer system. In the last ten years there has been a revolution in hardware, the principal result of which has been to reduce the size and cost of computers to the point where it is quite normal to see them standing in a small office instead of in a large, purpose-built computer room. A revolution is taking place in software: the means by which complex sets of instructions are fed into the computer has been simplified to the extent that it can often be handled satisfactorily by a nonspecialist person rather than a computer programmer.

A revolution in both hardware and software creates the need for a revolution in systems philosophy. To date, there is no indication that this is occurring. Computer projects are still being handled in the traditional fashion with all the well-known pitfalls. This chapter continues by discussing firstly hardware, secondly software, and thirdly systems philosophy. The section on hardware begins with a description of the old type of systems and contrasts them with the modern ones. The section on software reviews the gradual development that has taken place, and assesses where it is leading. The section on systems philosophy describes the accepted view of the way systems should be designed and implemented, points to some reasons why it so often fails, and concludes with a discussion of the way developments in hardware and software could be used to revolutionize the approach to systems development, and so increase the chances of a successful outcome.

Hardware

The first computers were very large indeed. They would often occupy a whole floor of a building, and engineers would be permanently employed servicing them. Over the years their size was reduced as a result of technological advances, but even in the 1960s a computer was still normally a large machine, housed in a special room with purpose-built air conditioning and measures for eliminating dust.

These computers are known as mainframes, that is, they are principally large machines run by trained operators. Mainframes in use today are very powerful, and are normally designed to perform a number of different and unrelated tasks at the same time. For example, they might be updating the personnel records, producing monthly pay slips, restructuring a planning network, analysing market trends, and performing process design or engineering calculations, all at the same time. In fact, the computer only ever does one thing at once, but it does them so fast that they all appear to be happening at once.

Each task performed by a computer is stored within it as a set of instructions. When several tasks have to be performed at once it simply rotates through the sets of instructions very rapidly, performing part of one followed by part of another. This is known as time sharing. Essentially it is CPU time that is being shared. As the number of tasks to be performed increases, the time taken to perform them becomes longer. The speed of performance is known as response time, and is a function of the amount of processing power available and the number (and complexity) of the tasks being performed.

Mainframes and time sharing tend to go together. A mainframe is so expensive in terms of original purchase cost, special housing conditions, and back-up staff that it is normally only possible to consider using it if it can handle a large number of tasks at once. For this reason in-house mainframes are not suitable for small companies. If they wish to use a mainframe, their needs are best served by a computer bureau which operates a mainframe and sells its services to a wide variety of clients. A company can be connected to a bureau over a telephone line, and will normally be charged on the basis of the length of time for which it is connected, the amount of processing power used (expressed in CPU seconds), and the amount of storage space required inside the computer. Bureaux tend to be very expensive, but in the era of the mainframe they made computers available to people who could certainly not justify purchasing one themselves.

Traditionally, then, processing power has been provided through time sharing on a mainframe, in many cases via a telephone connection to a bureau. Originally almost all these tasks were performed by means of what is known as batch processing. This means that work is gathered together into batches which are processed at regular intervals (a month, a week, or a day, for example) in a form convenient for the computer, as

21

opposed to processing things as they occur in a form convenient to the user. The conversion of work from the form in which it exists naturally into a form that is convenient for the computer is known as data preparation. Data preparation is, therefore, inseparable from batch processing. What does it involve?

The first stage is to write out the information to be fed into the computer on specially designed forms. Each letter has to be written in a square box with a number above it. These forms are known as key punch forms, the point being that they are to be used for key punching. Key punching is a process whereby a written document is converted into a punched card by means of a keyboard resembling a typewriter.

A punched card is about the size of an ordinary office envelope, and it has eighty columns across and twelve down. Each time a key on the punching machine is pressed, holes are punched in one of the columns. The pattern of these holes down the twelve rows corresponds to a given character. Key punch operators are often extremely fast, but naturally they make mistakes. One of the means by which mistakes can be detected at an early stage is known as 'verification'. Two people punch the same thing, and a machine compares the results by shining a light on the cards and checking the patterns. Any discrepancies result in the appropriate cards being rejected for checking and recycling.

When the cards have been punched they are made up into a batch and fed into a device known as a card reader. This, as the name suggests, reads the cards and feeds their contents into the computer. The fact that cards can be read much faster than they can be punched highlights one of the supposed advantages of batch processing: it does not waste the computer's time. Naturally, this is an important consideration when time on the computer is purchased from a bureau at a high rate. However, it does have an absurd side to it. Why should the entire operation be arranged to suit the computer? Batch processing may avoid wasting the computer's time, but it certainly wastes everyone else's.

In addition to carrying out work in the normal way (for example, writing notes on bits of paper or logging events in a book), specially designed forms have to be completed, and someone has to key punch them, before they can be fed into the computer. In fact, there is a great deal more to data preparation than this. It is normal to set up a series of controls to check, for example, that the cards are all read and that they are in the right order. A large system requires a whole army of people for data control, data preparation, and data entry, and this has the effect of widening the gulf between the computer and the person using its services.

It has been suggested in this chapter that there is a link between mainframes, time sharing, bureaux, batch processing, and data preparation. This link is not inevitable; mainframes may offer alternatives to batch processing, and they will not always be housed in bureaux, but it gives a reasonably accurate picture of data processing up to about 1970. It is now time to consider the changes that have taken place since then.

The great change has been the introduction of the mini computer. As the name suggests, a mini is much smaller than a mainframe. It is also designed to operate in a normal office environment without the assistance of full-time operations staff. A word of caution is appropriate here. Computers do not take kindly to large fluctuations in temperature or humidity, or to excessive amounts of dust. A clean, air-conditioned office should be all right. What is perhaps more important to realize is that they are quite noisy, and produce a considerable amount of heat. The noise argues in favour of a separate room, but the heat problem may mean that a special extractor fan is required if excessive temperature fluctuations are to be avoided.

Minis came into being because advances in technology made it possible to provide a significant amount of processing power in a machine the size of a filing cabinet. The advent of the micro chip has revolutionized computers, and the so-called 'micros' which are now on the market can be astonishingly powerful in terms of processing power. This revolution is still going on, but it has already gone far enough to transform the business of data processing. The price of minis is in the range that makes it economic for any company or department with a significant data processing requirement to buy one for their own use. For example, it is certainly possible at the time of writing to purchase for £50 000 a mini that will handle all the requirements of a personnel department in a company employing 3000 people. The indications are that these figures will be going down over the next few years.

The fact that purchasing a mini is often more economic than using a bureau, together with the fact that it does not require specialized conditions or operators, undermines the argument for batch processing. If the machine is purchased outright, cutting down the amount of computer time required is no longer a key requirement. Instead of filling in special forms, and going through all the paraphenalia of data preparation, data control, and data entry, it makes more sense for the person doing the work to put the data into the computer as well. Finally, if the person doing the work is going to put it into the computer as well, the question arises whether any of the work normally performed can be dispensed with in favour of direct interaction with the computer.

The mini computers have exploited this possibility very successfully, and in so doing have transformed the nature of data processing and its efficiency in terms of manpower. The essential change has been a switch from batch processing to a mode of operation in which the user is in constant communication with the computer. Systems that enable information to be updated as it changes, in other words, that perform an update at the precise moment when it is input, are known as real time systems. The important point is that there is no artificial time cycle for

23

updating. The significance of this is that, if it is possible to update information as it changes and to examine what you have at any time, there is no need to keep any independent notes or records of your work. A batch processing system requires manual back-up, because it is always out of date, but a real time system does not. Instead of writing on bits of paper, and completing special forms at a later date, the user can simply input the information as it becomes available. The manual system is no longer required.

Direct communication with a computer is obviously impossible by means of punched cards. They introduce an intermediate stage which slows the process down. Instead the user must be linked straight into the computer, and this is done by means of a peripheral known as a terminal. Some terminals are just keyboards that operate like typewriters, typing out the information as it goes in. A more popular type of terminal is a visual display unit (VDU), which displays information on a screen as it is typed in, or in answer to an enquiry. A VDU screen is typically 80 characters across and 20 characters down. It can sit on an ordinary desk in an office and can be used by anyone.

Two other types of terminals should be mentioned: fast printers and high quality printers. A mainframe computer produces its output on a device known as a line printer. These are large and expensive, and operate at astonishing speeds, for example, 600 lines per minute would be considered quite unremarkable for a line printer. Some of them operate so fast that gathering the paper up as it emerges is a major problem. A mini computer is normally capable of being linked to a line printer, but it is more likely to have a small device, costing perhaps £3–4000, known as a fast printer. This could be expected to operate at around 180 characters per second (cps), which is quite fast enough for most purposes. Some terminals operate as both a keyboard and a printer, this being a particularly useful and economical arrangement.

A high quality printer is one which operates at a much slower speed (50 cps, for example), but which produces a high quality of printing, similar to a typewriter. This can be used for producing documents or letters which would normally be typed. Producing letters on a mainframe at 50 cps would be unacceptably expensive, but it makes sense on a mini, and is part of the process of eliminating manual tasks. The facility to produce documents and letters direct from a computer system is undoubtedly a significant advantage of the minis.

When a mini computer is installed in a department to service the requirements of that department alone it is said to be a 'dedicated' system. If it is unconnected to any other system it is described as 'stand-alone'. A possible objection to the proliferation of minis is that they make coordination of systems more difficult. If all a company's systems are running on a mainframe, those that can benefit from being linked together (personnel and payroll, for example) are at least in the same

24

physical location. How can they be linked together if they are running on separate computer systems?

The concept of distributed data processing offers a solution to this problem. The idea is that minis can be distributed over a wide area (they may even be in different parts of the world), but information can be passed to a central pool which might be a larger mini or a mainframe computer. Communication over the telephone lines is possible by means of a device known as a 'modem'. In other words, the individual minis must be capable of communicating with one another, or with a central pool, or both. Computer communication is a highly technical subject on which specialist advice is required. All that it is appropriate to say here is that it offers the possibility of a solution to the problem of achieving overall coordination of company systems, while exploiting the advantages of mini computers.

In summary, it may be said that the essence of the revolution in hardware has been to bring the computer to the user. Instead of a mysterious remote operation requiring the filling in of special forms and the employment of specialist staff, the user department has a mini computer with which individuals communicate by means of VDUs on their desks. Instead of sending work off in batches, and accepting that manual back-up is essential for urgent enquiries, the computer is used to update information as it becomes available, and to deal with enquiries as they arise. The mini represents a known expenditure because it can be purchased outright, so that there is no need to agonize throughout the day over how much the bureau will charge for processing a particular enquiry, and whether it is worth it. The mystique is dispelled, and the computer becomes just another member of the department.

Software

The terms hardware and software are intended to give an impression of the difference between that which is fixed and that which is variable. Hardware is fixed in that it determines the computer's potential for carrying out instructions. Software is variable in that it consists of the instructions the computer actually carries out. These instructions are fed into the system by a programmer, and are stored in what is known as 'machine code'. Machine code consists of electronic patterns, and it represents the most complete analysis possible of individual instructions into separate parts.

The problem with this is that it is so detailed. A seemingly simple instruction like, 'Compare the result of the first calculation with the result of the second one' has to be broken down into a complex series of instructions in machine code. Consequently, it is not practical to give a computer instructions in machine code. It was this difficulty that gave rise to the need for programming languages, that is, means of communicating instructions to the computer which bore some relation, even if a remote one, to the original form of the instructions. The first languages of this sort to be developed were not very sophisticated, and so are known as low-level languages, because they are relatively close to the form in which the computer carries out the instructions.

The next stage was the development of high-level languages: FORTRAN, COBOL, and ALGOL, for example. These languages are still widely used today, and are much closer to the way a human being would regard the instructions than to the way a computer would analyse and store them. Every instruction in a high-level language has to be translated into a series of instructions in machine code. This is done by means of a compiler, which is effectively a set of instructions stored within the computer for converting a high-level language into machine code. Instructions are written by a programmer in a higher level language, and then compiled into machine code.

At this point it is appropriate to consider what is meant by the term 'program'. Software consists of programs. A program is a set of instructions for performing a specific task. Software is a general term for all programs within a given context. Programs fall into various types. The sort of programs that a programmer normally writes when developing a specific system, personnel records, for example, are known as application programs, that is, programs designed for a specific application. There are other types of instructions that are strictly speaking programs, but they have a special status and are normally written by programmers of exceptional skill and experience who know the precise capabilities of a particular piece of hardware. One example has already been given: compilers.

Another important example is what is known as 'the operating system'. When a manufacturer markets hardware, it is sold with an operating system. This is the basic set of instructions enabling it to operate, that is, to comprehend some basic commands. If a computer system is running several programs at once, it will need to know how much time to allocate to each of them, and what to do with one of them while the other is being processed. The operating system controls this. It also does such things as taking the required action when a particular program is to be set in motion. The application programs concern specific tasks. The operating system controls the utilization of the system and the relation of the programs to one another. Such tasks as moving files from one location to another, optimizing the use of space inside the computer, and defining the areas within it are all part of the function of the operating system. An operating system that is capable only of batch processing will be very different from one that operates in real time. Hardware manufacturers normally supply an operating system with their equipment, although some ultraenthusiasts write their own. The writing of an operating system is a complex task, far beyond the horizons of an ordinary programmer. A computer's operating system is the foundation stone that is required before application programming can begin.

Operating systems and compilers are special types of software. The most common type is application programs. These are the programs that normally have to be written when a system is developed, and it is therefore relevant to consider them a little more closely. A programmer begins by constructing a flow chart, that is, a diagram of all the possibilities that may arise during the execution of the task in question and the action to be taken. The task must be broken down into a series of logical and sequential steps. Some of these will be processes, that is, things to do (for example, 'add this number to the last one you calculated'). Others will be decisions, for example, 'Is this number greater than 105?' (yes or no). The answer given will determine the next process or decision. This flow chart is then converted into a series of instructions in the appropriate programming language.

It is normal practice for programs to be divided into logical units known as subroutines, each consisting of a section of program code. This technique is known as modular programming, and is of particular value during conversion or testing, since it is easier to identify errors if different parts of the program can be tested in isolation from one another. Subroutines are also used to enable the same set of instructions to be executed several times in a single program. Instead of repeating the instructions on each occasion, they are put into a subroutine, which is referred to in the program code whenever they are required.

Application programs running on a computer normally fall into groups or systems. For example, there might be a payroll system, a personnel system, a recruitment system, a planning system, and a marketing system. A system of programs which operates successfully may be sold as a package. The advantages of buying a package are as follows:

1. It avoids the trials and tribulations of development work.
2. For the reason outlined in 1, it is substantially less costly.
3. It can be installed immediately.
4. Practical advice will be available from current users on implementation and operation.

The principal disadvantage is that a package will not be tailor-made. Users must either accept that it will fall short of their requirements in certain respects, or tailor it, which can be expensive. The decision whether or not to buy a package is a critical one, which should be made principally on the basis of how close any existing packages come to meeting the requirements.

This section has discussed the gradual way in which software developed from machine code to low-level and then to high-level languages, some special types of software (such as compilers and operating systems), and some basic terms used in connection with programming: flow charts, subroutines, application programs, and packages. This completes the picture of traditional programming, and it is now time to consider the changes that have taken place in recent years, and have revolutionized software.

The first major change was the introduction of what might be called very high-level languages. Traditional high-level languages enabled a large number of instructions in machine code to be condensed into a single statement; but the composition of these statements was nevertheless a technical matter, requiring a trained programmer. Very high-level languages are much closer to normal speech, and are designed to be used by a nontechnical person. The instructions must be given in a set format and must be definitive; they use abbreviations, but they are not in an obscure language. An instruction such as 'sort this report by name' might be communicated to the system as 'SORT, NAME' or even 'S, NAME'.

Very high-level languages are a breakthrough in that they enable users to modify their own systems. They therefore introduce a considerable degree of flexibility. The great complaint made against traditional computer systems is that they are too rigid. Every minor irritation has to be corrected by a trained programmer. Very high-level languages have changed this. Nevertheless, it would be wrong to paint too rosy a picture. At the present time they do not have the range and power of conventional high-level languages. It is still normal to find a complex system written in a language such as FORTRAN, COBOL, or ALGOL. These languages normally handle the mechanism for updating data. The contribution of very high level languages is principally in the area of formatting output, that is, determining the order in which items are to be printed out or displayed; they can also be useful for formatting input.

Facilities for formatting output without the writing of application programs are known as report generators. These are essentially complex pieces of software which enable a simple English-type instruction to be translated into a form which the computer understands. They are discussed in detail in Chapter 7. A considerable amount of the development work on conventional projects was connected with the writing of application programs for report production, and a considerable amount of the frustration involved in running these systems arose from the difficulty of getting the programs changed. Report generators have very largely eliminated these problems.

The formatting of input has undergone a similar development, although this is less advanced. Under some systems facilities can be made available to the user for specifying the way in which an operator is to be prompted for input when a particular command is entered. For example, the system can be instructed to ask certain questions in response to a command, indicating the form in which a reply is required. Alternatively, the VDU screen may be laid out in a set pattern with appropriate headings, and the operator guided through it to input the data.

The formatting of input and output by means of facilities such as report generators enables the user to undertake a substantial part of the work

28

involved in system development. Report generators, however, are nothing more than complex pieces of software that enable the existing file structure to be interrogated quickly and easily. The most significant software developments to have taken place are considerably more sophisticated than this. They represent a completely new look at the way data should be stored and retrieved within a computer system, and reflect a significant change in attitudes towards the applications for which computers can be of use. The change is so fundamental that it may reasonably be described as a shift in emphasis from data processing to information management.

The task for which computers are most obviously suited is the performance of calculations. They can carry out complex calculations very fast, and this is principally what the first ones did. They were soon extended to work which involved making decisions as well as performing calculations, for example, decisions like: 'Is this value greater than or less than 100?'. In this way, computer applications extended far beyond the range of mathematical calculations. However, it was still true to say that they were heavily process orientated. Information was fed in; it went through various phases of change; and out it came in a different form.

Information management differs from this in that it is not process orientated. Information is fed in, and is retrieved in various forms, but it does not necessarily undergo any intermediate process of change. For example, all the details of people working for a particular company may be fed into the system, and reports may be produced on qualifications, addresses, relations, employment history, and current details. The computer has output the information in a different form from that in which it was input, but it has not done anything to it in between.

In a traditional system the principal contribution of the computer was the processing: the work that occurred between input and output. Input was handled by batch processing and output by application programs. Input and output are, by contrast, the principal concern in information management.

This shift in emphasis led to the development of a new type of software. Systems that utilize these new techniques are known as data base management systems. As the name suggests, they are orientated towards managing a base of data, rather than towards processes or calculations. The important point is that it should be possible to input data in a variety of forms and to analyse, manipulate, and retrieve it as required.

What is a data base management system? This is a controversial subject. Specialists disagree over how they should be defined, and even over whether particular systems are correctly described as 'data base' or not. The first point to stress is that the term 'data base' is often used in a deliberately misleading way. People often talk of setting up a data base, when all they mean is storing a pool of information inside a computer. It is true that this is a base of data, but the term 'data base' in its strict sense should be applied only to a base of data which has been structured specifically for the purpose of rapid manipulation, analysis, and retrieval.

The essential point about data base management systems is that they are designed for information management. In practice, this means that the data is stored in a different way. In conventional systems, data is stored in files, which are rather like manual files in that the information within them is not joined together in any particular fashion. Reports are produced by means of application programs, which are specially written to link the information together in a particular way. Data base management systems are essentially a means of linking information together. They do this by maintaining an index of the data within them. It is the addition of this index which distinguishes them from a traditional file structure. In the ultimate form of data base, an index exists for every item stored within the system. For example, if one of the items stored is age, there will be an index for age, and this will contain references to every age existing within the system, so that when the question 'Who are we storing aged 55?' is asked, the answer can be given immediately; the index informs the system where to find all occurrences of item AGE equal to 55.

The difficulty with this approach to storing data is that the index soon occupies more space than the data itself. In most systems, it is not essential to have an instant index for every item. Consequently, most data base management systems represent a compromise, in which an index is maintained only for certain specified values. Purists deny that these are truly data base management systems. But there is a good case for saying that they are. They represent a significant departure from traditional file structures, and they have been designed specifically for information management.

There are many more problems associated with the definition of data base management systems. For example, the data base is not necessarily in one place. If software is written to combine data in one computer with data in another by methods which are designed for information management, there is a case for saying that it constitutes a data base management system. There is no point in pursuing these questions. The first point about data base management systems is that they must be specifically geared to information management by the provision of an indexing system. The second is that they must provide for easy restructuring of the data; items may have to be added or deleted, and they may or may not be part of the index. And, finally, formatting of output must be straightforward.

The last development should be mentioned in connection with user-orientated systems is the provision of dictionary facilities. This, again, arises from the need to increase flexibility. The idea is that items likely to change regularly should be stored in a dictionary which can be accessed and updated through a VDU by the user rather than being written into the application programs. Dictionary facilities are discussed in detail in Chapter 3.

Systems philosophy
The changes that have occurred in hardware and software have in common that they both bring the computer to the user. The hardware changes have brought the computer to the user physically through the development of mini computers, which can operate in a normal office environment, servicing the requirements of a particular department. Instead of filling in special forms, and sending them away for key punching and remote processing, the user can have a VDU for input and output, and a fast printer for producing hard copy when required. There may also be a high quality printer for producing any related documents, so that these do not have to be typed separately.

The software changes have brought the computer to the user in the sense that systems are easier to use and easier to modify than in the past. Instead of typing in data in predefined positions, formatted screens can be used, and the cursor guided through the appropriate positions for entering information. Dictionary facilities increase flexibility. Data base management systems provide a means of restructuring data when required, and of analysing and manipulating it. Report generators enable the format of output to be defined by the user at the terminal, instead of requiring a specially written application program.

The result of all these changes has been to change the computer from a large and expensive machine shrouded in mystery at a remote location, and serviced by armies of specialists, to a normal piece of office equipment assisting a wide range of people in their jobs. Remoteness, mystery, and rigidity are replaced by physical presence, simplicity, and flexibility. Updates are processed as they occur by the people who initiate them; and reports are written as required without the need for specialist programming. Above all, there has been a shift from calculations and processing to information management. It is not just the scientist or the engineer who uses a computer. The personnel manager has a use for one as well.

A revolution has occurred in hardware and software, but it has not yet been fully exploited. The reason for this is that attitudes have not yet caught up with the changes. Users frequently fail to take the initiative to the extent that they should, and feel nervous about getting on with running a system themselves. Computer specialists, on the other hand, sense that the ground is crumbling beneath their feet. It is clear that computing is a boom industry but what, if anything, is to be the role of the specialist within it? Certainly not the same as in the past. If computers can be run by users, and a substantial part of application programming replaced by report generators, the computer department in its old form ceases to exist. After years of telling themselves how much they will be in demand in the future, computer specialists have suddenly been struck by the thought that they may not be needed at all because technological advances may result in their being phased out.

In many cases the reaction to this worrying thought has been an attempt to modify traditional roles to suit the new climate. Arguments are put forward for sharing a large mini between several departments, under the control of a central computer group, or for introducing strict controls on development work, so that it is handled centrally rather than by the users themselves. The questions of operation and development need to be dealt with separately.

There is no reason why users should not operate a mini computer entirely themselves. What kind of skills are required? It is necessary to undergo some basic training on the correct procedures to follow and what to do when problems arise, but this should not present any great difficulty, and it all helps the user to understand the computer and use it intelligently. Procedural training will be largely concerned with providing adequate back-up. Since there is always a chance that a problem may occur which corrupts the data in the system, it is essential to provide a means of recovery. This is done by taking regular back-ups of the system; these are effectively snapshot pictures of the data at a given point in time. Normally this is done by copying the data on to magnetic tape (in modern computers it is normal for live data to be stored on disc). If back-ups are taken every day, the worst possible situation is for the data to become corrupted at the end of a day, so that all the transactions for the day are lost when the back-up from the previous night is restored. Some systems have a facility to log all transactions as they occur, so that after a corruption problem it is possible to restore the back-up of the previous day, and then run the transaction file against it to restore the data to the state it was in immediately before the problem occurred. If transaction logging is not available, operators must repeat all the day's transactions after the back-up has been restored.

Knowing what to do when problems occur requires more skill than carrying out standard procedures, such as back-up. The important point is to decide what sort of a problem it is. First of all, is it hardware or software? This is not normally very difficult. Equipment failure is often obvious, although there are some borderline cases. If the problem is software, then an attempt must be made to decide what sort of software is at fault, for example, the operating system, the data base management system, the report generator, one of the reports, or an application program. Faults in an operating system should be extremely rare. Most users will probably never encounter one, and if they do, are most likely to be led towards it by a process of elimination—it cannot be anything else, so it must be the operating system.

In order to detect faults in the data base management system it is necessary to understand the way data is structured and linked together. Since the structure of the data should reflect the user's requirements, there is no reason why this should be unattainable. Problems with the report generator or with the reports themselves are best dealt with by the user since they are entirely user-orientated. Finally, problems with an application program should not be too difficult to spot. It is normally possible to devise some test cases which will help to pin-point the problem. Once the problem has been identified, the program should be modified by the person responsible for maintaining it, who, in some cases, might be the user.

These are some examples of the kind of skills users will need to acquire to run a system. Operating a system and sorting out problems as they arise requires a greater depth of knowledge than simply typing in commands at a terminal. However, a user benefits from acquiring this knowledge, and will be able to use computers more effectively as a result. The understanding required to make full use of data base management systems and report generators is inseparable from the knowledge required to run a system and diagnose problems. These points take on a greater significance in the context of system development.

System development can mean anything from making minor modifications to an existing system to writing an entirely new one. Since the principles of development are the same throughout, it is best to concentrate on the more substantial case—writing an entirely new system—since it demonstrates these principles more clearly. For many years there has been general agreement amongst computer specialists about the way system development should be tackled. Naturally, there is disagreement over precisely how the principles should be applied, but the broad outline is the same. These principles may reasonably be referred to as traditional systems philosophy. The purpose of this section is to explain what traditional systems philosophy is, to offer a critique of it, and to propose an alternative: one which suggests itself as the natural response to the revolution that has taken place in hardware and software.

The most important point about traditional systems philosphy is that it draws a clear distinction between users and specialists. Certain documents are produced by the user, others by the specialist; some are approved by the user; others are approved by the specialist; certain tasks must be performed by the user; certain other tasks must be performed by the specialist. The user is held to be responsible for defining the requirements. The specialist is held to be responsible for working out how to meet them. The user is held to be responsible for testing and accepting the results.

At first this sounds perfectly reasonable. The specialist does not presume to tell the user what the requirements are and the user does not presume to tell the specialist how to meet them. Indeed, often the first two stages go quite well. The problems occur at the third stage, when the user and the specialist are unable to agree over whether or not the requirements have been met. The user claims that the requirements have been misinterpreted, and the specialist retorts that the point at issue was not included in the specification. The user feels that it is absurd for anyone to be so totally lacking in common sense. The specialist reflects on the difficulties of dealing with people who do not know how to write a proper specification.

The difficulty is that an unequivocal specification would have to be very detailed indeed, much more detailed than anything which a person with no 'specialist' knowledge of computers could write. The stock answer to this is that the user is not expected to write such a document. The user supplies a user specification. The specialists examine the requirements, investigate everything that is unclear or insufficiently detailed, decide how the computer could help, and then produce a system specification. The user is not expected to write the system specification, but merely to approve it.

The problem with this is that the user is approving something without fully understanding it. Again there is a stock answer. The system specification should not contain any technical terms that will confuse the user. However, this is not really the point. The point is that the detailed specification of systems is a skill in itself. Someone who has never worked on the production of such a specification is not in a position to approve one. The mass of detail will be confusing. A user reading such a document will be able to spot mistakes, but what about omissions? The system specification might be deliberately vague over certain points, because the specialists are not yet sure how much they will be able to do. A user who has never worked on the production of a system specification will have no way of detecting such omissions. How much detail should there be about response times, for example?

It is no answer to say that the user approves the system specification. The user is being forced to play the specialist's game, and is bound to lose. The principle is wrong, but the practice is even worse. System development normally requires a great deal of systems analysis. This, as the name suggests, means analysing the existing systems. Manual procedures are investigated and flow-charted, and the results incorporated into the system specification. This is done by specially trained people called systems analysts, and the theory is that they know how to set about uncovering all the details of the way a system works.

In the past there may have been some truth in this. If a system is to perform calculations or process input in a clearly defined way, a logical approach to the problem should be adequate. However, logic is only of use in determining how to get from A to B. It does not provide any insights into the deviations which may occur *en route*. In practice, this means that a systems analyst is dependent on people giving a full and clear description of what they do; not only what they normally do, but what they do in special cases, and even what they would do if certain sets of circumstances were to arise.

34

The analyst's logical skills will enable gaps in the information to be identified, but there is no means of detecting total omissions. Many first attempts at computerizing accounting systems have come to grief because of this problem. It is one thing to describe the normal flow of work through an accounts department, and quite another to take account of all the deviations from the norm that occur. Manual systems have an almost infinite degree of flexibility built into them. If something unusual occurs, a note can be written on the appropriate piece of paper, card, or file. Once these have been computerized, the writing of notes is impossible; all eventualities must be foreseen.

According to the traditional view, the answer to this problem is that the user must take full responsibility for approving the system specification. One reason why this does not make sense has already been given: the user has no conception of what a system specification ought to look like, and so is not in a position to approve one. A further difficulty is now apparent. The systems analyst is held up as a specialist who knows how to carry out a full analysis of the existing system, but at the end of the day the user is expected to say whether or not the job has been done thoroughly. Traditional systems philoscphy casts the users in the role of ignorant onlookers and then expects them to take full responsibility for everything which the specialists do.

It should be clear by now that the traditional approach was determined not by any desire to find the most efficient means of developing systems but by a concern on the part of the specialists to avoid any responsibility in the event of failure. A great deal of system development is undertaken by systems houses. Their primary concern is to ensure that they make a profit, and given the high failure rate of computer projects, they can only do this by defining responsibilities on the project in such a way that they always emerge on the winning side. The most difficult part of any computer project is to get the system specification right. Provided that the user has full responsibility for approving this specification, the systems house can only lose money through incompetence in carrying it out.

Some companies do not use systems houses. They have their own computer departments. But the same problem arises. The nature of conventional computer operations with batch processing and teams of specialists for operating the computer and writing programs leads to a gulf between computers and users, both physically and mentally. Computer departments are consequently regarded with suspicion and fear, and so feel the need to protect themselves against possible reprisals. The systems philosophy developed by systems houses has come in very handy here for it ensures that the computer department can never be responsible for the failure of a project, except through total incompetence.

Traditional systems philosophy is supposed to have arisen as the most effective way of managing a computer project. Its real purpose is to vindicate the specialists and to ensure that responsiblity for failure is seen to rest with the user. The user is discouraged from acquiring specialist skills such as systems analysis and programming in order to protect the specialists from criticism, but is expected to be responsible for the way these tasks are performed.

At one time there was some excuse for maintaining a clear distinction between users and specialists. The computer was a remote machine, requiring interim stages of data preparation before it could be accessed. All programming was a specialist task. This is no longer the case. It is time to realize that the task of analysing jobs in detail is not a specialist activity, but one which is best performed by someone who is familiar with the jobs. It is true that the user is the only person who can be sure that the systems analysis is correct. But to do this, the user needs training in the disciplines and possibilities of computing. In so far as specialist skills are required, the user must acquire them.

This view is certain to meet with the objection that users do not have the time to acquire these specialisms. Three things need to be said in response to this:

1. It is impossible to use mini computers to their full potential without knowing anything about them. If full use is to be made of the technological advances, users will have to get more involved.
2. Much more time is wasted if computer projects fail altogether (as so many do) than if adequate time and consideration are given to user training in the first place.
3. The problem involved in systems analysis being carried out by people who are effectively outsiders to the user operation are bad enough in the more traditional computer applications; they are insurmountable in the development of systems which revolve around information management.

This last point requires explanation. The difficulties of systems analysis in an environment such as an accounts department, where there are many deviations from the norm, have already been discussed. However, although there may be many hidden complications in the way an accounts department performs its work, at least the overall objectives are clear. Accounting procedures have been developed over a long period of time, and there are generally accepted principles.

This is not the case with all disciplines. It is not the case with personnel management, for example. There is no generally accepted body of opinion, even in broad terms, as to what a personnel department ought to do. Although attempts have been made over a number of years to improve the situation, it is fantasy to suppose that the objectives and principles of personnel management can be defined with anything like the clarity of accounting principles. Carrying out a systems analysis of a personnel department is inseparable from attempting to define its role within the company.

Most personnel managers, when they talk of computerizing their records, have an idea that the current system is holding them back, and that if the immediate problems could be resolved, they could concern themselves with more worthwhile matters. In other words the value of computerization lies for them as much in the provision of totally new facilities as in the resolution of existing problems. The systems analysis they require is not just an analysis of the existing systems within their department, but an analysis of all the systems that they feel could or should exist. The definition of their role within the company, and the identification of problems and objectives, take precedence over the analysis of existing systems. For this reason it cannot be tackled by someone from outside the department. The work must be done from within. To a large extent information management is inescapably a computerized activity. It cannot be done manually except in a very limited way, so there are no manual systems to analyse.

This chapter has discussed the revolution in hardware and software, and suggested that a revolution in systems philosophy is required to exploit these advances to the full. Where should a personnel manager who wants to investigate personnel computer systems begin? Who can he turn to for help or advice? An attempt must now be made to answer these questions.

Where to start

The discussion of systems philosophy concentrated on the case in which an entirely new system is developed. In fact, systems development is normally confined to modifying existing systems. Entirely new work is expensive and time-consuming, and also very risky, no matter how it is tackled. Developing a personnel computer system *ab initio* is certainly not to be advised. The sensible course is to buy a package, and tailor it if necessary.

The advantage of buying a package is that it can be seen in operation, tested out, and evaluated in the light of a company's requirements. The tests performed should be comprehensive and this is discussed in detail in Chapter 9. The organization selling the package should also be prepared to offer training, advice, and support during implementation, along the lines discussed in Chapter 10. It is part of the purpose of this book to evaluate what a system should do, and to identify the services that should be supplied with it.

The alternative to buying a package is to develop a system. Some systems houses undertake what are known as turnkey projects for systems development, that is, they arrange the purchase of the hardware, supply the project team, advise on installation of the equipment and the means of getting existing records into the computer, and undertake to provide training. This sounds marvellous. In practice it is normally not so. Systems development is too dificult and risky to be undertaken on a turnkey basis. It requires a much longer term commitment, and a degree of involvement from the user which the concept of turnkey projects is supposed to avoid.

The only way to measure whether a systems house has provided what was expected on a turnkey project is to measure the results against the system specification. But a major part of the development work on the project is directed towards preparing the specification. Hence the user has no real idea what the system will eventually look like. Under these circumstances it is almost impossible to prove that a systems house has failed to meet its commitments.

The most important single piece of advice offered in this book is: buy a package. The key questions which now arise are: what should the package do and how should the implementation be tackled? That is what the rest of this book is about. The salient features of a personnel computer system were discussed in the last chapter. The next chapter deals with two of these features: the letter writing and dictionary facilities.

3. Letter writing and dictionary facilities

A personnel computer system must have facilities for letter writing and dictionary handling. They are fundamental elements in each of the principal programs within the system, and it will never achieve the objectives identified in Chapter 1 without them. Why are they fundamental? Letter writing is fundamental for two reasons:

1. A substantial part of any manual system is concerned with the production of letters and documents, as opposed to the updating of records and reports.
2. Only by combining the process of producing a letter (or document) with the process of updating records can the possibility of discrepancies between the two be eliminated, and a definitive check be maintained on the accuracy of the records.

Dictionary handling is fundamental because it is the only way of introducing the necessary degree of flexibility into a large and complex system. A great many elements in the system will be subject to change, some on a regular and some on an irregular basis. These elements may vary from the code assigned to a training course to instructions on the way the recruitment system is to behave under given circumstances. If such things are written into the programs, the system's life will be measured in days. Instead, they need to be contained in a dictionary, which can be updated quickly and easily by the operator, when required.

This chapter deals with the letter writing and dictionary facilities. It therefore differs from the next three chapters, each of which is concerned with the requirements in a specific area of the system. Letter writing and dictionary facilities cut across and underly all areas of the system. Letter writing will be discussed first, but references to the dictionary will be unavoidable, since the two facilities overlap. These references should become clearer in the second half of the chapter.

Letter writing facilities

WHAT LETTER WRITING MEANS

It is easy to say that a personnel computer system should enable all letters and documents to individuals to be produced automatically as a result of a person's record being updated, but it is difficult to appreciate fully what this means. There is a common misconception in connection with the idea of automatic letter writing which must be dispelled at the outset. The letter writing in question here has nothing at all to do with word processing. It is not being suggested that the computer should double as a word processor. The claims of word processing have already undergone demolition work in Chapter 1. What must now be stressed is that the objective of word processing—whether or not it is satisfactorily achieved—has no place in a personnel computer system.

The great strength of a word processor lies, or should lie, in its ability to reformat text. If the operator indicates that an extra sentence is to be inserted in the middle of the text, the word processor will take the sentence, insert it, and reformat the rest of the text, so that retyping is not required to maintain an acceptable layout. This is a highly specialized operation, and its advantages are most readily apparent in tasks such as the revision of manuals. Often a minor modification to a passage in a manual will require extensive retyping. A word processor removes the need for this.

A personnel computer system does not need to reformat text. It does need to handle standard letters, but the complexities involved lie not in the reformatting of text but in the diversity of sources from which the information to appear on the letter may be drawn, and the way in which these sources need to be processed. For example, the system will be required to produce an assignment letter, whenever an employee is to be sent on assignment. The trigger for producing the letter is simply that an individual's record is updated to indicate a revised location, an assignment job title, and the date, length, and status of the assignment. The letter produced as a result of this simple operation may be three or four pages long, and will consist of a number of parts:

1. The text itself.
2. Entries from the data base.
3. Entries from the dictionary.
4. Insertions specified by the operator.
5. Results of calculations performed by the system on the basis of values obtained from the data base, the dictionary, and the operator, either separately or in conjunction with one another.

Insertions from the data base will include such things as name, address, department, employee number, salary, members of family included (name, relationship, and, in the case of children, date of birth), date of assignment, length, and status.

Entries from the dictionary may be of three kinds:

1. Expansion of codes stored on the data base. Examples of this would be location and job title.
2. Pieces of information that are linked to location by virtue of being standard conditions for anyone in a particular place, for example, client, percentage uplift on salary, standard working week, hours for which overtime will be paid, location allowance and medical cover.

3. Interpretation of instructions passed by programs on the way certain parts of the letter should be completed, for example, deducing from the initials of the originator of the letter the reference to appear at the top, the extension number to print, and the signatory and job title to appear at the bottom.

Items supplied directly by the operator will be both peculiar to the individual and of a kind that is not considered useful to store on the data base. The obvious example is special conditions, such as 'subject to the discretion of the resident manager, all reasonable expenses incurred by way of accommodation and travelling will be met by the company, until it is possible to arrange normal accommodation, as specified in the rest of this letter'. The data base should store an indicator that special conditions apply for this individual, but it will not be practicable or economical to store the full details.

Facilities for arithmetic are required because an assignment letter will normally contain calculations based on current salary. In the simplest case, the letter will state current salary, percentage uplift, the amount that this represents, and the assignment salary (the total of current salary and the amount of uplift). A more complicated letter might involve two uplifts, and the second one might apply either to current salary or to salary as modified by the first uplift. The system must be capable of accepting instructions on the kind of calculations to perform within a standard letter in a given set of circumstances.

It should be clear from this brief analysis of the constituents of an assignment letter that the facilities required for letter writing in a personnel computer system are complex, and that they bear no relation to word processing. A word processor could never meet these requirements, because it is a general purpose tool, and the facilities required in a personnel computer system are inextricably linked to the management of personnel records. The letters can be produced from the system only because it registers such things as current transactions and standard assignment conditions. In other words, the letter writing system is an integral part of the personnel computer system, and not something coupled onto it.

The discussion that follows will be split into three main parts: the mechanism for triggering the production of a letter; the system for running letters off; and details about the way the letter writing system should work, including the facilities which should be available to operators for setting up new standard letters within the system.

TRIGGERING THE PRODUCTION OF A LETTER

A personnel computer system consists of a collection of interrelated programs. To perform a given task—updating personnel records or updating recruitment records—the operator must use a particular program. The first question to be asked when considering the mechanism for triggering the production of a letter is, therefore, 'Which programs will be required to generate letters?' Clearly the reporting programs will not need to produce letters; their task is solely to produce reports. Nor will the requirement be connected with housekeeping, since this is linked not to changes in individual circumstances, but to general decisions about system management. In general, the programs concerned will be those that update one of the data bases, because they are the programs that change an individual's details, and so require the generation of a letter. These programs, which are discussed in detail in later chapters, are concerned with recruitment updating, personnel records updating, salary reviews, and redundancies. There is also a potential requirement connected with the main enquiry program since it may be necessary to find everyone who satisfies certain criteria and to send them a predefined letter. For example, a company may need to identify everyone who has a company car, and write to them about a change in policy.

The second question to be resolved is what information the operator will need to pass to one of these programs in order to generate a letter. The individual concerned and the details updated will already be available to the program by virtue of the fact that an update to the records is being made. The letter writing program should supply standard inserts and operations. All that the operator should need to provide is the code for the letter to be produced, and the initials of the signatory. There is no other source from which these can be derived.

The question now arising is how the letter and signatory should be supplied to the letter writing program. This point is dealt with in detail during discussion of the individual programs but, in summary, the provisions are as follows:

1. In the recruitment system, the letter to be sent is indicated by an operation number, which is the basic update made to an applicant's record on every occasion to indicate the stage that has been reached. There is a unique relationship between operation number and letter type. Each applicant's record will store the initials of the recruiter dealing with the application. This entry should default to the recruiter whose initials have been associated with the vacancy concerned via the job title dictionary, but the operator must be able to update it.
2. In the personnel records system, the operator will need to supply the letter type. A simple command (for example, 'LT') entered at the bottom of an individual's screen can indicate that a letter is required. The program should store a default value for the signatory (probably the personnel director), but a quick and simple facility should be available for changing it.
3. The salary review program should store letter type and signatory on the workfile used for experimentation. Facilities should be available for providing this information in the same way as salary updates,

either as a bulk update concerning a group of people or as an individual update.

4. Redundancy letters can be dealt with in the same way as salary review letters. However, it may be considered sufficient to provide a simpler facility whereby everyone to be made redundant will receive the same letter from the same signatory. In this case it will simply be a matter of the program asking the operator once and for all which letter is to be sent and who the signatory is.

5. Letter writing facilities are required in the enquiry system to send letters to individuals who meet a given set of criteria. All that is required is that the enquiry system should identify the individuals who qualify in the normal way, and then ask the operator for the letter and signatory to be used.

This is an outline of the way letters will be triggered from the programs that need to produce them. Essentially, the question resolves itself into one of how the operator causes a given letter and signatory to be associated with the individuals to whom a letter is to be sent. The details will become clearer in the chapters dealing with these programs. It is now necessary to consider the other end of the process, that is, how will the letters be run off?

THE SYSTEM FOR RUNNING OFF LETTERS

Generating letters from an application program is a separate process both logically and physically from running them off. The operator should be able to update a person's record at any time without having to check that the printer is available and loaded with the correct paper. To achieve this separation, the program that generates the letter should write it to a file, and the letter writing program should access this file for the purpose of printing the final product.

It is most important to consider the type of device on which the letters will be printed. They must look reasonably like typed letters, rather than a computer product. The obvious solution is to use a daisy wheel printer. This is a printer which produces output reasonably similar to that produced by a typewriter. It is specifically designed for printing high-quality texts rather than lengthy reports. There are some problems associated with daisy wheel printers. They are much slower than the type of printer normally linked up to a computer system. They contain more mechanical parts, and so are less robust. Finally, the supposed high quality is not always what it is made out to be, and finding suitable stationery to use can be a problem.

With regard to speed, it is most important to time the printer printing the letters which it will be required to produce. This test must be carried out with the printer linked to the computer system which is to drive it, because its speed is determined by the hardware, software, and interfacing as well as by its own design. Quality can be greatly improved by the use of carbon ribbons, even though they have to be changed frequently. Finally, some firms that deal in computer stationery have facilities for mounting a company's headed paper on a backing sheet in a way that enables it to be fed continuously through the printer and yet to be torn off with a quick movement leaving no jagged edge. It is possible to mount paper in this way with carbon sets in between. Another possibility is to use a device known as a cut sheet feeder. This feeds single sheets of paper through a printer from a stack at the back. It can provide a simple and economical solution to the problem, but cut sheet feeders do not normally work with multipart stationery.

The alternative to using a daisy wheel printer is to print the letters on the fast printer. This will not produce the same quality, and it will be obvious that it is a computer produced letter, but it will be much faster. If there is no objection to a letter which looks obviously computerized, this is probably the best solution. However, most companies attach considerable importance to the appearance of their letters, and in this case a daisy wheel printer is to be recommended.

So far, attention has been directed towards the hardware required for letter production. Thought must now be given to the means for running letters off once a program has written them to a file. The first point to make is that it is sensible for different programs to write to different files. If this is not done, letters produced from different programs will be muddled up together, and this is most inconvenient, especially if they need to be run on different paper. It must also be possible to rerun letters, in case a problem arises with the printer, or the wrong paper is inserted. This is best done by numbering the letters. The numbers should print out, and the operator should be able to set the letters back if required.

The two aspects of letter writing covered so far are the mechanism for triggering the production of a letter and the system for running them off. It now remains to discuss the central issue: the way the system should work, and the means for creating new standard letters.

HOW THE LETTER WRITING SYSTEM SHOULD WORK

The example of an assignment letter that was adduced earlier in this chapter indicated that letter writing in a personnel computer system was a complicated matter. The emphasis lies not on the reformatting of text but in the manipulation of standard components. Standardization is the crux of the matter. Can it be achieved, and if so, how? The first point to recognize is that a high percentage (anything from 50 to 80 per cent) of the letters which a personnel department produces will undoubtedly be standard. Most departments recognize this fact by using preprinted texts to which names and addresses are added by a typist. Recruitment is very largely a repetitive operation, and no one pays too much attention to the precise wording of such things as a salary review letter.

The majority of letters, therefore, pose no great problem. Nevertheless, the minority can cause difficulties that are out of all proportion to their volume. It is not enough for a system to cope with 80 per cent of letters. Anything under 99 per cent is unacceptable. The strength of the system lies in its comprehensiveness. There should be a clear philosophy that all letters are produced through the system. The problem, then, is how to deal with the less standard cases. This problem resolves itself into two parts. The first part is well illustrated by some examples from recruitment. If an applicant is to be sent a regret letter, the wording may be varied slightly to reflect differences in the route by which the application was made and the extent to which it may be of interest in the future. The letter may need to reflect whether it refers to a normal interview, an open house, or a visit to a university for graduate interviews. It may be intended to discourage the applicant altogether from applying again, to be polite but conclusive, to suggest that there may be an opening in the future, or even to request the applicant to make contact again at a later date.

All these possibilities affect the wording of the letter, but the best way to deal with them is to treat each one as a separate standard letter, rather than as a variation on the same one. It is much simpler to operate in this way, both for the operator and for the computer. Naturally, it imposes a heavy burden of analysis on the people who set up the system, but it is not an impossible burden. Once the essential differences have been identified, it is a matter of self-discipline for the personnel department to filter out the inessential ones. Therefore, the first aspect of standardization is concerned with the definitive analysis of standard tasks, operations, and circumstances, and with agreement within the department to work in an organized and disciplined manner.

The second aspect is concerned principally with contracts of employment, whether it be the initial contract, a modification to it, or a document such as an assignment letter. These documents differ from ordinary letters in that they are concerned not with communicating a basic message but with detailing a set of conditions. Although each individual condition may be standard, the number of possible permutations is vast, and it would be absurd to treat each possible combination as standard. Certain combinations will be standard, but it is the elements of the document rather than the total product which are standard in this case.

The letter writing system needs to recognize this fact. It should handle two types of components: standard letters and standard clauses. A letter will normally be complete by itself. A clause will be designed for use in combination with other clauses, strung together so as to appear in the form of a letter text. Letters may be indicated by a two character code, and clauses by a three character code (there are more of them). Combinations of clauses that are likely to be used may be strung together and referenced by a single code, known as a clause combination. For example, clause combination 12 might consist of clauses 2, 7, 9, 27, 136, 212. It should be possible for the operator to request the printing of these clauses either by giving the clause combination or by quoting the individual clause numbers. The latter technique would be used only where there was no standard clause combination in existence. The clause combinations should be stored in the dictionary, so that they can be created and altered at will.

Would clauses or clause combinations ever be used in conjunction with standard letters? In one sense they certainly would be. A contractual document would normally have a covering letter of a standard type. The clauses that followed would comprise an attachment to the letter, and so would be part of it in a sense, although printed on a separate sheet or sheets of paper. There might also be a requirement for clauses to be interspersed in a letter text. However, this can be complicated both for the operator and for the computer. It is simpler to have several standard letters. Unless a department has specialized needs which involve this facility, it is best avoided. The point must be considered, but it should not be pursued without good cause.

A need has been identified for standard letters and standard clauses, and for a means of putting clauses together in clause combinations. These are the basic components of the system, but the question of how they are to be manipulated has still to be considered. It is best tackled by breaking it down into parts: the text, standard additions (for example, signatory), basic options (such as the number of copies to be produced), and variable additions (that is, everything else). The last two are dealt with together in the section entitled 'Letter Parameters'.

THE TEXT

The part of a letter or clause referred to as 'the text' is the part that is entirely standard, in other words, the part that will remain unchanged whatever operator, data base, dictionary, or program insertions may be made. In the case of a standard letter it may conveniently be stored as a normal file within the system. Manufacturers of mini computer systems should supply standard programs for creating and modifying such files quickly and easily in any application. In principle there is no reason why clauses should not be stored as files as well. But it could result in a confusing and uneconomical use of space. If there were 500 clauses, the system would have to handle 500 files. There is, therefore, an argument for putting them all in one file, with a specially designed program to create, access, and update them.

The words of text should be entered in the file precisely as they are to appear in the letter or clause. Spaces will have to be left where insertions are to be made from one source or another, and it may be necessary to put an indicator for an insertion (inverted commas, for example), and possibly also a symbol for its length. If an insertion is to be of unspecified length, it must occur in a place where there will always be space for it to print out without overprinting something else or going off the page. This normally means placing it at the end of a paragraph, and paying careful attention to the possible length of the insertion.

STANDARD ADDITIONS

Every letter contains parts that are peculiar to its originator. The letter should end with the name of the signatory and the appropriate job title. It is useful to print the extension number of the signatory in the top right-hand corner. Also, a single system may be providing a service to several different companies within the same organization, and in this case the company name printed out at the end of the letter will need to be different. Again, this is an area in which the greatest possible flexibility should be provided, and this is best achieved through the dictionary. Earlier in the chapter, consideration was given to the way in which basic information necessary for the production of a letter could be passed to the letter writing system. Signatory was one of the items to be passed across by all programs. Signatories should exist as dictionary entries, and the following information should be attached to them: name of signatory, job title, extension number, and company. These additions can then be made automatically to the standard text, with a substantial saving in time, and one that would not be possible in a word processing system.

LETTER PARAMETERS

The aspects dealt with so far have been those that are fixed either by reference to the letter text or by reference to the signatory. This still leaves the most complicated parts: those that vary from individual to individual. There has to be a method for the operator to indicate to the system how the variable parts of the letter are to be handled, when the standard letter is originally introduced. This may conveniently be referred to as a letter parameter, or in the case of clauses, a clause parameter. Clause parameters are similar but do not need to duplicate information that has already been supplied in a connected letter parameter, for example, number of copies. Letter parameters are sets of instructions to the system about the way to compile a given letter. The parameter should be stored in the dictionary, to provide the required flexibility, but it will need to be generated by means of a special program. This program must ask the operator all the questions that need to be resolved to provide the system with a complete set of instructions for producing the required letter.

There are three questions that this program will need to resolve at the beginning: the number of copies to produce, the data base to access, and the type of salutation. The number of copies is as much a part of the standard letter as anything else. If the letter is standard, the number of copies should be standard as well, and it is a waste of time for the operator to specify it at the time the letter is written. Of course, the question being asked is not so much 'How many copies are to be produced?' as 'How many times is this letter to be printed?'. The actual number of copies will be determined also by the stationery in the printer, for example, each printing may produce several copies. The data base to access is a straight-forward input, since the answer will be either recruitment or personnel.

TYPES OF SALUTATION

The type of salutation is more complicated. Several different sorts of letter will need to be produced. The most common sort will begin 'Dear Mr Smith' and end 'Yours sincerely'. However, there will be occasions when the company wishes to address members of staff in a less formal fashion, for example, when congratulating them on 35 years service with the company. On these occasions 'Dear Fred' will be more appropriate than 'Dear Mr Smith', and it is stored on the personnel data base as name known by (see page 83). These two forms of address may be referred to as formal and informal.

A further complication is that the system will not be writing exclusively to applicants and employees. References for employment or for building societies will be addressed to third parties who have no connection with the company, and so are not stored on either data base. In these cases the operator will need to tell the system who to send the letter to, supplying both the address block and the words to appear after 'Dear'. The letter should end 'Yours sincerely'. This may be referred to as the blank saluta-tion. A variation on this is the impersonal salutation. This would be used, for example, when writing for an employment reference to a personnel manager whose name was not available. In this case, the operator will need to supply the address block, but the letter should begin 'Dear Sir' and end 'Yours faithfully'.

The last type of salutation refers exclusively to letters to agencies which supply staff at an hourly rate. Agency employees are stored on the system with a code to indicate the agent who employs them (see page 85). The dictionary should store the full name and address for each agency code. When letters are written in connection with agency employees, they will need to go to the agent rather than the employee (letters about a change in the hourly rate, for example). When a letter is generated from an agent's record, the system should send the letter to the name and address stored in the dictionary against the code found in the relevant record. The name in this case will be the name of the company, the letter should begin 'Dear Sir' and end 'Yours faithfully'.

In summary, there are five basic types of salutation.

1. Formal: letter to employee or applicant beginning 'Dear Mr Smith'.
2. Informal: letter to employee beginning 'Dear Fred'.
3. Blank: system asks for details of addressee and what is to appear after

'Dear', and ends 'Yours sincerely'.

4. Impersonal: system asks for details of addressee; begins 'Dear Sir' and ends 'Yours faithfully'.
5. Agency: system reads agency code in individual's record, derives address block from agency dictionary, begins letter 'Dear Sir' and ends 'Yours faithfully'.

These salutations will be written into the parameter for the standard letter. In general, a standard letter will always require a given form of salutation. If exceptions were found—and this should be very rare—there would have to be two standard letters with identical texts and insertions but different salutations. One final point should be made in connection with this subject: letters to employees can normally be addressed to their department, but occasionally they may need to go to their home address. This could be handled by duplicating the first two types of salutation: formal and informal. However, this becomes a little unwieldy. An alternative is to say, for example, that all letter codes beginning with a given character or range of characters will go to the home address and the rest to the individual's department.

When the operator creating a new standard letter has indicated the number of copies to be produced, the data base to access, and the type of salutation, the system will need to be told where to find the insertions for the blank spaces in the letter text. The operator must therefore supply an insertion string, and this may be composed of four elements: data base items, free entries, dictionary insertions, and arithmetic operations.

DATA BASE ITEMS

In the simplest case, the letter will require the data base item value to be printed in the letter text in exactly the same form as it is stored on the data base. The letter text may say 'your salary has been increased from £ . . . . . to £ . . . . .'. The letter parameter will only need to know which data base item to look at for the value to be inserted. These might be LASTSAL and BASESAL. These data base item names must therefore be supplied to the letter parameter generating program by the operator at the time when the new standard letter is added to the system. The parameter that is produced will then be used by the letter writing program, whenever this standard letter is called, to find out what to insert in the blanks.

Some data base items will require editing before they are printed. For example, dates should be turned round the right way (the system will store them backwards to facilitate sorting) and slashes should be inserted, that is '801225' becomes '25/12/80'. Times (such as interview times) should be converted from, for example, '1030' to '10:30'. If an item requires editing, '(E)' can be added after the data base item name when the parameter is generated. The system can store the way in which each item that may require editing should be edited.

49

FREE ENTRIES

A free entry is an insertion that has to be given in full by the operator at the time when the letter to the individual is written (written to the file, that is, it will not necessarily be run off on the printer at the same time). An example of this might be an interview letter. The text may conclude 'when you arrive in reception, please ask for . . .' If the interviewer varies from letter to letter, the operator will have to supply the appropriate name in full whenever this letter is used. The way to achieve this is to get the parameter to ask the operator a question when the letter is used, and to insert the reply in the blank space. The question could be 'Who is interviewer? (answer in maximum 20 characters)' and the answer might be 'Mr D. Reynolds.'

How can the letter parameter do this? The answer is to assign a question to each free entry, and to store the text of the question in the dictionary with a question number. All that the parameter need store is the question number. Question numbers will need to be flagged as such, so that they cannot be confused with other types of inserts, for example, 'Q12'.

DICTIONARY INSERTS

The dictionary is used to store the expansion of codes on the data base, and information related to these codes. For example, the location dictionary will store such things as standard assignment conditions in addition to the expansion of a location code. Any of this information might be required in a letter, so the letter parameter will need to know which part of the dictionary entry is to be retrieved. The starting point, however, is to recognize that all dictionary entries are related to data base items, and that the first thing the letter parameter will need to know is which data base item to read in order to find the code to reference in the dictionary.

Different data base items will need to have their codes referenced in different parts of the dictionary, but this is not a problem that need concern the operator. It should be handled by the letter parameter generating program itself, and the necessary additions should be made automatically to the letter parameter as it is created. The dictionary will be storing a string of characters, and the answer to the problem of how to decide which part of them should be used in the letter is for the operator to give the number of the character from which the letter writing program is to start reading the insertion, and how many characters it is to read. The finished product will look like this: 'LOCATION (22,40)' meaning take the code stored in the data base item LOCATION on this individual's record, find out what the dictionary is storing between characters 22 and 40 of the entry for that code, and insert it into the blank space in the letter.

ARITHMETIC OPERATIONS

Arithmetic is required in personnel letters in connection with salary, particularly when an employee is given an assignment that involves special adjustments to overall pay. The arithmetic operations that will be required in these cases are: addition, subtraction, multiplication, division, and percentages. The most common case would be for a data base item (salary) to be uplifted by a percentage stored in the dictionary (the location dictionary stores standard assignment conditions) or for values already calculated in the letter to be added together. These are not the only possibilities, however. A data base item might be multiplied by a constant or by a free entry. Any of the components discussed so far could participate in an arithmetical operation, either with another component of the same type or with one of a different type.

On this basis, there are five possible components of any arithmetical operation, and this results in 15 permutations of elements, ranging from the essential to the highly unlikely:

Data base item value	by dictionary insert	
Data base item value	by calculated value	essential
Dictionary insert	by calculated value	
Calculated value	by calculated value	
Data base item value	by constant	highly desirable
Data base item value	by free entry	
Free entry	by calculated value	desirable
Constant	by calculated value	
Dictionary insert	by free entry	
Dictionary insert	by constant	unlikely
Free entry	by constant	
Data base item value	by data base item value	
Dictionary insert	by dictionary insert	highly unlikely
Free entry	by free entry	
Constant	by constant	

An example of the four essential ones (in the order in which they are listed above) would be provided by an assignment letter that provides for two uplifts, the second of which is to be applied to the salary as uplifted by the first one. The text of the letter would show the following (the first line is a straightforward insertion from the data base without any arithmetic).

Base salary	10 000
Uplift 1 (20%)	2 000
Uplifted salary	12 000
Uplift 2 (25%)	3 000
Assignment salary	15 000

If standard arithmetical notation is used, and the elements of the calculation are specified in the way suggested above in the sections on data base items, free entries, and dictionary inserts, there is no difficulty in specifying to the letter parameter generating program what is to be done.

Constants can be written exactly as they are. Values that have already been calculated will require a cross referencing system. The simplest solution is to assign an alphabetic character to each calculated value that is to be referenced later in the parameter. It may be distinguished by inverted commas (commas and brackets are already in use). Using this system of notation, and assuming that the relevant percentage uplifts are stored in positions 25 to 29 and 31 to 35, respectively, of the location dictionary, the arithmetical operations to be performed would be specified to the letter parameter generating program as follows:

SALARY, SALARY % LOCATION (25,29) 'A'
SALARY + A 'B', B % LOCATION (31,35) 'C', B + C

Translated this means that the insertion values are:

1. Data base item SALARY.
2. Data base item SALARY multiplied by a percentage stored in positions 25 to 29 of the dictionary entry corresponding to the code in the data base item LOCATION. Call the result of this calculation 'A'.
3. Data base item SALARY plus 'A'. Call the result of this calculation 'B'.
4. 'B' multiplied by the percentage value in positions 31 to 35 of the dictionary entry for the code stored in the data base item LOCATION. Call the result of this calculation 'C'.
5. 'B' plus 'C'.

In summary there is no difficulty in defining a simple form of arithmetical notation to indicate to the letter parameter generating program the operations that are to be performed.

A letter parameter is a set of instructions to the system about the way to derive the values to be inserted in a letter. The parameter is generated by a program that elicits the instructions from the operator when a new standard letter is introduced into the system by asking a series of questions:

How many copies?
Which data base?
What type of salutation?
Which data base items (and edit forms)?
Which free entry questions?
Which dictionary inserts? (Referenced by data base item names and the range of the characters to be read from the dictionary entry.)
What arithmetical operations?

A program that works logically through these questions will enable parameters to be generated quickly and easily, and so will provide the required flexibility for introducing new standard letters.

In conclusion, it is perhaps worth remembering that the greatest strength of the letter writing system is the extreme ease with which letters may be sent to individuals, once the text and parameters have been introduced into the system. In any one of the programs that write letters, the operator has only to supply the letter code and signatory (for example 3M, AI), and in many cases the program handles even this automatically. In recruitment, for example, the letter code is linked via the dictionary to the operation number to which the applicant has been updated, and the signatory exists as a default value for each vacancy (a default value is one which is allocated by the system in the absence of instructions to the contrary from the operator). In personnel records, the signatory is set to a default value whenever the program is run, and only the letter type need be set. The salary review program is designed to assign letter codes and signatories to groups of employees, with individual changes as an option. The redundancy program uses default values for letter and signatory, and the enquiry program assigns the same letter and signatory to all members of a group selected by a single procedure.

The production process has been reduced to the absolute minimum, taking all the strain from the operator, and greatly increasing the speed at which tasks can be performed; the recruitment process is on average ten times as fast. It is to be expected that providing facilities so fast and flexible will involve a degree of complexity at some point. That point is the generation of letter parameters. Consequently, this process requires a special program, and the person responsible for introducing new standard letters into the system must become familiar with a special type of notation. It is the concept of letter parameters and the means for generating them that extends the letter writing facility in a personnel computer system so far beyond the boundaries of word processing.

Dictionary facilities
The use to which the dictionary may be put extends well beyond the straightforward translation of codes to such things as standard assignment conditions for the production of assignment letters, and instructions to the recruitment update program about the way to behave under given sets of circumstances. Items that need to be coded are discussed in the What to store sections of Chapters 4 and 5 on recruitment and personnel records (see pages 61–64 and 82–90 respectively). In summary, the dictionary should store the following things:

Locations (including standard assignment conditions)
Job titles
Qualification and institute levels
Qualification subjects
Institutes
Courses
Languages
Fluency

Staff category
Department
Salary grade
Nationality
History comment
Vaccinations/immunizations
Agency
Rejection comments
Recruitment ratings
Notes for recruitment reports
Signatory/interviewer
Question texts
Recruitment operation levels
Letter parameters
Clause parameters
Clause combinations
Errors.

The purpose of this chapter is to clarify the nature of the dictionary, to describe the facilities required for maintaining it, to consider the way in which it will be used by interactive and reporting programs, and to examine some special sets of circumstances which have a bearing on dictionary management.

THE NATURE OF THE DICTIONARY

The dictionary is nothing other than a file that may be accessed by means of an interactive program enabling the operator to create, delete, or update entries. These entries will all be the same length, whether or not the available record space in the file is used, and they all need to consist of two parts: the key and the data. The key must obviously contain the code for which data is to be supplied, but it does not only contain the code. Many codes in the system will be two characters long, and several at least will be four characters. Thus the job title code BACA may mean production manager, and the qualification code BACA may mean philosophy and psychology. In order to distinguish between the different meanings of identical codes, the system will have to prefix them with an indicator of the item or task to which they relate. This means that within the dictionary there are a number of subdictionaries, each referenced by an identifier, which is prefixed to the code. So, for example, if the job title subdictionary is to be prefixed JT and the qualification one QU, the codes cited above will become JTBACA and QUBACA, respectively, when they are stored in the dictionary. These prefixes will never be required in the data bases themselves. The adding and interpreting of prefixes should be handled by the application programs. However, the operator will need to use these prefixes when updating the dictionary. The length of the key will be determined by the length of the longest code in use in the system. If the location code is six characters long, the dictionary key will need to be eight characters to allow for the addition of a prefix. Two character codes will then need to be padded out between the prefix and the code, for example, 'RC****CA' for 'Rejection Comment CA'.

The rest of the entry will consist of data. Eighty-eight characters has been found to be a suitable length. A dictionary entry, then, consists of a total of 96 characters, eight of which comprise the key, and 88 the data. The key consists of a prefix and a code, and may be padded out if necessary. Codes with the same prefix may be referred to as a subdictionary, and all the subdictionaries exist within a single dictionary file. The next question to consider is how this dictionary is to be accessed for adding, updating, and deleting entries.

UPDATING THE DICTIONARY

A special program is required for accessing and updating the dictionary. It is clear that the operation of this program will be dominated by three commands: create a new entry, update an existing entry and delete an entry. A single character can be allocated to each of these operations. Deletion is straightforward. The entry is simply called up, and the deletion command invoked. In the case of creating or updating a record, however, consideration must be given to the format in which the data is to be supplied. It is critical to enter each item of data in the correct position, since the programs will expect to find them there. If the 88 characters contain a string of diverse information (as in the case of standard assignment conditions, for example), the operator will need help in making the appropriate entries.

The simplest solution is for the system to format the data so that each piece of information can be supplied on a new line. The system should take care of the spacing, and ensure that it all ends up in the right place. For example, the operator might have to make an entry that would be stored in the system like this:

Position   1 2 3 4 5 6 7 8 9 10 11 12 13 14 15
           S A U D I   2 5 %   N O

If an irregular format of this sort extended for 88 characters it would be very difficult to remember, and consequently putting in new data would be a slow process. The system should accept the data in this form:

SAUDI
25%
NO

It should manage the spaces itself.

The layout of the spaces may be referred to as the format, and therefore it can be said that each subdictionary has a format. It is a logical extension of the flexibility provided by the dictionary that it should be possible to alter the subdictionary formats. There is no reason why they should not be stored as dictionary entries themselves, with padding in place of a code, for example, JT******. Subdictionary formats can then be altered like any other dictionary entry to suit the operator. Altering a format will not upset an application program which accesses the subdictionary, unless the distribution of data between the 88 characters is altered.

It is also important that there should be a facility for listing subdictionaries, so that an up-to-date list of the contents of the file can be maintained. When the program is run it should first enable the operator to enter either the listing command or the name of the subdictionary to which additions, deletions, and updates are to be made.

One of the subdictionary types should be a format which enables the entry to be made simply as a string of 88 characters. This will be used mainly for creating new subdictionary formats. If the listing command is entered, the subdictionary should list to the printer. If the name of a subdictionary is given, the system should then ask for the key. Data for the key supplied should be displayed or, if the key does not already exist, it should be requested. It should be displayed or requested in the format for the appropriate subdictionary. Under this system there is complete flexibility about the codes stored in the dictionary, the nature of the subdictionaries, and the structure of the data.

USE OF THE DICTIONARY BY APPLICATION PROGRAMS

As far as application programs are concerned use of the dictionary is very simple. They take a code from the data base, add the appropriate prefix for the subdictionary to which it belongs, read the appropriate part of the data for the given entry from the dictionary, and print or display it in the specified position. A program will need the following information in order to do this:

1. Which items to expand.
2. What prefix to add to the code stored in a given data base item.
3. Which character positions of the dictionary entry to read.
4. Where to print or display them.

It should be a straightforward matter to include this information in a program, or to reference it in a report generating mechanism. Programs that use formatted screens on which codes will appear should always be designed so that there is space for the codes to be expanded.

DICTIONARY MANAGEMENT IN SPECIAL CIRCUMSTANCES

The use of a dictionary introduces immense flexibility into a system, and enables coding to be used without the presentation of data becoming unintelligible. However, coding can also give rise to problems when a

56

company revises its coding structure. The revision of coding structures is highly undesirable. When the system is set up, the greatest care should be devoted to designing structures which will stand for all time. However, it is unrealistic to ignore the possibility of restructuring altogether. A personnel computer system will contain about thirty subdictionaries, and any one of these may require restructuring for a variety of reasons. For example:

1. The coding structure may be common to several in-house computer systems, and one of these may require restructuring to be carried out.
2. There may be a change in company organization which makes restructuring unavoidable.
3. The structure originally drawn up may turn out to be unsatisfactory in practice.

The revision of coding structures should be avoided wherever possible, but it must nevertheless be catered for within the system. What are the problems? When a coding structure is revised, two things have to be done: the keys of certain entries in the dictionary have to be changed and all occurrences of the old code on the data base need to be updated to the new code. It is important that these two operations should be linked, so that discrepancies cannot arise between the two.

The best solution is for the operator to create a file giving the old codes and what they are to be changed to, for example:

AAAA, BBBB
XXXX, YYYY
etc.

As was mentioned earlier, mini computer systems should provide a simple means for an operator to create files of this type. This file should be used by two separate programs, one to update the dictionary keys and one to update the data base. The one updating the dictionary will need to know which subdictionary to address, and the one updating the data base will need to know which item is involved. Both programs should report on errors (such as codes not existing), and should provide a listing of the changes they have made. In the case of the program updating the dictionary this will be a replica of the file created by the operator, except that any errors or omissions will be reported. In the case of the program updating the data base, the employee numbers or applicant numbers of every record updated should be reported after each code change is listed in case any queries arise in the future.

This may seem an elaborate facility. However, it is indispensable. A system without a dictionary is both inflexible and unintelligible. One with a dictionary facility that does not cater for the modification of coding structures is vulnerable in the extreme. The restructuring facility should never be used with any regularity, but it should be there for when it is needed.

The letter writing and dictionary facilities described in this chapter are complex to design and manage, but only because the system is being made to do a substantial amount of work to make life easier for the operator. Members of the department who use the system regularly but are not involved in its management are provided with facilities that are flexible and readily comprehensible. It is the extension of the system into the areas of letter writing and dictionary handling which makes it so much more than a straightforward information system—makes it, in fact, a production system at the heart of the department's operation. As such, it saves a substantial amount of time, and ensures that there can never be used should become clear during the next three chapters, which concern is only necessary here to note how it will fit into the recruitment system.

This chapter has been concerned with two facilities that are fundamental to a personnel computer system. The way in which these facilities are used should become clear during the next three chapters, which concern the detailed operation of specific areas of the system: recruitment; personnel records; salary reviews and redundancies.

4. The recruitment system

Recruitment systems are much more difficult to design than at first appears. This is partly due to the complexity of the tasks that they need to encompass, a complexity that only becomes apparent when the requirements of a system are specified in detail. But it is also due to the danger of getting sidetracked. It is easy to concentrate too much on the process of selection, rather than on the recruitment process as a whole. The idea of computerized selection has a strong intuitive appeal, and there is a tendency for the system to be centred around selecting suitable applicants from a comprehensive base of information rather than around the total requirements of a recruitment campaign. This approach is misguided for two reasons. Firstly, the process of selection within a given company (as opposed to within a recruitment agency) can be made relatively simple, at least, the part that lends itself to computerization can be. Secondly, selection is not the major problem associated with the recruitment process, and therefore not the aspect around which the system should be designed.

The problems associated with recruitment and the objectives which a system should meet were discussed in Chapter 1. The overriding need was to ease the administrative load, in particular minimizing the effect of fluctuations in the level of activity. This could only be achieved if the system had the overall effect of speeding up the processing of applicants by a factor of about ten. This should be the prime consideration in the design of the system. A second requirement was to eliminate duplication, and this was to be achieved partly by combining the process of producing a letter for an individual with the process of updating his record, and partly by producing reports direct from these records without any additional input. Letter writing was dealt with in the previous chapter, and it is only necessary here to note how it will fit into the recruitment system.

This chapter begins with a brief description of the way a recruitment system should work, and goes on to give a detailed analysis of the critical design points. When a system is being designed, hundreds of decisions have to be made about the way it is to operate. Some of these are minor; some are not. A mistake on a critical decision can cause considerable delay and expense, and may even render the system unusable. Unfortunately, however, it is not always clear at the outset which of the decisions are critical to the success of the system. The purpose of the analysis in this chapter is to highlight the critical issues, and explain why they are important. The question of recruitment reports is not dealt with here. It is discussed in full in Chapter 8, together with the other reports required in a personnel computer system.

Brief description

A computerized recruitment system should completely replace all manual systems. Secretaries should be able to perform their work at a VDU rather than at a typewriter, and the process of producing a letter for an applicant should automatically update the records. It follows that the system should be simple to operate and sufficiently flexible to accommodate a wide variety of paths through the recruitment process. It should also be available throughout the day to as many members of the personnel department as may need to use it. There should be no intermediate documents between the instructions written on the application form by the recruiter and the processing of work on the VDU. In other words, the application form should be the base information document used by the secretary when processing work at the VDU. If any codes are used, the system should be capable of translating them both when they are entered or displayed on a screen and when they appear on reports. Above all, the system must be fast.

The basis for such a system is the reduction of the recruitment process to a series of standard operations, each of which is represented by a code (1A, 2A, 3A, etc.). Every applicant is allocated a number by the system when their details are first entered, and this number is written on their application form. All subsequent operations are performed simply by supplying to the system their applicant number and the number of the operation to be performed. In many cases this will be all that is required. The system will update the appropriate record and combine the relevant details for the applicant in question with the standard letter indicated by the operation number.

In some cases the system will require additional details and it should elicit these from the operator at the time the operation is performed either by means of positioning the cursor on the formatted screen or by means of direct questions asked through the letter writing system. For example, if a new applicant is being put on to the system, it will ask for their basic details (name, address, vacancy, source, and recruiter). If an interview letter is to be sent, it will ask for interviewer, time, and date. In the case of an offer, it will require salary, salary grade, hours, pay period, notice period, department, location, and start date.

There are three things above all else which are critical to the successful operation of a recruitment system:

1. The vacancy structure, that is, the means of indexing applicants, so that they can subsequently be grouped together and retrieved in whatever way may be required.
2. The operation levels, that is, the reduction of the recruitment process to a series of standard operations which encompass all possible processing routes, but which are nevertheless flexible and able to be adapted to any reporting requirements.

3. The update mechanism, that is, a means of updating applicants, under varying circumstances, about ten times as fast as a manual system.

These three aspects will be dealt with in turn, but initially it is necessary to consider the foundation of the system: what to store. Here again, an oversight can have unfortunate repercussions.

What to store

In specifying any system, the first task must be to identify the items to be stored, whether they need to be coded, and how many characters they require. This is not as straightforward as it sounds. On the one hand, the list of items must be sufficiently comprehensive to replace all existing manual systems. But on the other hand, it should only include an item if it is strictly necessary for the system to meet its objectives. The storing of redundant information wastes space, impedes the operator, and encourages opposition to the system because it is creating work rather than saving it. To take a simple example, it sounds reasonable to suggest that a recruitment system should store an indicator of whether a vacancy is technical or nontechnical. On careful consideration, however, this is clearly unnecessary. Every recruiter knows which vacancies are technical and which are nontechnical. If a report is required on the technical vacancies, the recruiter will simply specify the appropriate range. Every proposed item must be subjected to close scrutiny. What, then, is it really necessary to store?

To work at all, the system will clearly need to store an applicant's name, initials, title (Mr, Ms, Dr), address, and telephone number. Applicants will have to be allocated to a vacancy, a vacancy group (this distinction is explained later in the chapter), and a recruiter. There will also need to be an indication of the source of the application. This is all basic information, which will be relevant to every applicant without exception. How much additional information is required will depend on the stage of the recruitment process which the applicant reaches. At interview stage, it will be necessary to add interviewer, interview time, and interview date. At regret stage (or in the event of an applicant withdrawing), the system should store the reason for rejection or withdrawal and the date until which the applicant should be kept on file. When an offer of employment is made, details of the offer must be added: salary, salary grade, hours of work, pay period, notice period, department, location, and start date. If the offer has to be chased, a close of offer date will be appropriate. If it is declined, the reason and hold date should be stored (as in the case of a regret); and if it is accepted, medical and reference clearance will be required, and in some cases (if the individual is to work on a client's project) client approval. All it is necessary to know about medical clearance and client approval is whether it has been received, but in the case of references, more detail is useful, so that an offer report from the system can supply detailed information on the status of each offer. The relevant information is the number of references required and the number of references received.

A key piece of information on any applicant going through the recruitment process is the name of the person currently in possession of their papers. An application form normally has to be sent out of the personnel department to various managers or section heads, and it can easily go astray unless a close watch is kept on its movements. The system should store the name of the person to whom it was last sent and the date on which it was sent. This is all processing information.

A system should also store selection information—those items which will enable the applicant to be picked out in the future if a suitable vacancy arises. These items should include alternative vacancies for which the applicant could be considered (three should be sufficient, if the system is used sensibly), an overall rating in the applicant's main vacancy, and date of birth (this last item is only necessary if someone is going to insist on a specific age range for a job, because the relevant information on qualifications and experience is implicit in the combination of vacancy and overall rating). In addition, there are two items of information which are useful in the case of staff who may be assigned overseas: whether a single status assignment would be acceptable, and whether there are any countries to which the applicant either would not or could not go.

The system must store details of progress through the recruitment system: when, for example, was the applicant sent an application form, an offer, or a regret? This information can only be stored if the recruitment process is reduced to a series of operations, each occurring on a specific date. A way of doing this is described later in the chapter. If all potential reporting requirements are to be met, provision must be made for each applicant's record to store nine operation numbers and dates. Finally, it is useful when removing applicants from the data base to know the date of the last operation. This completes the catalogue of information about applicants.

What should the system store in connection with sources and vacancies? The only information required about sources is description, date, and cost. This, like any details of coded information common to a number of applicants, is best stored in the dictionary. The only information about vacancies which is of any real interest is how many people are required for the job title in question. It is not practical to store this in the dictionary. Changes are too frequent. There needs to be a facility within the program for updating vacancy requirements. The difficulty is that all the other items to be stored belong in an applicant's record. Vacancy requirements have nothing to do with individual applicants. Therefore, a special file is required for storing the information. This file will simply contain a list of the vacancy codes and the numbers required.

Here is a list of the items required, as they emerged from the foregoing analysis, with the suggested number of characters which should be allocated to each one indicated in brackets, and with an asterisk against items which should be coded (the implications of coding are discussed later in the chapter).

Basic details

Surname and initials	(20)
Title	(2)
Address line 1	(30)
Address line 2	(30)
Address line 3	(20)
Postcode	(10)
Telephone exchange	(16)
Telephone number	(12)
Vacancy group	(2)
Vacancy	(4)*
Recruiter	(2)*
Source	(2)*

Interview details

Interviewer	(2)*
Interview time	(4)
Interview date	(6)

Regret/withdraw/decline

Comment on rejection	(2)*
Hold until date	(4)

Offer details

Salary	(5)
Salary grade	(2)
Hours	(4)
Pay period	(1)
Notice period	(1)
Department	(3)*
Location	(8)*
Start date	(6)

Chase offer

Close date	(6)

Confirm Offer

Medical cleared indicator	(1)
Number of references required	(1)
Number of references received	(1)
Client approval indicator	(1)

Internal processing

Initials of person to whom application form sent	(2)*
Date sent	(6)

Selection information

Alternative vacancy 1	(4)*

Alternative vacancy 2	(4)*
Alternative vacancy 3	(4)*
Overall rating	(1)
Date of birth	(6)
Whether single status assignment acceptable	(1)
Countries of assignment not acceptable 1	(2)*
Countries of assignment not acceptable 2	(2)*
Countries of assignment not acceptable 3	(2)*
Operation levels	
Operation 1	(2)*
Date of 1	(6)*
Operation 2	(2)*
Date of 2	(6)
Operation 3	(2)*
Date of 3	(6)
Operation 4	(2)*
Date of 4	(6)
Operation 5	(2)*
Date of 5	(6)
Operation 6	(2)*
Date of 6	(6)
Operation 7	(2)*
Date of 7	(6)
Operation 8	(2)*
Date of 8	(6)
Operation 9	(2)*
Date of 9	(6)
Date of last operation	(6)

The items marked with an asterisk need to be coded. The definition of a coded item for this purpose is that it is validated against the dictionary. There are other items that contain codes of a sort, for example, 'M' for 'monthly' in pay period and 'Y' for 'yes' in client approval, but these are abbreviations or conventional signs rather than codes. As far as possible, codes should be both displayed and translated on the screen, subject to the restrictions imposed by the limited space available.

The vacancy structure

Why should the vacancy structure be difficult to define, and why should it be fundamental to the success of the system, as was suggested earlier in the chapter? The reason is that the concept of a vacancy is not clearly defined, and however straightforward it may appear from a human point of view, distinctions have to be drawn which, if they are ignored, will lead to serious practical difficulties in a computerized system.

The problem with the word 'vacancy' is that it is used to describe a requirement for manpower, regardless of the level of detail to which that requirement has been specified. For example, when a manager says, 'I need a recruitment status report on piping engineers', he may mean that he needs a report concerning only those people who have applied for a job with the precise title 'piping engineer'; but he may mean that he needs a report on any engineer who has applied in the piping discipline. This might include such job titles as: chief piping engineer, assistant chief piping engineer, principal piping engineer, senior piping engineer, piping engineer, and trainee piping engineer. The contents of the report will be totally different in the two cases. What is required depends on the circumstances. If the intention is to recruit someone for a specific job, the first type of report will be relevant. But if the intention is to review the overall recruitment situation in the piping group, the second will be required.

It is a simple matter to say 'the system must be capable of producing vacancy status reports'. But it is essential to add that the definition of a vacancy may vary from the requirements for a specific job title to those for a function, a discipline, a department, or even some more general category. It would be possible to specify a recruitment system in considerable detail, and yet to render it useless by omitting this point. How can the system be given the necessary flexibility? Two things are required: one directly concerned with the definition of the vacancy structure, and the other with the facilities for generating it.

The point about the definition of the vacancy structure needs to be settled first. There has to be a link between applicant and vacancy, and there has to be a series of vacancies. The important decision is the definition of the individual members of the series. Clearly there must be considerable flexibility in this respect, since no vacancy structure is fixed. But a decision must be made as to whether the vacancy structure should look like this, for example:

Vacancy number 1   Procurement
Vacancy number 2   Construction
Vacancy number 3   Engineering
Vacancy number 4   Design and draughting
Vacancy number 5   Process design

or like this:

Vacancy number 1   Chief cost engineer
Vacancy number 2   Assistant chief cost engineer
Vacancy number 3   Lead cost engineer
Vacancy number 4   Senior cost engineer
Vacancy number 5   Cost engineer

The decision should be made on the basis of which vacancy structure will enable all the information requirements to be met, and all the different types of vacancy status reports to be produced. In fact, once the nature of the problem has been recognized, the answer is obvious. It is possible to generalize from specific details. But it is not possible to be specific if only generalized information is available. Therefore, the vacancy structure must define a vacancy as the most specific level of information, namely individual job titles, and this amounts to saying that the vacancy structure in the recruitment system should be identical to the job title structure in the personnel records system.

The point about facilities for generalizing the vacancy structure is simply that it must be possible to regard several vacancies as one for certain purposes, such as reporting. There is a fundamental difference between producing a recruitment status report on a series of vacancies to be treated individually, and on the same series treated as one vacancy. The same sort order will produce different results in the two cases, and in the second case all summaries and totals for individual vacancies will be combined into one.

How is this facility to be provided? The mechanism is straightforward. Group number exists as an item on the data base. It is also stored in the job title dictionary. When an applicant is allocated a vacancy code, the group number corresponding to it is written to the data base from the dictionary. When the more general type of report is required, the system searches and sorts on group number instead of vacancy code.

In summary, then, the vacancy structure must be identical to the job title structure, and the best way to ensure that it is, is to use the same code. Instead of linking applicants to both a vacancy number and a job title code, they are linked only to a vacancy code, which is identical to the relevant job title code. It follows that there is no need to store the applicant's job title as a separate item.

This discussion of vacancy structures leads naturally to the question of selection. The chapter began with a warning about the danger of getting side-tracked when designing a recruitment system, and of paying a disproportionate amount of attention to computerized selection. It was also suggested that a company can make computerized selection relatively simple. It is now possible to clarify these points.

A distinction must be drawn between the kind of computerized selection in which a company might be interested, and the kind which is appropriate to a recruitment agency. An agency is not in a position to impose any uniformity on the requests it receives for manpower. The job title 'senior buyer', for example, means totally different things in different companies, and the agency will only be able to identify what is required or available in any particular case if a substantial amount of additional information is supplied: age, experience, salary, qualifications, and an assessor's comments. But a company is in a different position. Job titles are used, or should be used, in a consistent fashion. All the recruiter needs to know is the applicant's job title, and how he or she rates amongst other holders of that job.

To say this is not to suggest that job title and rating are the only items relevant to selection, but merely that they are all that an experienced recruiter will need to produce an initial shortlist. For any vacancy that exists there are likely to be several specific job titles from which a suitable candidate might be drawn. For example, a candidate for the job of proposal engineer may currently be working as a project or process engineer. Provided that these job titles have been used in a consistent way throughout the system, they provide a basis for selection.

Some individuals have experience in a wider range of areas than would normally be suggested by their job title, and therefore it will be necessary to store alternative job titles for them in addition to the basic title. The recruiter should be able to express the requirement in the form 'find everyone who has applied to us over the past six months as an X, a Y, or a Z or who has alternative experience as an X, a Y, or a Z and whose overall rating is P or more'. The computer can then produce a shortlist of application forms to be extracted for scanning by the recruiter. More sophisticated types of selection are counter-productive for two reasons: they involve the inputting of a large amount of information which may never be used, and they attempt to mechanize the process of selection, which is necessarily an individual business and which, except in broad outline, is rightfully carried out by a human being rather than a machine.

Operation levels

A key feature in the design of a system is the reduction of the recruitment process to a series of standard operations. Clearly a large number of possibilities must be catered for, because the routes that applicants follow are so various. Furthermore, it must be possible to change the operations or add to them from time to time as requirements change. But the difficult point is to decide how to group them together to provide a logical basis of operation of the system. If the operation code consists of a number followed by a letter (for example, 6A) the number can indicate the level of operation (for example, interview) and the letter can specify the particular type (for example, graduate second interview). The range A–Z within each level will allow for as many operations overall as the operator and recruiters can conveniently deal with. The number represents the stage in the recruitment process which the applicant has reached.

The simpler the system of operation numbers can be the better it is both from the point of view of the system and from the point of view of the operator or recruiter. If the system is to produce standard reports on such things as the number of applications, interviews, and regrets, it will need to know which operations fall into which category. If there is no simple correspondence between the operation number and the report group, the system will have to know which group every single operation code falls into. This is cumbersome, and has the added disadvantage that the information will need to be supplied whenever an operation code is added or modified.

However, the real difficulty arises in the processing of *ad hoc* reports and enquiries. Efficiency, economy, and simple physical limitations dictate that there is a limit to the number of items which can be stored on each applicant. It is not practical to store an item for every operation code (especially since these are likely to be variable). But it is practical to store one for each basic level. Nine items are acceptable, but ninety are not. When an *ad hoc* report is produced, the operator will effectively be saying, for example:

Report anyone at level 3 under regrets.
Report anyone at level 6 under offers.

The objective must be to have the same number of operation levels as logical report groups. If there are more, there may be difficulties in combining them in a simple *ad hoc* report. If there are less, the system will be unable to distinguish the required groups within a level.

One possible approach is to define each level as a range of alternatives through which each applicant must necessarily pass. This is an example of an approach which prevents critical distinctions from appearing on *ad hoc* reports. It looks like this:

1. Application form sent.
2. Application received/hold.
3. Regret/interview.
4. Regret after interview/hold after interview/offer/chase offer.
5. Accept/decline/withdraw offer.
6. Confirm offer.

This arrangement is useless for *ad hoc* reporting, because there is no way of distinguishing between regrets and interviews, regrets and offers, or offers that are going ahead and those that are not, all of which is basic information.

An obvious alternative would be to have a level for each separate type of operation listed above. But this is unnecessarily complicated, considering that what is required is that the overall recruitment status can be adequately reported. For applicants who have returned their forms, for example, it is not necessary to distinguish between those who have been informed that there is a delay in recruitment for their vacancy (that is, they have been sent a hold letter) and those who have not. The only important point for overall statistics is that they have all returned their forms and are awaiting the next stage. Similarly, there is no need to distinguish between interview and hold after interview or between offer and chase offer. It is vital when dealing with an individual applicant to know that his offer has been chased, and this will be apparent from the full two character operation code, but it is irrelevant for overall statistics.

Finally, decline and withdraw offer do not need to be separate, although it might at first seem so. If the distinction is required, it could be achieved on an *ad hoc* report by printing out the rejection/withdrawal/decline comment, which is there for that purpose. This information is required for answering the question 'Why are offers not going ahead?', but it does not affect the fact that for the purpose of quickly communicating the overall recruitment picture all these applicants are in the same class, that is, the class of offers which are not going ahead. The recommended way to organize the operation levels is, therefore, as follows:

1. Application forms sent.
2. Applications received/hold.
3. Regret.
4. Interview/hold after interview.
5. Regret after interview.
6. Offer/chase offer.
7. Accept offer.
8. Decline/withdraw offer.
9. Confirm offer.

An additional advantage of limiting the number to nine is that they are easy to remember, and the operation code only needs to be two characters long.

This is satisfactory as an analysis of operation levels, but when the progress of an applicant through the system is taken into consideration, a flaw emerges: there is a tacit assumption that an applicant will always be moving from a lower operation number to a higher one. If the applicant were to repeat an operation level or move from a higher one to a lower one, the problem would arise that the data base items required already contained information. There are two situations in which this can happen, and if they are not allowed for, they can undermine a recruitment system. They are:

1. Duplicate operations.
2. Going back down the operation ladder.

These situations are different, but the solution to them is the same.

A duplicate operation occurs when an applicant has more than one operation at the same operation level. The obvious cases are a second interview or a re-offer. It is clearly desirable to store both sets of details, but how is this to be done? Interview and offer details occupy a major part of the space in the record. If two sets of each were to be allowed for, the size of the record—and hence of the data base itself—would be significantly increased for the sake of a minority of applicants. And why should two be the limit? What happens if an applicant has a third interview or a second re-offer? Expanding the size of the record is clearly uneconomical. A more satisfactory solution is to create a second record when a duplicate operation occurs, and link it to the first one. In this way, the record size is kept to a minimum, but applicants with duplicate operations have more than one record. There need be no fixed limit to the number of linked records possible; an applicant could have three interviews and two re-offers, if required.

Going back down the operation ladder is a similar but more complex problem. This occurs when an applicant goes, for example, from level six (offer) to level one (initial contact). Why should an applicant go back down the operation ladder? There are three possible reasons:

1. A genuine progression of the application. Perhaps the applicant is being recontacted, despite initial rejection, because of a change in vacancy requirements.
2. The operator has updated the record with erroneous information, and is now correcting it.
3. A mistake. The operator did not intend to put the applicant back down the operation ladder.

Unfortunately the system will need to recognize these three cases, and respond accordingly. The first one is the only genuine case of going back down the operation ladder. The applicant is in fact progressing through the recruitment process, and therefore the existing information should remain intact. This can be dealt with in the same way as a duplicate operation. Instead of storing additional items on the record to cope with rare occurrences, or overwriting existing information, an additional record can be created and linked to the original one. In this way the existing information is stored on the old record and a new one is created with the same potential for storage. This would be simple enough if all cases in which an operator entered a lower operation level than the existing one were genuine cases of going back down the operation ladder. But this is not the case. If the operator is deliberately correcting a mistake, the existing record must be overwritten; and if a mistake is inadvertently being made, the system must reject it and neither overwrite the existing record nor create a new one. How is this to be achieved?

The first point to recognize is that it will be extremely rare for an operator to be systematically correcting operation levels lower than the current one. It is easy to make a mistake on the current operation level—and it must be easy to correct this—but something very odd is going on if there is a mistake lower down. Why was it not spotted at the time the operation was current? Was the applicant actually sent the wrong letter? If so, it was indeed a mistake, but the system is correctly recording what happened, and should not be tampered with. In view of the rarity of the occurrence, and its potentially serious implications, it is both reasonable and sensible to make this an operation that can only be carried out at a higher level of security. In other words, the system treats it as a mistake, and will not allow the operator to overwrite the record. However, someone in possession of the higher level password can overwrite records even when the system thinks that a mistake has occurred. The three possibilities are therefore reduced to two as far as the system is concerned, and the remaining problem is how to distinguish mistakes from genuine cases going back down the operation ladder.

These genuine cases are fairly limited. They are all in a sense duplicate operations. The obvious one is a repeat of the initial contact letter. In all cases of going back down the operation ladder the repeat letter will need to be slightly different from the original one. These operations will therefore necessarily have distinct operation numbers (for example, 1E recontact). Consequently, they can be flagged as ones which are not mistakes, but which should result in the creation of a second record. Where will this information about operation numbers be stored, and how will it be given the required flexibility? The answer is that it can be stored in the same place as all such information about operation numbers, the dictionary. The way in which the dictionary interacts with the update mechanism via the operation number is dealt with in the next section. The point to note here is that the dictionary should carry a flag for operations which require the creation of a new record. This mechanism can be used to generate the additional record both for duplicate operations and for going back down the operation ladder. Details from the old record (number, name, vacancy, source, etc.) should be written from the old record to the new one, except that, when going back down the operation ladder, information relating to operation levels equal to or greater than the current one should not be carried across. For example, if an applicant has been regretted and is now being recontacted, the comment on rejection and hold until date must clearly not be written to the new record, as all these things are now being reconsidered. They remain intact for historical purposes on the old record.

It should now be clear that these special situations, though they only apply to a minority of applicants, give rise to some complex problems which could cause endless confusion if they were not adequately dealt with.

Update mechanism

Speed is the most important requirement of a recruitment system, and the design should reflect this. In every case the number of key depressions by the operator should be reduced to the minimum possible for performing the operation in question. There are a number of features that can contribute towards this end, and they will be considered in turn:

1. A select screen for indicating the type of operation to be performed.
2. A formatted screen for updating individual items of information.
3. Cursor positioning linked to operation levels, so that input required from the operator is reduced to an absolute minimum.
4. Fast update facilities for dealing with special circumstances.

SELECT SCREEN

A select screen is one on which the main update options are listed with a code for each one (for example, 'CA' standing for 'create applicant'). At the top is an action box in which the appropriate code is entered. When the program is run, the operator is presented with the select screen, and the cursor sits in the action box waiting for a code to be entered. The options required in recruitment are given below, and are explained in the rest of this section.

Create applicant
Update applicant
Display applicant
Chain through applicant
Chain through vacancy
Hold vacancy
Terminate vacancy
Update vacancy.

In other words, the options on the select screen are the general categories of option available, rather than the specific operation levels which are subsequently applied to individual applicants.

The first three options are self-explanatory, and indicate to the system the way in which it is to behave. If an applicant is to be created, the system will need to allocate a number and then request the operator for all the new details. If an applicant is to be updated, the system will need to ask which one, and then to present the operator with the appropriate record and request an operation level. If an applicant is to be displayed, 'Which one?' is the only relevant question. No further operator input should be required.

The next four options are fast update facilities, and are explained below. After the option code has been entered in the action box, it will always be necessary to identify the applicant or vacancy in question. It should be possible to access applicants either by number or by name. Number is quicker, because it is shorter and avoids the difficulty of accessing the wrong person if several applicants have similar names. However, name is essential, because number will not always be available. There is often some doubt about the correct way to spell a person's name, or even what exactly it is, therefore the system should be capable of accepting a partial name (for example, Brown) and listing all names which begin in the way specified so that the operator can indicate which one is required. Vacancy options should work by reference to the vacancy code.

When the option code has been entered, the system should request the applicant number, applicant name, or vacancy code, as appropriate. This is best done by means of a permanent format on the lower part of the screen.

Vacancy code . . . .   Applicant number . . . . .
Name . . . .   No. Required . . . .

If the option specified relates to a vacancy, the cursor should go straight to the vacancy code box and await input. If the option relates to applicant, it should go to applicant number. The operator can either enter the number followed by carriage return, or press tab to go to name and enter full name or as much of it as is known. The last facility (update vacancy) should simply cause the system to request the vacancy code, followed by the number required.

Since the select screen should have plenty of space on it, it can also be used for displaying error messages, or asking the operator questions (as is necessary when an applicant is sent a letter which contains information not stored on the data base). Error messages cannot be displayed on a formatted screen, because the format breaks them up and makes them unintelligible.

FORMATTED SCREEN

A recruitment program can operate entirely by alternating between the select screen and a formatted screen for applicant information. Once the nature of the operation to be performed (for example, update applicant) and the applicant number have been given, a formatted screen should be displayed with provision for displaying all applicant details stored within the system. The items on the screen should be arranged into logical groups, just as they were in the discussion of what the system should store.

Basic details
Interview
Regret/withdraw/decline
Offer
Confirm offer
Other information (internal processing and selection information)

In the normal course of events these items will be updated as the operations are performed, but it is also necessary to have options displayed on the screen to enable the items in these blocks to be updated independently of the performance of a specific update. This is necessary both to correct errors, and to provide for the updating of items which are not linked to a specific operation (in other words not linked to the sending of a letter), for example medical clearance, reference clearance, and client approval. The formatted screen should have the applicant number at the top and an action box at the bottom. Next to the action box should be a list of the logical groups, and the commands necessary for updating them. A normal update would conclude with the cursor residing in the action box, so that the operator can signal either a further update or a return to the select screen.

Cursor positioning is the most important of all the time-saving devices in a recruitment system. The idea is that the system takes the operator to the items which are to be updated, without passing through fields which are not directly relevant. If the operator has indicated on the select screen that applicant number 2039 is to be updated, the details of applicant number 2039 should be displayed on the formatted screen, and the cursor should position itself at the box for operation number. Supposing that the operator enters 2A for application received, then no further information is required, and the cursor should go straight to the action box without passing through any more items. But if a 6A were entered for offer, the cursor would need to go to all the items in the offer box, so that the operator could enter the relevant information.

To achieve this the system will need to know the cursor positioning appropriate to each operation. It might at first appear that each of the basic operation levels should have a specified set of cursor behaviour linked to it. But this is not so. Level 6, for example, is used for both offer and chase offer, but the cursor positioning required in the two cases is entirely different. The first requires all the offer details, whereas the second requires only a close of offer date. However, although there is not a one to one relationship between the two, it is possible to distinguish eight basic sets of cursor positions, which between them cover all the operation levels. (It should be remembered that operation levels do not include such items as whom the application form has been passed to, or whether references have been cleared; these items are updated by means of the options at the bottom of the formatted screen.) The eight possibilities for cursor positioning with the items to be updated, are as follows:

1. Create applicant
   Name, title, vacancy, recruiter, source, operation number, address, action box.
2. Straightforward update
   Operation number, action box.
3. Regret/withdraw/decline
   Operation number, comment, hold until, action box.
4. Interview
   Operation number, interview date and time, interviewer, action box.
5. Offer
   Operation number, job title, department, salary and grade, location, hours, pay period, notice period, date of birth, start date, action box.
6. Chase offer
   Operation number, close date, action box.

7. Offer accepted
   Operation number, start date, references requested, references cleared, medical clearance, client approval, action box.
8. Confirm start
   Operation number, start date, action box.

There is not a relationship between operation level and cursor positioning, but there is a relationship between operation number and cursor positioning. The system must be aware of this relationship, in order to save time on the operation. But since operation numbers (being linked to standard letters) are to be flexible, this facility must be flexible too. It must be possible to introduce a new operation number, linked to the appropriate standard letter and cursor positioning. The only way to achieve this is to store them in a dictionary. Therefore, there must be a dictionary entry for each operation number, storing what it is, letter or letters to send, and cursor positioning (1–8). In fact, this dictionary will store other information as well. The need for it to store a flag against certain operation numbers to indicate that a second record must be created was discussed in the section on duplicate operations and going back down the operation ladder. The next section (fast update facilities) mentions some further information which it should store.

The result is that, when the operator enters 3D at operation number, the system will look in the dictionary entry for 3D, see that it requires a comment on rejection and a hold until date, will position the cursor in the boxes for these items, awaiting operator input, and will then go straight to the action box without requesting any further information. This will all happen without any delay being apparent to the operator. Consequently, the number of key depressions per applicant update will be reduced to an absolute minimum, and a significant saving in time will be achieved. Most applicant updates should only take about seven and a half seconds from start to finish, so any unnecessary operator input will have a significant effect on timing.

FAST UPDATE FACILITIES

It might appear that the mechanism described above reduces updating to the minimum possible. However, there are several circumstances—some of them perhaps frequent occurrences—in which further reduction of operator input can be achieved, and special facilities are required to exploit them to the full. First of all, there are two ways in which applicants can be said to be in natural groups: one is unavoidable, the other depends on internal procedures.

The first one is this: when the operator sits down at a VDU to work through a batch of work, the new applicants created will have sequential numbers (1039, 1040, 1041). Since they have all applied on the same day, there will be a tendency for them all to pass through the recruitment system together. If this is so, the numbers that need to be called up on subsequent days will be to a large extent sequential, and it is a waste of time to call them up. The system should do it. When applicant number 1039 has been updated, the system should automatically present the operator with 1040, without it being necessary to return to the select screen, indicate that an applicant update is required, and enter 1040. Provided that it is easy to skip applicants, for example by pressing carriage return when they appear, this can save a significant amount of time. It is also worth making the operation number given to the last applicant the default value for the next one, as some operations (such as application returned) will be particularly widespread at certain stages. This facility—which is extremely useful in practice, however unlikely it may sound—saves an immense amount of time, and may be referred to on the select screen as 'chain through applicant'. When it is used, the system will only need to know the name of the first applicant.

The second fast update facility is similar, but depends on procedural considerations. A recruiter is normally liaising with a manager over a particular vacancy. On large recruitment campaigns it is not practical to deal with applications in a piecemeal way. Instead, as each stage is reached, the forms will be collected together and discussed with the manager, after which the appropriate records will be updated. If this procedure is followed, as opposed to piecemeal treatment of applications, the operator will find that all the forms for the vacancy need to be updated together, and so, again, provided that they are put into numerical sequence and that it is easy to skip unwanted records, the system can do the work of calling them up. The operator will simply indicate on the select screen that the chain through vacancy facility is to be used, and enter the vacancy code and the applicant number from which to begin. The system will respond by presenting the operator with all applicants in that vacancy in sequence. These two facilities—chain through applicants and chain through vacancy—cover the two most common natural groupings of applicants within the system.

The second set of circumstances in which fast update facilities can be utilized is when a change occurs to the status of a vacancy. This can occur in two instances: a hold may be put on recruitment for a vacancy (perhaps because the job for which the requirement exists has been delayed) or recruitment for the vacancy may be terminated altogether (perhaps it has been filled). In both cases it is necessary to send letters of a similar type to a large number of applicants, and it is clearly desirable to have a means of producing these in bulk rather than calling up each applicant individually. However, this is not as simple as it at first sounds.

First of all, not everyone in the vacancy should receive a letter since some of them will have received regrets already, some will doubtless have dropped out at some stage of the recruitment process (not returning their application form, for example, or not turning up for interview), and one at least has already accepted the job. Secondly, different hold or terminate letters are appropriate at different stages. A letter to an applicant who has just been in for interview will need to be worded differently from one to an applicant who has not; it should begin by making reference to the interview.

The system must be capable of distinguishing between these cases and taking the appropriate action. How is this to be done? Essentially this is the same as the problem of cursor positioning. The need there was to inform the system of the cursor positioning appropriate to each operation number. The need here is to tell it which hold or terminate letter is appropriate to the stage that the applicant has reached, if the vacancy has to be held or terminated. The solution is the same: store the information in a dictionary, the same dictionary as for cursor positioning. Each operation number in the dictionary will, therefore, have a description of what it is, the letter or letters to send, cursor positioning (1–8), the letter to send if a hold is put on the vacancy, the letter to send if it is terminated, and a flag when required to indicate that a second record needs to be created.

Hold vacancy and terminate vacancy should exist as options on the select screen. When one of them is selected, the vacancy number will have to be specified, and the system will then send the appropriate letter automatically to every applicant in the vacancy, by checking the current operation number on the record and reading the appropriate action from the dictionary. In this way a hundred or so letters can be produced in a couple of minutes, the task of holding or terminating a vacancy ceases to be a tedious clerical ordeal, and applicants are told where they stand promptly and efficiently.

This concludes the question of fast update facilities. Between them, chain through applicant, chain through vacancy, the hold and terminate facilities can save a substantial amount of time.

Housekeeping

Housekeeping is the name given to the tidying up of files. Some of this may be of a semitechnical nature, and full instructions should always be provided with a system as to what is required in this respect. However, the major housekeeping activity in the case of data bases is the removal of unwanted records, for example, in this case, applicants whom it is no longer necessary to keep on file. Considerable flexibility is required here, as requirements regarding the length of time applicants should remain on file will vary from time to time, and some people will always be exceptions.

The exceptions can be dealt with by means of the hold until date, which was discussed earlier. When applicants are sent a regret, or when an offer is declined or withdrawn, a hold until date should be entered. The system can have a default date written into it, being the period of time for which applicants would normally be kept on file. But it must be possible to override this. Care must also be taken that applicants do not get removed shortly before they are due to start; if the appointment was arranged in advance, the time period can be unusually long. With these two exceptions, most applicants can be removed when a given period of time has elapsed since their last operation (say 18 months).

The program for removing applicants from the data base should therefore ask how many months are to be kept on file, and should translate this into a last operation date. It should then check:

1. That none of the applicants to be deleted has a hold date equal to or greater than the current month.
2. That none of them has a start date later than the last operation date under consideration.

The system of working on last operation date has the advantage of providing a mechanism for the removal of applicants who are in a permanently unresolved state, for example, those who never returned their application forms. If deletion was related primarily to hold date, these applicants would remain on the data base indefinitely.

Finally it is essential that the system should produce a full report on applicants who have been deleted. This report should include applicant number, name, vacancy, source, hold date, start date, and all the operations with the dates on which they were performed.

In summary, if a recruitment system is to achieve its objectives—the sort of objectives which make a real difference to the running of a personnel department, as discussed earlier in this book—it must satisfy certain criteria.

1. It must store the right information; this must be enough to completely replace the manual records, but not so much that it gets bogged down.
2. It must have an adequate vacancy structure, so that selection information is readily available, and reporting requirements can be met.
3. The recruitment process must be reduced to a series of operation levels which realistically reflects the reporting requirements. The operation numbers must be comprehensive, flexible, and able to cope with such occurrences as duplicate operation and applicants going back down the operation ladder.
4. The update mechanism must be very fast, including such facilities as: a select screen, a formatted applicant screen, cursor positioning, and the ability to chain through applicants, chain through vacancies, and hold or terminate a vacancy.
5. Standard reports must be provided at various levels of detail (for discussion, see Chapter 8).
6. The housekeeping procedure must be flexible, and must take due account of special situations in which an individual applicant may need to be kept on the data base longer than usual.

These are not the only points to be considered in the design of a recruitment system. But they are the critical ones. A wrong decision here or an oversight will result in an unworkable system. And of course, even if all these points are satisfactorily covered, the system will only achieve its objectives if it is placed in the right context as far as the wider system is concerned. It depends for its success on the prior existence of sophisticated facilities for letter writing, handling dictionary codes, and generating *ad hoc* reports.

5. The personnel records system

Personnel records systems have to service a wide range of activities. Nevertheless, they are not as hazardous to design as recruitment systems. The problem is one of size rather than degree of difficulty or obscurity. Recruitment systems have to deal with a number of problems that can easily be overlooked, but which will render them unusable if they are not adaquately dealt with. A personnel records system can turn out to be unusable, but it is more likely to suffer from limitations of scope and minor irritations than from total failure. However, a sufficient number of limitations of scope and minor irritations add up to total failure, so here again it is worth beginning with a recapitulation of the objectives of the system, and considerations of the problems that are likely to arise.

The most important objective of a personnel records system is that it should completely replace the manual records. If this is not achieved, the manual records will have to be kept going alongside the computerized system, and so all hopes of saving time will be shattered; running two systems is necessarily more time-consuming and complex than running one. Obvious though this sounds, it is a fact that most personnel records systems in existence at the present time have fallen into this trap. It is one of the problems that was discussed in Chapter 1 under 'Solutions that only make it worse'. Why does it happen? It happens because the scope of a personnel records system is so wide that a substantial number of points are likely to be overlooked. The only way to cope with such oversights on a day to day administrative basis once they have occurred is to keep the manual system going alongside until the computer system is modified, assuming that it is modified.

Two types of oversight are liable to occur in the design of a personnel records system. Specific facilities may be overlooked, particular reporting requirements, for example, or the ability to perform certain kinds of salary calculations. Alternatively, a complication in the composition of the data may be overlooked. For example, insufficient attention may be given during the systems design to the fact that different types of staff will be stored on the system: permanent, agency, and assigned from an affiliated organization. The second type of oversight is much more serious, because it cuts across all the basic facilities provided by the system. It is not possible, for example, to produce sensible salary reports from a system that is unable to distinguish annual salaries from hourly rates.

The success of a personnel records system depends, in the first place, on the meticulous analysis of a wide range of activities and information requirements. The pitfalls are not hidden, as they are in recruitment, but there are many of them, and it does not take many mistakes to wreck a system. In the second place, success is dependent upon the provision of the generalized facilities discussed earlier in the book. Letters to individuals concerning such things as promotions, salary increases, and assignments must be produced automatically by the system when the records are updated. This is the only way to ensure the accuracy of the information stored; it also eliminates a substantial amount of duplication of effort. Dictionary facilities must be provided. The considerable volume of information to be stored will be unwieldy and inaccessible unless it is coded, and the codes will be unintelligible unless they are translated from a dictionary wherever they occur. Finally, a personnel records system without a powerful report generating capacity is nonsensical. This is one of the areas in which the benefits of a computerized system should be most apparent.

Letter writing, dictionary facilities, and report generating are prerequisities of a successful personnel records system, and are dealt with elsewhere in the book. This chapter is concerned with aspects of design that are specific to the personnel records system. The starting-point is consideration of what to store. This will be followed by a discussion of the update mechanisms, and the facilities for housekeeping. Inevitably, the precise requirements of a system will vary from company to company. However, the basic requirements are the same, and the system discussed in the rest of this chapter represents a coherent structure to replace a manual system. It would satisfy the requirements of many companies exactly as it stands, and would be a firm foundation for any personnel records system.

Brief description

The personnel records system, like the recruitment system, should operate by means of a select screen, presenting the operator with the main options available. When the option to be used has been indicated, the current details of any employee to be updated should be displayed. However, it is clearly not practical to display all the information concerning an employee on a single screen. Therefore, there must be a selection of screens, each storing logically related information: main details (name, man number, department, and salary, for example), history, relations, addresses, training, and medical. There must be a rapid process for passing from one screen to another as required, and for updating information when necessary. If an update is of a kind that requires the production of a letter to an employee, the system should produce it automatically, asking for any information that may be required in addition to the data stored in the system. The system should also produce all employee-related reports required within the personnel department. It must have a flexible facility for removing leavers from the data base when a specified period of time has elapsed since their departure.

What to store

The items that need to be stored in a personnel records system fall into six logical groups: main details, history, addresses, relations, training, and medical. Each of these can conveniently comprise a data-set. Other sections could be added, but these are the ones that will normally be required to replace the manual records. There is an important difference between the main details and the other groups. The length of the main details data-set can be fixed without difficulty. A certain number of items are relevant. Most employees will have entries in the majority of them, and there is no need for more than one entry against any particular item; if the old value needs to be recorded when it changes, it becomes history, and so is no longer a matter of concern in the main details data-set.

The length of the other files cannot really be fixed. How much history do we allow for each employee? What is the maximum number of entries that might be relevant under training? The answer will vary depending on the individual concerned, company policy, and external events. In 1974, most companies with computerized personnel records found their systems collapsing as a result of threshold payments. It had widely been assumed that five years of salary history was sufficient, and on the basis of one review per year, most systems had the capacity to store only five salary changes. In many cases, threshold payments had the effect of reducing five years' salary history to one. Limiting history means limiting the scope of the system, and so effectively relying on a manual system as a back-up. If the system is to store all an employee's transfers, promotions, assignments, and salary increases, it may well need to record as many as fifty separate historical events.

The training file should include qualifications, institute membership, courses attended, language ability, and information about trainees. Again, an employee might have anything from no entries to 20. How many addresses should be allowed for? An address is much the most space-consuming item on the system, so economy is essential. Some employees will have just a permanent address. For many the company will need a bank address. If the next of kin address is different, it must be stored; and if the employee is at a temporary address, it will be necessary to store that as well. Relations (meaning next of kin, spouse, and children) present a similar problem.

Once the maximum likely size of each of these data-sets has been considered, it will rapidly become clear that any system with fixed space allocated to each employee will be immensely wasteful. The only practical solution is to make the space allocated to each individual variable. If the employee has no details to be entered in a data-set, no space will be allocated. For the rest, the data-sets must be analysed into entries, with the employee having one record added to his data for each additional requirement. To put it another way, an employee is only allocated a record when it is required. For every additional requirement, another

82

record is created and linked to the previous one. An employee might have 40 history records, 4 address records, 12 relations records, 15 training records and 8 medical records. Only by adopting this principle can a system be designed which is both comprehensive and economical. The exception to the principle of record linking is the data-set storing the main details. This can be of fixed length, and must have the capacity to store a wide range of information.

MAIN DETAILS

The first thing to consider when looking at an employee's current details is what kind of employee they are, for example, permanent or agency. This may reasonably be referred to as staff category, and it may be convenient to refine it further to indicate such things as which payroll the employee is on and which office they report to. In short, it may be used for any peculiarity in conditions that may be of interest when interpreting the basic record.

Next the employee must be identified by name and number. The question that inevitably arises is how many names should be stored. It is essential to know a person's surname and initials, and whether they should be addressed as 'Mr' or 'Ms', but is there any reason to waste valuable computer space with christian names? It is difficult to think of any report that will require christian names; on the other hand, it is sometimes useful to know what a person is called. An interesting point arises here. A significant number of people are not called by their christian names. Many names are abbreviated by friends and colleagues, some people are called by their second christian name in preference to their first, some have adopted a quite different name, and others are commonly referred to in terms that bear no relation to any real name at all. If it is of interest to know what a person is called, the relevant item to store will be not christian names but name known by. This will have the additional advantage of enabling the computer's letter writing facility to be used for letters that require an informal mode of address, service awards, for example.

The system should then store the basic facts about the position that the employee occupies within the company: department, job title, salary, and location. In respect of these four items, it is most useful to include in the main details data-set the date on which each of them last changed, and what they were prior to the change. How long has the individual been on this salary? doing this job? in this department? at this location? What were they doing before? Although the full history is stored within the system, it cannot be displayed on the same screen, and it is useful to have the last change immediately accessible. It is simplest to do this by storing it in the main details data-set. Provision should also be made for storing salary grade and the date on which the individual's salary would normally be reviewed (this information is essential in companies operating a rolling review system). Pay code and cost code are normally required as accounting information.

The storing of location requires special consideration. If the individual is in a home office location, it may be convenient to store extension number—this will enable the system to produce the internal telephone directory. If the location indicates that the individual is on assignment abroad, then further information will be required: the date the assignment began, its anticipated length, any uplifts in salary connected with it, and whether it was a single or married status assignment. Length of assignment must be stored in standard units (months is the only practical one), and six characters should be allowed so that indefinite periods can be catered for: '12–18', for example. The system should also calculate the date of return, using date of assignment and approximate length, as the reporting mechanism will then be able to search for people with a specified date of return.

As far as uplifts in salary are concerned, some distinctions must be drawn. Most foreign assignments include a number of special benefits (location allowance, different overtime rules, etc.). There is no need to store this on every individual's record (they should be standard for the location), although it is worth storing an indicator to be used if the basic conditions are nonstandard; the indicator would say, in effect, 'Look at the detail of this individual's assignment letter; there is something unusual about it'. However, it is worth storing any simple percentage uplifts on basic salary that the individual is entitled to for the purpose of the assignment, because these are of fundamental importance when reviewing the record. Since such uplifts should normally be standard, they may be written into a location dictionary, and appear as the default value. However, it must be possible to override them, which is why they should be stored as items on every individual's record.

Finally, in connection with assignments, it may be necessary to store an assignment job title. This is essential for companies that have to assign staff into a client's job titling structure. The client insists that a scheduler grade 9 is required. The company has no such job title, but recognizes this as a requirement for lead planning engineer. It is totally wrong to change the person's job title; it would upset salary surveys and confuse everyone who saw it. The individual's substantive job title should be retained but an assignment job title must be allocated in addition.

The next group of items to store in the main details data-set is that of information related to the basic contract: pay period, conditions, hours worked, eligibility for overtime, eligibility for a company car, holiday entitlement, staff status (for the purpose of benefits), and the date from which these benefits became effective. In the case of permanent staff, conditions may simply indicate notice period (staff status is a separate item). For agency members of staff it may well indicate different sets of conditions, depending, for example, on where they are working. Companies that run a private medical insurance scheme (as many do), providing cover on the scale appropriate to provincial teaching hospitals, and giving employees the option of increasing to the London scale at their own expense, will find it useful to store scale of cover, as this will enable the breakdown of costs to be computerized (see pages 155–156).

The main details data-set should also store personal information about the individual: start date, continuous service date, number of years with the company prior to continuous service date, number of years in the industry, birth date, sex, marital status, number of children under 21, nationality (the AA system of codes for countries may be used), and National Insurance number. For government purposes it is necessary to record whether an employee is a registered disabled person.

It is also useful to store an indicator of the individual's performance and promotability. This assumes that the company has a performance appraisal system, and that anything to be stored has already been discussed and agreed with the individual. This information must be kept simple: an overall rating of 1 to 5 for performance, for example, and 'yes' or 'no' for promotability. The system should also store an overall indication of the individual's qualification level. The details will be in the training data-set, but it is useful to have a quick reference indicator of approximate level of education or qualification: chartered, institute membership, and degree, for example.

Additional items may be required for different types of staff. Records for agency staff, for example, will need to include the name of the agent, the order number, National Insurance rate paid (this may be stored in the space allocated for National Insurance number in permanent staff records), and name of supervisor.

Finally, thought must be given to leavers. It makes no sense to store information on leavers in a separate type of record. To do so introduces additional complications into the system, and imposes unnecessary restrictions. All sorts of searches and reports may be required in relation to leavers since they cannot all be specified in advance. It is essential for manpower planning purposes to have full records available. Rather than transferring leavers' information into a new format, a leave date should be added to their records, with an indication of whether the company would re-employ them. Every search or report can then either include or exclude them by reference to leave date. No extra parameter will be required. It will not be economical to keep them on file indefinitely. When a reasonable period of time has elapsed, their records can be transferred from the live data base to magnetic tape (still in the same format). This is discussed later on in the chapter in the section on housekeeping.

HISTORY

Many items of current information discussed above are only of interest while they are current. Others, such as salary history, dates of promotions, transfers and assignments, and the locations in which a person has worked are of historical interest. They help to build up a complete picture of the individual, and are of use in manpower planning. It has already been suggested that the only way to make the capacity for storing history sufficiently flexible is to reduce it to a series of events, each occupying one record, with the ability to join records together.

The important question, then, is which items of information comprise a historical event. Changes of historical significance generally involve a change in department number, location, job title, or salary. Therefore, the record should contain the date of the change, the department number, location, job title, salary, and reason for the change (engage, review, promotion, transfer, assignment, leave, etc.). Since more than one change may occur at the same time (assignment and promotion, for example), it is advisable to allow for two reasons to be stored. By storing these events together a succinct outline picture of an employee's career with the company can be presented, and the system will be able to answer questions such as: 'Who have we got who has worked as a project manager? As a project manager in Saudi Arabia? How many salary increases have there been in the last six months? How many transfers? How many promotions?'. In this way a considerable body of historical information can be stored in an economical fashion. It is important to store a transaction date in addition to the effective date of change. The transaction date is the date on which the event was processed on the system. Many changes have to be back-dated or fore-dated, and so the question 'What changes have gone through the system in the last month?' can only be answered if a transaction date is stored.

RELATIONS

This data-set is used to store details of family and next of kin. When someone is sent on an extended assignment abroad, it is sometimes necessary to know the nationality of all members of their family, and it will certainly be relevant to know the ages of their children; this is useful in any case for other purposes. Therefore, the record must store the relationship (husband, wife, son, daughter) and the relation's name, their date of birth, and nationality. It should also have a flag to indicate its type, for example, whether this child is a next of kin. As in history, any number of records may be linked together.

ADDRESSES

Again, records may be linked together, but in this case four is the maximum: permanent, temporary, next of kin, and bank address. There should be a flag for record type to indicate which is which. Three lines should be allocated to address, with 30 characters each for the first two, and 20 characters for the third. Ten characters should be allowed for postcode (this can then be used for country in the case of foreign addresses). It may be necessary to allow space for storing telephone exchange. Finally, 12 characters should be allocated to STD code and telephone number.

TRAINING

This data-set has to store a mixture of details: institute membership, qualifications, courses, language ability, and information about trainees. The difficulty is to reduce the differing requirements in each area to a standard format, so that each institute, qualification, course, language, or training scheme can constitute one training record as far as the system is concerned, linked to the other training records for the individual in question.

There must be a flag for record type, so that reports will have a simple means of identifying the type of training records required. Each record may then be analysed into two main parts, which for convenience may be called level and type, although this is not an accurate description of what they are to store in every case. Level can store the level of membership of an institute (fellow, member, and associate, for example), the level of a qualification (PhD, BA, and ONC, for example), the organization running a course, the fluency with which a language is spoken and written, or the year of a training scheme. Type can store the name of an institute, the type of qualification, the nature of a course, the language spoken or written, or the name of the training scheme concerned. Both level and type will need to be coded for convenience of entry and enquiry, and expanded from the dictionary.

Additional information may be required on institutes and courses. Many companies pay an individual's subscription to an institute if they feel it to be relevant to their work. It is therefore useful to store an indicator of whether the company pays the subscription, and the date on which it was last paid. As far as courses are concerned it is useful to know the date of the course and its length. It makes sense, therefore, to allocate space for a date in the record, and to use it to store date subscription paid in institute records, and date of course in course records. Similarly, the space allocated for length of course can double as an indicator of whether an institute subscription is paid by the company. A four character space is required so that a character can be entered to indicate whether the course length is measured in days, weeks or months, followed by a space and the number of units (for example, 'W 10'). The advantage of storing it this way round is that a report sorting on this field would enable courses of a few days duration to be separated from those lasting several weeks, and those measured in months. The subscription paid indicator need only be 'Y' for 'yes' or 'N' for 'no'.

MEDICAL

It is not the purpose of a personnel records system to store extensive medical information. The application should be strictly practical. Apart from showing when employees have medicals (if they have them), it should be confined to detailing the immunizations and vaccinations that people have had, the dates on which they had them, and the dates when they are due for updating. This is important when sending them overseas, and once the information has been collected, it can be used to produce reports for checking that staff who may have to travel overseas have the requisite immunizations, and for prompting updates. Cases of people being found to be medically unfit are, like many aspects of employee relations, individual matters, and should be dealt with as such. There is nothing to be gained from storing such information on a computer system. The period of time for which an immunization is effective should be stored in the dictionary, so that the system can calculate when immunization is required, and store it in the individual's record.

This completes the discussion of items to be stored. Here is a checklist with the number of characters required for each item in brackets, and an asterisk against coded information (coded, that is, in the sense that it is expanded from the dictionary).

Main details

Staff category	(2)*
Employee number	(5)
Surname and initials	(20)
Title	(2)
Name known by	(10)
Department number	(3)
Date department number last changed	(6)
Previous department number	(3)
Job title code	(4)
Date job title last changed	(6)
Previous job title code	(4)
Salary	(5)
Date salary last changed	(6)
Previous salary	(5)
Salary grade	(2)
Review month	(2)
Pay code	(3)
Cost code	(4)
Location	(6)*
Extension number	(4)
Date location last changed	(6)
Previous location	(6)*
Assignment status	(1)

Length of assignment	(6)
Calculated date of return	(6)*
Assignment job title	(4)*
Uplift 1	(4)
Uplift 2	(4)
Nonstandard conditions indicator	(1)
Pay period	(1)
Conditions	(1)
Hours worked	(4)
Eligibility for overtime	(1)
Eligibility for company car	(1)
Holiday entitlement	(2)
Staff status	(1)
Effective date for staff status	(6)
Medical insurance scale	(1)
Start date	(6)
Continuous service date	(6)
Number of years prior to continuous service date	(2)
Number of years in industry	(2)
Birth date	(6)
Sex	(1)
Marital status	(1)
Number of children under 21	(2)
Nationality	(2)*
National Insurance number	(10)
Registered disabled indicator	(1)
Overall performance rating	(1)
Promotability indicator	(1)
Qualification level	(1)
Name of agent	(2)*
Order number	(10)
National Insurance rate paid	(see National Insurance number)
Name of supervisor	(2)*
Leave date	(6)
Re-employability indicator	(1)

History

Transaction date	(6)
Date of change	(6)
Department number	(3)
Location	(6)*
Job title	(4)*
Salary	(5)

Reason 1	(2)*
Reason 2	(2)*
Relations	
Record type	(2)
Name of relation	(20)
Relationship	(2)*
Date of birth	(6)
Nationality	(2)*
Addresses	
Record type	(2)
Address line 1	(30)
Address line 2	(30)
Address line 3	(20)
Postcode or country	(10)
Telephone exchange	(16)
Telephone number and STD code	(12)
Training	
Record type	(2)
Level	(2)*
Type	(4)*
Course length/subscription paid	(4)
Date of course/subscription paid	(6)
Medical	
Immunization/vaccination or medical	(2)*
Immunization/vaccination or medical date	(6)
Date when update due	(6)*

Update mechanisms

The efficiency of a personnel records update program is determined to a considerable extent by the update mechanisms it utilizes. The facilities required will be discussed in turn. Briefly, they consist of the way in which data is divided between screen formats on the VDU, the options available on the select screen, the provisions for updating the main screen, the letter writing facilities, the deletion facilities, the provision for updating other screens, and the means of transferring starters from the recruitment system.

DIVISION INTO SCREENS

The amount of information that needs to be stored in a personnel records system is too great to be displayed on a VDU all at once. It therefore has to be split into logical sectors, and the system must be capable of moving rapidly from one to another. The logical sectors are the ones already identified above in the discussion of what to store: current details, history, relations, addresses, training, and medical. Each of these can conveniently occupy a separate screen . In the recruitment system, only two screens are used (select screen and applicant screen), and it is therefore possible to store the format for each of them in the memory of the VDU. Although it is possible to handle the screens required in a personnel records system in a similar manner, it is neither necessary nor economical. The two screens that will be used most of the time are the select screen and the main details screen (hereafter referred to simply as the main screen). They are also the most complex. The main screen has to store a large number of items, and if it is to be readily comprehensible, it must be formatted.

It is sensible, therefore, to store the format of these two screens in the memory of the VDU (the system should build the screens whenever the main personnel program is run). The other screens do not need to be formatted. It is sufficiently clear for the system to write the data to the screen with headings where necessary. An address is self-explanatory. In the case of all other screens, the data stored should be broken down into records, as described in the discussion of what to store, and each record will fit on one line, so that headings can easily be provided. A screen should always display both the code (where appropriate), and the expansion read from the dictionary. In the case of history, where there are a large number of coded items, it is worth highlighting the expansions so that they are naturally separated from the codes on the screen.

There is no guarantee that all the items required will fit on to one screen, nor is it desirable that they should do so. The system has to write the data to the screen, and this takes time. Naturally it should do so very fast, and this must be one of the criteria for evaluating a system. But however fast it is, it will delay an efficient operator, and it is therefore important to display only as much data as is likely to be required on most occasions, together with a simple facility for requesting more.

SELECT SCREEN

The purpose of the select screen is to present the operator with the basic functions available in the main personnel records program. Nearly all functions will be concerned with displaying or updating employee records, and since a record should be displayed before it is updated, there is no need to distinguish between the two. Updates can be of two basic types: individual ones and bulk ones. The principal cases of bulk updates are salary reviews and redundancies. These are dealt with in the next chapter. Other than these, bulk updates are rarely required, and may reasonably be handled by the use of the update facility provided with the data base management system, rather than by specially written application programs.

Therefore, bulk updates do not need to be handled by the select screen, and attention can be focussed on selecting the employee to be updated. It should be possible to select an employee for updating by reference to number, name, or partial name. Number and name are straightforward;

the appropriate code (NO or NA) is entered, and the number or name supplied. Partial names were explained in the discussion of the recruitment system. The idea is that the operator enters as much of the name in question as is known (for example, 'Kinn'), and the system then displays the names of people who qualify one by one in alphabetical order together with their name known by, employee number, department number, extension number and, if they have one, leave date. The operator must be able to indicate to the system when the correct person has been found, and the system will then proceed as for the NO and NA options.

Once the person to be accessed has been identified, the system should display the formatted screen stored in the memory of the VDU, and fill it with their main details. The options for accessing other screens should be displayed on the bottom of the main screen, together with the update options. There are two reasons for invariably displaying the main details of a person before providing the option to access another screen. Firstly, many people have similar or even identical names, and displaying their details is a way of checking that the right person has been found. Secondly, the majority of the updates made will concern the main screen either partially or entirely, and therefore it is simpler—and so ultimately quicker—to access it as a matter of course, rather than providing a bewildering list of update alternatives on the select screen.

The suggestions made above have the advantage of simplicity. The operator decides whether to select an employee by number, name, or partial name, and supplies the appropriate input. The system then displays the main details of the person selected on a formatted screen. At the bottom of this screen a series of commands are listed which enable the operator either to update the screen or to pass to another one. In addition to updating facilities, the select screen must include options for putting new members of staff on the system. Two of these are required: one for permanent staff and one for agency staff. In both cases, default values should be written to the current details screen where possible to speed up the entry of information by the operator. The option for putting on agency staff does not need to access all the items on the screen. The relevant ones are given in the section on agency updates below.

This section began with the observation that nearly all functions on the select screen will be concerned with updating or displaying employee records. It is now necessary to consider the exceptions. They are easy to overlook. There are only two exceptions, and they are both connected with the letter writing facility, that is, the ability of the system to produce letters to employees automatically when critical items on their records are updated. The system needs to know the signatory for the letter and the operator (this should be included in the reference at the top of the letter). Both of these can be set as default values in the program. However, since there may be different signatories and operators for different purposes, it is essential to be able to change them, and this facility is best provided on the select screen. A code may be entered—SG for signatory and OP for operator—followed by the initials of the person concerned, to be read from the dictionary.

To summarize, the options required on the select screen are: select employee by number, select employee by name, select employee by partial name, put on new member of permanent staff, put on new member of agency staff, set letter signatory, and set operator.

UPDATING THE MAIN SCREEN

The main screen has to display a large amount of information, and to provide facilities for updating it. The simplest facility for updating is for the cursor to pass through each field in turn, allowing the operator either to leave it as it stands or to change it. If the means of leaving it as it stands is simply to press carriage return, then the operator can cause the cursor to move through the screen very fast just by keeping the carriage return key depressed. Nevertheless, this is not an efficient way of updating items which constantly need to be accessed. The operator should be able to go straight to them.

The opposite technique is to number all the items on the screen and specify the numbers of the ones to be updated. This has two disadvantages. The first and overriding one is that there is no room to fit the numbers on the screen. It is difficult enough to display all the items required with an explanation of what they are alongside. The addition of numbers would necessitate abbreviating the explanations to the point of incomprehensibility, and would make the screen look unacceptably cluttered. The second disadvantage is that the operator has to find the item numbers on the screen and then type them in. This can easily take longer than tabbing through all the fields.

It appears, then, that neither approach is satisfactory. An intermediate solution is required. The answer is to identify the update paths that will be used most frequently and to supply them as specific update options. To update any other items, by definition those that are not frequently accessed, the full update can be used, passing through all fields on the screen. The full update has to be provided. The important decision is which short update options to provide, and which items they should access. Naturally, it should be possible to make partial use of a short update option by pressing carriage return to pass over some fields, in the same way as in the full update.

The exact constitution of the short updates will depend upon the procedures in force in the environment in which the system is installed. However, it is likely that six particular situations will lend themselves to short updates: salary changes, assignments, changes in staff status, leavers, agency updates, and some combination of these. Between them these cover the majority of items that will be updated frequently on the main screen. Each short update should have a code for initiation by the operator in an action box at the bottom of the screen. The comprehensive short update may be referred to as the short update (SU), and the others as salary (SA), assignments (AS), staff status (ST), agency (AG), and leavers (LV). The items that they should update are as follows:

Short update (SU)
    Department
    Department date
    Job title
    Job title date
    Salary
    Salary date
    Salary indicator
    Adjustment amount
    Adjustment salary
    Salary grade
    Pay code
    Cost code
    Hours
    Location
    Extension number
    Location date
    Length of assignment
    Status and indicator
    Assigned job title
    Uplifts
Salary (SA)
    Job title
    Job title date
    Salary
    Salary date
    Salary indicator
    Adjustment amount
    Adjustment salary
    Salary grade
Assignments (AS)
    Department
    Department date
    Pay code
    Cost code
    Hours
    Location
    Location date
    Extension number
    Length of assignment

Status and indicator
Assignment job title
Uplifts
Staff status (ST)
Notice period
Staff status
Medical insurance scale
Effective date
Agency (AG)
Staff category
Agency name
Surname and initials
Title
Department
Department change date
Job title
Job title change date
Hourly rate
Rate change date
Cost code
Conditions
Leavers (LV)
Leave date
Re-employability

These are the short update facilities that should be provided on the main screen in addition to a full update. In each case the cursor should go only to the fields specified, in order to save as much time as possible. It is now necessary to consider the repercussions of updating some of these fields in other parts of the personnel records system.

The history data-set records changes in critical items, that is, department, location, job title, and salary. It therefore follows that a change in one of these items on the main screen is certain to require the addition of a history record. There is no reason why this cannot be done automatically by the system, with the operator being prompted for any additional information required. The trigger for generating an automatic history is that one of the critical items changes. The system can take the values for all items in the new history record from the main screen with the exception of the reasons for the change (even the effective date is stored on the main screen, and the transaction date is, of course, today's date). As soon as the record has been created, which should take place immediately after the updating of the main screen, the system should present the operator with the last five lines of history to check the new record and to enter the reason for the change.

Although a change in one of the critical items must always result in the creation of a history record, it should not be concluded that these are the only historical events that can or should be recorded. The 'reason' columns can be used to indicate other types of changes, for example, an employee leaving or a change in staff status, even though the critical items remain unchanged. Therefore, the system should create an automatic history and present the operator with the history screen in these cases as well.

Two points should be noted in connection with automatic histories. Firstly, whenever a critical item changes, the system has to do two things: it must create a history line, and it must post the value of the existing item to the field for previous department, previous job title, previous location, or previous salary, as appropriate, in the main details data-set. Secondly, it is a fundamental procedural point that two changes to critical items with different effective dates must never be processed together. There is no reason why they should be. Changes with different effective dates should come through as separate documents. But if they were to be processed together, the history data-set would become inaccurate since only one line would be generated, and, therefore, the two events would be allocated a single effective date (the first one the system encountered). All the critical items may change at once, and the operator can process all the changes in one pass through the screen, but only if they all have the same effective date.

LETTER WRITING

The operation of the letter writing system has been discussed in detail in Chapter 3, and all that is required here is a note on the way it should be integrated with the updating of the personnel records system. It should be possible to generate a letter from any of the screens by entering the command LT. However, some situations will almost invariably require a letter and in these cases the system should prompt the operator with the words 'Do you require a letter? (answer Y or N)'. These situations all occur on the main details screen. They are:

1. Change of salary.
2. Change of job title.
3. Change of location.
4. Change of staff status.

When the operator has indicated that a letter is required (by answering 'Y'), the system should ask any questions which may be necessary for the production of the letter. It is best for these questions to be written up on a blank screen, as the other screens will not all have enough room (especially the main screen, which is the one most likely to be in use). Since changes that prompt for letter writing are generally the same ones as those requiring automatic histories, it is necessary to decide the order in which these operations should be performed. There is something to be said for answering the letter questions before editing the automatic history, because they are a direct extension of the main update.

DELETION FACILITY

The ways of updating the main screen have been discussed. The creation of new members of staff is initiated from the select screen. What about deleting people? In the main this will be dealt with by means of housekeeping procedures, which are discussed later in this chapter. However, there are bound to be cases when it is necessary to remove a person from the system, other than in the normal course of housekeeping, for example, perhaps they were put on by mistake. For this purpose a deletion facility should be provided. It is sensible to provide this facility on the main screen, because although all records belonging to the person will have to be deleted in every data-set, the operator is less likely to delete a person accidentally if their current details are displayed at the time. In response to the command to delete the individual displayed, the system should first ask 'Are you sure?'.

This completes the discussion of the facilities to be provided on the main screen. In summary, they are:

Full update
Short update
Salary update
Assignment update
Agency update
Leaver update
Staff status update
Write a letter
Go to history screen
Go to addresses screen
Go to relations screen
Go to training screen
Go to immunization/vaccination screen
Go to select screen
Delete a person's record

UPDATING OTHER SCREENS

The main screen requires some refined updating mechanisms because it is storing so much information. The other screens are simpler. The operator needs to be able to create a new record, update a record, delete a record, display more records, write a letter, or go to one of the other screens.

The creation of new records can give rise to a problem. Each of the data-sets relating to the screens now under consideration consists of a series of records linked together. In a data base management system they will be linked together to form a chain, and each new record will be added on to the end of the chain. The order of records in the chain will determine the order in which they appear on the screen, and (in the absence of a specified sort) the order in which they appear on reports.

This can sometimes lead to problems. In the case of history, the last record added to the chain will normally be recording the last chronological event. But what happens if an event is missed some way back in a person's history? It clearly must not be added on the end of the chain, because this would put it out of chronological sequence. One possibility would be for the operator to delete all history records since the one that is missing, put it in, and then recreate all the others. But this is a laborious process, and the potential for error is high.

In the case of the other data-sets, it is perhaps not essential for records to be in any particular order, but it certainly helps if they are. It is confusing if a person's training details (institute, qualifications, courses, and languages) are jumbled up together, if the next of kin record is in the middle of the children, or if the permanent address is displayed before the temporary one (a temporary address is always likely to be overlooked).

The solution to this problem is to provide a facility for inserting records in a given position. Every record displayed on the screen should be numbered, and the operator can then indicate the insertion position by quoting the record numbers between which the new record is to be inserted ('4, 5', for example). The system will then have to go through the same process as the operator would have had to perform if an insertion facility were not available, that is, make a note of the record contents above the insertion point, delete them, write the new record and put the old ones back again. However, the system can naturally do this much faster than the operator, and without any errors.

Two options are therefore required: create a record and insert a record. The mechanism for entering new data should be for the cursor to pass through the appropriate positions on the screen, awaiting operator input.

The update facility should work in a similar way: the number of the record to be updated is given, and the cursor goes to each item for operator input. The delete facility must not be confused with the one on the main screen. The purpose of that one was to delete an entire person (it could never be necessary to delete the main details alone, since everyone on the system must have an entry here, and no one has more than one record). The purpose of the delete option on the other screens is to delete a single record, specified by number. The command for displaying more records does not have any complications associated with it. Options for writing a letter or going to another screen should be the same as on the main screen.

TRANSFER OF STARTERS FROM RECRUITMENT

Everyone who goes on to the personnel records system should have passed through the recruitment system. It is therefore possible to have an automatic mechanism for transferring details from one to the other. This has two advantages: it saves time, and it ensures that the information on the personnel records system tallies with the individual's offer letter. The details common to both systems are:

Surname and initials
Title
Address line 1
Address line 2
Address line 3
Postcode
Telephone exchange
Telephone number
Job title (stored as vacancy in recruitment)
Salary
Salary grade
Hours
Pay period
Conditions (notice period in recruitment)
Department
Location
Start date
Date of birth

A special program will be required to pass these details across. The operator should have the same kind of flexibility for selecting people to be passed across from recruitment as in running reports. This is discussed in Chapter 7. It would be normal to select applicants by reference to start date or applicant number. Once they have been passed across, the operator will need to add the missing details using the main personnel program in the usual manner.

Housekeeping

All that happens when a person leaves is that a leave date is entered on their record. Their details are not removed from the data base. Leavers need to be kept on the data base for reporting purposes, especially manpower planning. How long they remain is a matter of company policy, and must be determined by weighing the value of retaining leavers' information for a given period against the cost of the disc space, and, when the numbers become very large (as large as current staff, for example), their effect on the system's speed and performance.

When leavers are removed from the current data base, they should not be lost irretrievably. Instead, their details should be transferred to a leavers' data base, which can be kept on magnetic tape; this is an economical means of storage which removes them from the immediate vicinity of the live system. It will still be possible to access their details by special arrangement when the need for long-term leavers' information arises.

Thus, three requirements may be defined in relation to housekeeping on the personnel data base:

1. It must be possible to remove all people who left prior to a given date from the current data base.
2. Their details should be printed out in full when they are removed.
3. They should be transferred to a leavers' data base, stored on magnetic tape.

The most convenient format in which to print out all their details is the one in which it appears on the screens used to access current employees. These screens include headings for all information, and codes are expanded. If the housekeeping program operates in the same way, it should be easy to understand. It is worth adding that the facility to print out every single detail stored on an employee in an intelligible fashion is useful for purposes other than recording the final details of leavers at the time they are removed from the current data base. Therefore, this facility should be provided as an independent option, which can be utilized without deleting the person concerned.

This concludes the discussion of personnel records systems. It should be clear by now that there is nothing very complicated about them. However, a workable system requires a vast number of facilities, and the potential for errors and oversights is considerable. If any of the items to be stored are missed, a manual system will be required to supply them. If the arrangements for displaying information are not carefully thought out, it will be necessary to type in a cumbersome succession of commands to extract the required data. If the update mechanisms are not fast and efficient, the system will be unacceptably slow to use. And if there are inadequate facilities for letter writing, transferring starters from recruitment, and housekeeping, the system will suffer from serious limitations which will eventually cripple it.

A successful system depends upon exhaustive and meticulous analysis. Maintaining adequate personnel records sounds easy, but designing a system which will have the comprehensiveness and flexibility to satisfy all the demands to be made upon it is a difficult task. This chapter has attempted to show how it can be done. The next chapter looks at some special types of changes: those that concern the personnel records system, but are not in the nature of individual updates, that is, changes of a particularly dramatic and demanding kind.

6. Salary reviews and redundancies

Two situations exist that are intimately connected with personnel records but are best dealt with outside the main personnel records program. These are salary reviews and redundancies. The salary reviews in question here are not individual adjustments—these are handled by the main personnel records program—but companywide reviews. Regardless of whether a company operates an annual review or a rolling review, these changes involve special problems, and require a special program to handle them. The essential feature that distinguishes salary reviews and redundancies from other types of personnel records updating is that they involve bulk changes rather than individual ones. In both cases, a set of parameters is defined which determines the way in which a large number of records will be updated. In the case of a salary review, the minimum degree of similarity between the increases will be that they all occur on the same date; often the common factors will extend further to include a set percentage or amount for specified groups, or perhaps, in the case of a rolling review system, a common month of start for all employees under review.

In the case of a redundancy, the common factors are largely determined by law: the method for calculating statutory redundancy payments. Many companies will be offering compensation over and above the statutory requirements, and there will undoubtedly be an agreed formula for determining this. Finally, the date of the redundancy may be a common factor.

Both salary reviews and redundancies, then, involve bulk updates, that is, adjustments to the personnel records involving the application of common factors. They also involve the performance of calculations, and here again they differ from the mainstream of work processed by the personnel records program. Both of them, therefore, require specially designed programs, and to determine the way in which these programs should operate it is necessary to perform a careful analysis of the problems with which they will have to deal. This chapter considers each of the two programs in turn.

Salary reviews

An annual salary review is often a chaotic event. The reason for this is that a large number of separate tasks have to be performed very fast, and are supposed to be internally consistent. Calculations have to be performed to determine the effect of carrying out the review in various ways, and adjusted until a satisfactory course is identified. Letters have to be produced for individuals. The personnel records must be updated, and payroll and pensions need to be informed. The extra burden of work on the personnel department whilst these tasks are performed is considerable. The task of checking that the increase finally agreed for Mr Smith is the one that appears on his letter, that his manager receives a copy, and that payroll and pensions are notified of the correct final figure provides considerable potential for error, and this is greatly magnified by any last minute changes of mind.

Most personnel managers will be familiar with the frustrations involved in producing several sets of salary review letters, because a policy change occurs each time the task is completed. The danger then is that someone will receive the wrong letter, or payroll will be asked to pay them the revision two increase instead of the revision three increase.

There is only one way to deal with these problems and that is to design a program that performs all the required tasks from a common base of information; it must be designed to operate fast. In the first place it must provide extensive facilities for experimenting with different kinds of adjustments, and examining the results. In the second place, it must carry out all tasks associated with the review as an automatic extension of the first part of the process, producing the letters, updating the personnel records, and generating reports for payroll and pensions. These two requirements will be analysed in turn.

EXPERIMENTING WITH SALARY ADJUSTMENTS

The information used for experimenting with adjustments must be drawn from the personnel data base. However, it is essential that the experiments are not performed on the data base. If they are, all the records will be updated in error. The first requirement of a salary review program is that it should have the capacity to extract the records of a specified group of individuals from the data base. The second requirement is that there should be extensive facilities for performing different types of adjustments to the records that have been extracted. And the third requirement (as far as salary experimentation is concerned) is that it should be possible to print out or display the results. In other words, consideration of the mechanism for experimenting with salary adjustments subdivides further into: creating a workfile, updating it, and displaying it.

CREATING THE WORKFILE

The mechanism for selecting the employees to be included in the workfile should be exactly the same as the mechanism for selecting the employees to be included in a report (see pages 120–121). It should be possible to specify the values required for any relevant data base items. For example: salary grades 6–10, month of start May, and staff category permanent. The program should then set up the workfile, which should contain only those items that will be required by the program for experimenting with and processing the review. The items that need to be extracted from the personnel data base are given below. The reason why they are required will emerge from the discussion of the operation of the program which follows:

Employee number
Department number
Job title
Current salary
Salary grade
Performance indicator
Promotability indicator

Space must also be allocated on the workfile for items that do not need to be extracted from the personnel data base but are to be fed into the program for use either in generating letters or in updating the personnel records. Again, these will be discussed below.

Letter type
Letter signatory
Reason 1
Reason 2
Increase amount
Increase percentage
Proposed salary

UPDATING THE WORKFILE

Some companies have developed sophisticated programs for experimenting with salary adjustments. The mechanism discussed here is relatively simple. The reason for this is that the overall complexity of a review should not be reflected in a complex updating mechanism, but in the application of complex procedures. A review may require employees to be considered in a large number of categories, but this does not mean that the workfile updating mechanism should be capable of making all these distinctions. It should be capable of making the obvious distinctions—those relating to salary, department, or job title—but distinctions based on such things as age, length of service, staff status, or staff category should be handled by the setting up of separate workfiles.

When setting up the system, it is necessary to decide how the parameters for the review are most likely to be specified, and to build a means of handling them into the workfile updating mechanism. The system as a whole must be able to cope with cases in which unlikely parameters are used in carrying out the review, but to allow for them in the workfile updating mechanism would merely confuse the operator and slow down the program.

Example: 'Give 5 per cent to everyone in departments 302–320, and $6\frac{1}{2}$ per cent to everyone in departments 321–340. Give an extra £100 to

103

anyone whose job title is in the range DAAA to DZZZ.' This is a likely way for the basis of a review to be specified, and it should therefore be handled by the workfile updating mechanism. A much less likely, but yet not impossible specification, would be this: 'Give 5 per cent to everyone under 40. Give 6½ per cent to everyone over 40 or having more than 10 years experience with the company. Give an extra £100 to anyone having senior staff status.' It is uneconomical in every way to cater for a requirement like this in the workfile updating mechanism. If it did occur, the way to handle it would be to create three workfiles as described below.

1. Employees under 40 who have less than 10 years experience with the company and are not of senior staff status.
2. Employees over 40 or having more than 10 years experience with the company who are not of senior staff status.
3. Employees of senior staff status.

All that the updating mechanism would need to do would be to give the appropriate increases to each workfile. The parameters set for carrying out a review might well be a combination of the two examples given above. The first step would be to define the workfiles required and set them up. The second step would be to use the updating mechanism in the usual way. Thus the program can provide all the flexibility required without an over complex workfile updating mechanism.

Now that the scope of the requirements for the workfile updating mechanism has been identified in outline, the details of the facilities to be provided must be discussed. As with all programs in which a number of options are provided and speed is essential, a formatted screen should be presented to the operator, and the cursor should pass only through those fields that are required for the execution of the required action.

Although the program is designed for bulk updates, it must be able to cope with exceptions. Most reviews include some special cases, and there must, therefore, be a means of performing individual updates as well as bulk ones. In fact, even if every individual were a special case (in other words, reviews were being carried out on an individual basis instead of by reference to fixed parameters), the program would still be needed. There are two reasons for this:

1. The workfile provides a means of looking at the overall effect of reviews before they are put into effect.
2. A program written specifically for salary updating purposes is bound to be quicker than one which has to provide facilities for updating any item on the data base.

Individual changes could be required in two different circumstances:

1. To enter special cases that were exceptions to the bulk update rules (that is, the main parameters for the review).

2. To enter the revised salary of every individual on the workfile in cases where each review had been decided on an individual basis.

These two cases require different facilities. If the individual change is an exception, the individual must be identified by employee number before being updated on the workfile. However, if everyone is to have an individual change, there is no need for this. The system can work through the workfile sequentially. In this way, the operator will never have to enter an employee number, or repeat the individual change option. Only salary will be required, and the process will be much faster. The operator will need to work from an input sheet sorted in the same order as the workfile, but there is no reason why this should not be done. This facility is analogous to the chaining options in recruitment. Therefore, the system should cater for three types of salary change option: bulk, individual, and chained. It is now necessary to consider in detail how each of these options will work, starting with the bulk change.

Earlier in the chapter it was pointed out that the workfile updating mechanism need only cope with changes relating to salary, department, and job title. A bulk change may concern a department, a group of departments, or the whole company. Therefore, the cursor must go to department. If no entry is made, the update involved affects the whole company. Alternatively, a number or a partial number may be entered. A partial number would signify all numbers in a given range. For example, '15' would mean 'all department numbers beginning with 15'. If there were exceptions within the range, they could be dealt with by means of further bulk changes. A similar mechanism can be used to specify job titles. If no entry is made, there is no job title restriction. Alternatively, an individual or partial job title may be entered.

Next, salary change data is required. The increase will be specified either as a percentage or as an amount. Therefore, both should be available on the screen, and the cursor should pass through them, TAB being pressed at the one that is not required. A bulk change may well apply only to a given range of salaries, and a limit may have been set on the resultant proposed salary. Therefore, the cursor should pass through positions for entering the salary range and limit, without any obligation to make an entry.

Finally, it is important to distinguish between two types of adjustments: those applying directly to current salary, and those applying to a previously determined proposed salary. The program is intended for experimenting with salary calculations, and any number of adjustments may be made. Therefore it is essential to specify to the system whether the bulk change currently being processed is to replace all previous ones or to modify them. A simple system is to enter 'P' after the salary change data to indicate that the last change is to be performed on proposed salary rather than current salary. Since this facility may often be used to adjust

105

previous salaries downwards, both the percentage and the amount fields in salary data should be able to accept minus values.

The 'P' option is a critical facility. It enables the personnel manager to cope with last minute changes of policy. An eleventh hour decision to take $\frac{1}{2}$ per cent off all reviews, merely requires ' $-\frac{1}{2}$' and 'P' to be entered in the appropriate places.

How will the individual change and chained options work? The individual change should be identical to the bulk change, except that employee number will be required instead of department or job title details, and there could be a requirement to make an entry against performance, promotability or grade, since exceptional performance and regrading are two of the most likely reasons for an individual change. Therefore, the cursor should pass through these fields. The salary data requirements are unlikely to be as extensive as those for bulk change, since an individual change will almost certainly be linked to specifying a percentage or an amount. However, the same screen layout and cursor behaviour can be used, since carriage return will terminate the process. The program should be written in such a way that TAB causes the cursor to pass over an item of salary change data, and carriage return signifies that the entries are complete. Provided that their order on the screen is percentage, amount, salary range, limit, and 'P' option, carriage return after amount will terminate the individual change and return the cursor to the action box.

The chained option should work differently, because it will always be used to process the workfile sequentially, entering a salary for each individual, and speed is the essential requirement. The system should write up the employee number of the individual under consideration, and the cursor should go straight to a position in which salary can be entered. The cursor should then pass to grade, performance, and promotability. Carriage return at any point here should signify that the record of the individual under consideration has now been fully updated. TAB can be used to leave an item unchanged and pass to the next one. Immediately the individual has been updated, the next employee number should be displayed and the cursor repositioned at salary. A code should be used for entry in the place assigned to salary to signify that the chained update is now complete. It must also be possible to specify the start point for a chained update through the workfile. When the code for the chained option is entered, the system should position the cursor for entry of a department number and employee number. It should then continue chaining from that point until the signal to end is given.

DISPLAYING THE WORKFILE

Since salary experimentation is performed in order for the results to be reviewed, it is important to consider how they should be displayed or printed out. The workfile should have the same sort order as the departmental salary report (see page 151), since the two are certain to be used in conjunction with one another. The suggested sort order for the departmental salary report is: department, job title, salary, name. Each department on the workfile print-out should begin on a new page, so that it can be circulated to the appropriate manager for review. The heading for the job title should be printed out, followed by the individual's details:

Employee number
Surname and initials
Age
Salary grade
Current salary
Proposed salary
Increase amount
Increase percentage
Letter type
Letter signatory
Reason 1
Reason 2
Performance rating
Promotability indicator

In some cases, totals for current and proposed salary may be required after each job title group. This will not always be required, however, and it takes up a significant amount of space. Therefore, two options may be provided—full and short listing—with the full one providing totals after each job title. Both options should give totals at the end of each department, and at the end of the whole company. A third option, the summary listing, should also be provided. This should omit all details of individuals, and give only the totals for current and proposed salary at job title, department, and company level.

All three options should be available in two modes: department and company. If the department option is specified, the system should ask for a department number (or partial department number) and then produce the report. If the company option is specified, the workfile should be printed out from start to finish in the format specified. The six options, therefore, are:

Full company salary listing
Full department salary listing
Short company salary listing
Short department salary listing
Summary company salary listing
Summary department salary listing.

These listings may be used to review the results of salary experimentation either on a VDU or on a print-out, and also, when required, to enter further adjustments.

This concludes the discussion of program design considerations involved in experimenting with salary adjustments. It is now time to consider how to process the review once it has been approved.

PROCESSING A SALARY REVIEW

Putting a review into effect normally involves carrying out three separate operations:

1. Sending letters to individuals.
2. Updating the personnel records.
3. Notifying payroll and pensions.

All the information required for these purposes is on the workfile set up for experimenting with salary adjustments, and it is possible, therefore, to use the salary review program to carry out all three of these operations automatically by reference to the workfile without any operator intervention. Each operation should be analysed in turn.

AUTOMATIC GENERATION OF LETTERS

The process by which letters can be generated automatically in a personnel computer system has already been dealt with in Chapter 3. It is a fundamental feature of any worthwhile personnel computer system, saving an immense amount of time and ensuring that the personnel records are never out of phase with documents sent to individuals. The use of letter writing in the salary review program is a natural application of this principle, but also perhaps one of the most dramatic. If a company decides to carry out an emergency review of four per cent across the board, the salary review program should take only a couple of minutes to set up a workfile and update it with all the revised salaries. If automatic letter writing is available too, it should require only a few seconds more to write the required letters to a file inside the computer. They would still have to be printed off, but the fact remains that the bulk of the work involved in the review—which might normally have extended over several weeks—has been reduced to a couple of minutes.

The only information that the computer requires, in addition to the data used for salary experimentation purposes, is which letter to send and who will be signing it. Options must therefore be provided on the formatted screen to enable this information to be entered. The two items required are letter type and signatory, but will this information be the same for everyone? In certain circumstances it could be, but it is more likely that the letter signatory will depend on the individual's department. The letter type should be the same for everyone on a given workfile (factors that lead to different letters are almost certain to have led already to different workfiles) unless they have been adjusted by the individual change option.

It is reasonable, therefore, to provide options to set letter and signatory for everyone on the workfile or for everyone in a given department on the workfile. The best way of dealing with the problem created by the individual change option is to say that whenever this option is used the cursor should request letter and signatory as well as salary change data. The same goes for the chained option: letter and signatory should be requested for each individual. However, it is reasonable to specify the letter and signatory allocated to the last individual as the default values for the next one, so that the operator is able to leave them as they are and save time by pressing carriage return. Similarly, grade, performance, and promotability should always default to the existing value on the workfile (as extracted from the personnel data base), since it is more likely that they have remained the same than that they have changed. These default values are essential to enable chained updating to proceed at maximum speed, but the operator must always be able to alter them.

UPDATING THE PERSONNEL RECORDS

The position with regard to updating the personnel records is analogous to that with regard to letter writing. The essential information required is already available on the workfile. However, there are once again additional items to be considered. Nothing has been mentioned yet about the date of the review, and clearly this information must be supplied. It is best provided at the time when the salary review program is run, immediately before the formatted screen is set up. If reviews are to be carried out on different dates, they should be treated as separate workfiles. There is no reason why the number of workfiles current at any one time should be restricted since the name of the one to be processed can be supplied at the time the program is run.

The other item of information that will have to be added before the records can be updated is the reason (or reasons) for the change. When a salary update is posted to the data base, two data-sets will have to be updated: main details and history. Main details will only require the new salary and the effective date, but the creation of a new history record requires, in addition, department, job title, location, and reasons for the change. Department, job title, and location will not have changed, because this is a program for handling salary reviews only. Any other updates, even if linked to the review, would have to go through the normal updating channels and be processed via the main personnel records program. Therefore, these items can be set in the new history record to the same value as they had on the last one.

Reasons for the change will have to be supplied from the workfile. It is not sufficient to set the comment automatically to 'review'. It is true that the majority of cases will be adequately described in this way, but further information will be required on occasions, to deal with cases where another type of salary adjustment coincides with the review, and affects the overall amount, for example, regrading or increased hours.

The means of dealing with this can follow the same pattern as arrangements for letter generation, and in fact is best combined with it. The command for setting the letter and signatory (either as a company or on a departmental basis) can also cause the system to ask for the reasons for the change. An individual change should automatically provide for re-entry, and the chained option should enable reasons to be entered, but provide a default value taken from the previous individual updated, which can be given effect simply by the pressing of carriage return.

Thus, all individuals on the workfile for whom salary change data has been supplied will also have details of the letter type and signatory required, and the reasons for the change as they are to appear in history, A single command can then be used to convert the workfile into a reality, transferring its contents to the personnel data base and writing the letters required to individuals. When this update is performed, the system should display or print out the names, employee numbers, and departments of all individuals updated, so that a trail exists of what the system actually did during updating. The letters must be written to a file, because the process of printing them out is necessarily much lengthier, and should not be allowed to delay the updating of the personnel records.

There is an important difference between companies operating annual reviews and those operating rolling reviews which should be allowed for in the system. In the case of an annual review system, the budget is set, experimental adjustments are performed, and the increases are processed, all within a short space of time. Since the main reviews all take place at one time, there is no necessary division between the setting of the budget and the carrying out of the review. This is not the case with a rolling review system. Under this arrangement, the principal adjustments continue throughout the year, and the first reviews to be processed against the budget will take place 11 months before the last ones. Therefore, the budget is set well in advance of the main body of reviews to which it relates, and monitoring actual increases as they take place throughout the year against anticipated increases is an important function.

How can it be done? The only way is to carry out a budgeting exercise before the year begins along the following lines:

1. Parameters are set for reviews over the next year.
2. Managers allocate the budget amongst their staff, predicting the increases they expect to award.
3. The budgetary salary for each individual is stored on the personnel records as 'proposed salary'.

Each month, when managers are notified of the staff they are to review, proposed salary is included in the report sent to them along with all relevant salary details. They must then either confirm or modify the proposed salary, so that the relationship of actual increases to budgeted ones is immediately apparent.

The clearest and most economical way to supply this information is in the form of a workfile print-out, as discussed in the section on displaying the workfile (page 106). This print-out has a column assigned to proposed salary, and the budgeted amount can be picked up from the data base at the time the workfile is set up. Workfiles should always be set up as close as possible to the date when they are to be used. Unlike the data base, they will not reflect changes to the personnel records which occur after their creation, and so they will become increasingly out-of-date as time passes, as a result of such things as leavers, transfers, and emergency salary adjustments.

This amounts to saying that, where a rolling review is in operation, a process analogous to an annual review has to be performed, with the difference that proposed salary is posted to the data base instead of current salary. Therefore, for updating the data base from the workfile two commands will be required: one to update current salary and one to update proposed salary. The latter will not affect any items other than proposed salary, and will not require the generation of a new history record. Corresponding to this, there must be two possible ways of creating a workfile: with proposed salary read from the personnel data base and with proposed salary left blank. The principal purpose of the salary review program is to experiment with and process salary reviews, but it must also be capable of performing the budgetary functions that are sometimes associated with them.

NOTIFYING PAYROLL AND PENSIONS

This is an important task, but also a simple one. The format in which the workfile should be displayed or printed out has already been discussed. A print-out will need to be produced before the data base update command is initiated. This print-out can also be used for circulation to payroll and pensions to notify them of the increases that have been processed.

Redundancies

Planning and carrying out a redundancy program has a certain amount in common with planning and carrying out a salary review. There is the same requirement to experiment with different policies before putting anything into effect, in other words, to extract data from the data base and manipulate it through a workfile. Then there is a requirement to update the data base from the workfile when a course of action has been agreed, and to generate letters for individuals. Once again, reports will be required on the state of the workfile, both to review policy decisions and

111

to notify interested parties (such as payroll and pensions) of the final outcome. Each of these areas requires consideration: composition of the workfile, format of the output, generation of letters and data base update. Consideration must also be given to the facilities that should be made available for calculating the redundancy payments. First of all, however, some points must be made regarding the scope of the program.

SCOPE OF THE PROGRAM

When defining the scope of a redundancy program, the most important points to stress are as follows:

1. It should use a workfile.
2. It should provide an automatic data base update facility.
3. It should handle the generation of letters to individuals.

However, within this framework two important decisions must be made: the extent to which the program is to handle documents other than letters connected with redundancy, and the facilities that should be provided for the calculation of optional redundancy payments.

The question of documents arises, because throughout discussions in this book the view has been taken that a personnel computer system should replace all manual systems and produce all documents. It is not possible to extend this attitude to all aspects of a redundancy exercise. Redundancy procedures are the subject of detailed legislation, and the documents that have to be produced do not lend themselves to computerization. If it were just a matter of supplying information, the computer could handle it. But the information has to be provided in triplicate on various forms, and the only way to handle this would be to have the forms specially mounted on continuous stationery. As a redundancy is necessarily an emergency measure rather than a regular occurrence, this is not worth considering. The forms must, therefore, be completed by hand.

The question of optional redundancy payments is the other area in which a decision must be made about the scope of the facilities to be provided. It is not unusual for companies to offer redundancy payments that are more generous than the statutory ones. It is clearly desirable that the computer should calculate optional payments as well as statutory ones, but difficulties arise over how this is to be done. A company might decide to award additional payments in a great many different ways, and it is impractical to design a program that will cater for all of them in advance. A decision therefore has to be made as to what the most likely methods are, and the program designed to cater for these. Some suggestions as to how this can be done are given later in the chapter in the section on optional payments.

COMPOSITION OF THE WORKFILE

As in the case of setting up a salary review workfile, complete flexibility is required in specifying the individuals to be included by reference to data base item values. The items that need to be extracted from the data base and put into the workfile are:

Employee number
Surname and initials
Department number
Performance rating
Current salary
Start date
Continuous service date
Years of service
Age
Sex
Job title code

Years of service should be calculated by reference to continuous service date when the workfile is set up. Age should be calculated by reference to date of birth.

Space must also be allocated on the workfile for:

Weekly salary
Statutory entitlement
Optional entitlement
Total entitlement
Notice period
Amount of pay in lieu of notice
Total of redundancy entitlements and notice payments
Letter type
Letter signatory.

The question of pay in lieu of notice is dealt with under the section on statutory entitlements.

FORMAT OF THE OUTPUT

A print layout must be designed which can accommodate all the items listed under composition of the workfile. This can only be achieved if job title is printed out as a group heading instead of appearing in individual lines. For this reason the sort order must include job title. Provided it is printed out in the column assigned to name it will not confuse the vertical column layout of any of the critical items on the report. Unfortunately, the government forms require further information on individuals in addition to this. It would not be possible to fit all the information which has to be supplied about individuals on a single line of print-out. The only way to handle this requirement would be to produce a sheet for each individual, and transcribe it onto the forms (one of the forms, for example, has to show details of the way the calculation has been performed). This is really a task for payroll. What the personnel department requires is a report that lists individuals, but enables the overall picture to be assimilated rapidly. To achieve this, it is necessary to confine the details of each individual to a single line, so that a report with intelligible vertical columns can be produced. The details listed under composition of the workfile are sufficient for this purpose.

There are advantages in sorting the report in the same order as the departmental salary report—department, job title, salary, name—as this always tends to be used as a basic reference document. Each department should start on a new page, and finish with totals for each of the entitlements and payments. Totals for the entire company should be provided on a separate sheet at the end of the report. The first line of the report should give the effective date of the redundancy, and the date when it is to be announced. These items are discussed further in the next section.

CALCULATING ENTITLEMENTS

As with the program for salary reviews, the redundancy program should be split into two parts, the first one creating the workfile, and the second one calculating entitlements. When this second program is run, it will first need to establish the basic facts about the redundancy: when it is to occur and when it is to be announced. This will enable the program to calculate 'the relevant date' for each individual's redundancy. 'The relevant date' is defined by law, and is the date which must be used when calculating any individual's redundancy payment. It is calculated by adding a person's statutory notice period on to the date when they are declared redundant. It is not necessarily the same as the effective date of the redundancy, that is the date when the person actually stops working, because pay may be given in lieu of notice.

For example, a company may announce on 1 June that 20 people (identified by name) will be made redundant on 1 July. What the company means by this is that they will not be required to work more than one month, so that if they are entitled to more than one month's notice, they will receive pay in lieu of notice for the outstanding period of time. The date of the redundancy announcement was 1 June. The effective date of the redundancy was 1 July. But 'the relevant date' for redundancy calculations may be different for each individual. For someone on three months notice it would be 31 August. The program will have to calculate 'the relevant date' for each individual in order to perform the calculations, and this is why it must begin by asking the operator when the redundancy is to occur and when it is to be announced.

114

The calculation of statutory entitlements is a good example of the kind of thing a computer does very easily, but which can be a 'nightmare' to perform manually. The rules for calculating payments are simply embedded into the program. First, a check is made to see whether anyone on the file has less than two years continuous service or works less than 21 hours per week. If so, their entitlement is zero. For all remaining employees 'the relevant date' is calculated by adding notice period on to the date the redundancy is to be announced. The system then works out how many complete years of service (counting backwards from 'the relevant date') they have in each of the following age categories:

1. 18–21 inclusive.
2. 22–40 inclusive.
3. 41–64 inclusive (men).
   41–59 inclusive (women).

The maximum number of years allowed is 20, and where this figure is exceeded, years in the lower age categories must be dispensed with rather than years in the higher categories. A weekly salary is then calculated, and the employee is entitled to half a week's salary for each complete year of service between the ages of 18–21 inclusive, one week's salary for each year in the 22–40 category, and one and a half week's salary for each year in the 41–64 (or 41–59) category. The weekly salary is subject to an upper limit but this is revised from time to time, and so should be stored as a dictionary entry.

A computer will perform a calculation of this sort in a negligible amount of time. There are exceptions to these rules, but they will only ever affect a minute proportion of employees, so it is reasonable to disregard them in designing a program the principal purpose of which is to provide information rapidly on the effect and cost of a given redundancy policy. The only provision that could cause significant distortions is the rule stating that employees are only entitled to statutory redundancy payments for years during which they were paying class 1 National Insurance contributions. This can be significant for companies that assign large numbers of people overseas for periods in excess of a year, since class 1 contributions do not have to be made after that. If a company felt that this could cause significant distortions in their case, it would be necessary to allow for it within the program. The difficulty would be getting the information. It would have to come from the payroll system. If the payroll system did not store the information, a substantial manual exercise would be required to extract the information from payroll records and feed it into the personnel system. Complications like this must be avoided unless they are absolutely essential.

When statutory entitlements have been dealt with, pay in lieu of notice must be calculated. This is simply a matter of calculating how much notice

115

will be outstanding when the redundancy becomes effective, and multiplying it by weekly or monthly salary as appropriate. It is most important to include facilities for calculating this, because in many cases the amount of pay in lieu of notice will be greater than the statutory redundancy entitlement.

OPTIONAL ENTITLEMENTS

When the program has asked for the effective date of redundancy, and the date when it is to be announced, it should go on to ask a third question: 'Are there to be any optional entitlements?' If the answer is 'No', it can go straight on to calculating the statutory entitlement and pay in lieu of notice, and produce the output on the printer without any further input from the operator. If the answer is 'Yes', the parameters for the optional payments will have to be defined, and for this purpose a formatted screen is required.

What facilities should this screen provide? The first point to recognize is that optional payments should always be made in addition to statutory payments, not instead of them. It is always desirable to know the extent of the statutory commitment, and the figure produced by the computer can be used as a check on the official forms completed by payroll. A decision therefore has to be made as to how a company is likely to specify additional payments. There is a virtue in simplicity. The possibilities are endless, but perhaps the most likely are these:

1. A percentage increase over statutory.
2. A lump sum.
3. A lump sum for each year of service.
4. A specified number (including fractions) of weeks salary for each year of service.

These are the possibilities that should be allowed for on the formatted screen.

The second point to recognize is that, whatever formula is agreed, it must be the same for everyone on the workfile. If optional payments are to be made, a consistent principle should be applied. If, for some reason, a company were operating more than one principle, it would have to use more than one workfile. Consequently, there is no need to provide elaborate facilities for updating groups or individuals as there is in the salary review program. Any payment data entered must apply to the entire workfile, and if further data is supplied, it should completely overwrite the existing calculations. The facilities required in connection with calculations are therefore: update payments, remove payments, and list payments. The cursor should pass through the four possibilities identified above, so that the operator can enter the required parameters. There is no reason why an entry should not be made against more than one of the options.

GENERATING LETTERS

An option is required on the formatted screen to enable the operator to indicate to the system which letter is to be sent to individuals on the file. This is analogous to the letter facility in the salary review program, except that here again everyone in the workfile can be treated together. The system only needs to know the letters to be sent and the signatory.It would be possible to provide a more elaborate facility, so that different signatories could be used for different departments, but this is not really necessary. This facility enables a letter and signatory to be allocated to each individual in the workfile. The letters do not need to be written until the redundancy is put into effect.

DATA BASE UPDATE

This, again, is the same as in the salary review program. When the reports have been discussed, and the policy agreed, a command should be entered to cause the data base to be updated from the workfile and the letters to be written to a file. In this case, there is no need for the program to ask for the reason to be written to history; it will always be the same, that is, redundancy.

This concludes the discussion of two special aspects of the personnel records system. Both of them involve bulk updates to the personnel records, and the production of a large number of letters. The programs proposed enable these two operations, which frequently pose a major administrative problem for personnel departments, to be carried out quickly and efficiently without the risk of errors or discrepancies. They also enable extensive experimentation to be performed off-line, so that policies may be investigated thoroughly, and implemented rapidly once they are approved.

The last three chapters have been concerned with specific areas of a personnel computer system: recruitment, personnel records, salary reviews, and redundancies. The emphasis has been on processing information, and storing it in a comprehensive data base which replaces the manual records. It is now time to consider how this information can be extracted. The programs discussed so far enable data to be displayed on a VDU in a predefined way, but it was pointed out in Chapter 1 that flexibility in manipulating data is one of the principal requirements of a personnel computer system. The means by which it is achieved may be referred to broadly as the enquiry system, and this is the subject of Chapter 7. Chapter 8 discusses some particular reports that are likely to be required.

7. The enquiry system

The basic outline of a computer system is determined by four things: what is to be stored, the manner in which it is to be updated, special features, and the output required. The middle two of these are the ones that cause the problems. Chapters 3, 4, and 5 were largely concerned with the way in which information would be updated in a personnel computer system. It is complicated, because the update mechanisms have to reflect the mode of operation in the given environment down to the last detail. If certain items are always updated together, the system must take account of this; the system must mirror the permutations and complexities of a department's procedures, and is also likely to be constrained by requirements as to speed of operation.

Special features are anything other than straightforward input, update, and output. Letter writing and dictionary facilities may be regarded as special features of a personnel computer system. They are highly complex, because they interact with all the other parts of the system. Output, however, is not a difficult area. There are two reasons for this.

1. It is much easier to determine the output required from a system than to predict all the ways in which the information held within it may need to be updated.
2. Computer systems can be more flexible about the way they format output than about the way they perform updates.

Facilities of the kind discussed earlier in this book for updating the recruitment and personnel data bases can only be provided by specially written application programs. The information could be updated without application programs but it would be too slow and difficult to operate. This problem does not arise to the same extent with output. Reports can be produced by means of report generators which enable output to be formatted as required without the need for additional programming. This means that reports can be written by the user, and do not all have to be specified in advance.

Flexibility in the production of reports is an essential feature of a personnel computer system. Circumstances will constantly arise which require the production of a special report. One of the greatest advantages of a computer system is the speed with which it can interrogate and reformat any of the information which it stores. By providing this facility it transforms the service that the personnel department can supply to the company, particularly in the area of management information, and consequently improves its image.

The design of report generators is, of course, very complex. But there is no need to design one. A great many exist on different computers with

118

different capabilities, and in developing a personnel computer system, it is important to select one that will be suitable. In other words, it is necessary to determine the facilities that will be needed for the generation of *ad hoc* reports. This is not as easy as it sounds. It entails trying to imagine all possible requirements and analysing their basic elements.

How extensive should a report generator be? If report generators with very considerable flexibility exist, there might at first appear to be a case for writing all the reports required in a personnel computer system by this means, and not using application programs for output at all. This approach is worth considering, but it is not necessarily the best answer. Although there are report generators available which could handle all output from the system, they would not normally be available on very small computers. If the personnel department wants to use a stand-alone mini computer (the ideal arrangement as far as security is concerned), it may have to settle for a report generator which, though providing extensive facilities, is not able to produce all the required reports.

A further consideration is that, if a report generator is powerful enough to produce all the reports required of the system, it is bound to be more complex to use than one with limited facilities. Simplicity is an advantage. It reduces training times. There is a great deal to be said for identifying output requirements that involve unusual facilities, and using application programs to handle them, so that a simpler report generator can be used for generating the main body of reports. The majority of reports produced from a personnel computer system are simply concerned with selecting the required information and printing it out in a given format. Arithmetical requirements rarely go beyond counting the entries in a set, totalling items (typically salary), and working out averages.

To summarize, flexible report generation is one of the keys to a successful personnel computer system. It may be used not only for handling *ad hoc* reports, but for producing many of the standard ones as well. There might easily be 80 standard reports produced by such a generating mechanism in a complete system. Some report generators would be capable of producing all the reports required from a personnel computer system. However, this is not necessarily the best approach. It is normally more sensible to identify reports with special features (there should not be more than a dozen of these) and write application programs to produce them. A simple report generator can then be used to produce the majority of standard reports.

Chapter 8, which is concerned with identifying the reports required in a personnel computer system, makes a point of highlighting those that might be outside the scope of a simple report generator. The next step in this chapter must be to decide what the minimum requirements of a report generator should be, bearing in mind that the objective is to select and reformat information, perhaps doing simple counts, totals and averages, rather than to perform complex calculations.

119

The demands made upon an enquiry system may be divided into three types: enquiries, reports and statistics, and it is now necessary to explain the distinction between them. An enquiry is something of the form, 'How many engineers do we have who are aged between 35 and 45, earn between £8000 and £10 000, and have been with the company for over five years?' The answer is given in a single word: '30'. A report always consists of two parts: selecting the people concerned, and displaying their details in a specified format. The mechanism for selection is like carrying out an enquiry. An enquiry simply requires the performance of a 'find'. A report involves the initial performance of a 'find', followed by the report itself. The mechanisms for dealing with these may be referred to as find procedures and report procedures. Statistics build on these techniques, but are more complicated. Therefore, they will be dealt with last.

Enquiries and reports

FIND PROCEDURES

For the reasons given above a report generator is no good unless it can handle find procedures. These should be simple, English-type statements which express precisely what is required. The words used should all be easily comprehensible, but their syntax will necessarily be strict. The computer can only understand what it is being asked to do if the words used follow a predefined structure. This is not difficult to achieve. A find procedure only needs to contain three types of words: item names, item values, and logical connectors. It is concerned with specifying which items the computer is to search, and what values it is to look for in each of these items. Logical connectors are required because a find procedure may have a complex set of parameters. An item name would be something like 'SALARY', 'LOCATION', or 'START DATE'. Item values corresponding to these might be '10000', 'H/O', and '750601'. Logical connectors are such things as:

$=$
$\neq$
$>$
$<$
$\&$
or

For example: 'Find job title $=$ process engineer $\&$ location $\neq$ H/O and salary > 8499 $\&$ salary < 10001 or job title $=$ thermal engineer $\&$ location $\neq$ H/O and salary > 8499 and salary < 10001'. This would find all process engineers and thermal engineers who are earning between 8500 and 10 000.

Great care must be taken with the logical connectors. Each enquiry system will have rules as to how they are to be used. It is easy to misplace

'&' and 'or' so that the parameters are wrongly specified. Depending on the rules in force the following two find procedures could specify a totally different selection of people.

1. Find job title = senior process engineer or job title = process engineer & salary > 8000.
2. Find salary > 8000 & job title = senior process engineer or job title = process engineer.

If 'or' is used to separate off distinct parts of the procedure (1) will find all senior process engineers and those process engineers who earn over 8000, whereas (2) will find senior process engineers earning over 8000 and all process engineers. Most report generators will include rather more logical connectors than those given above. The point to make is that find procedures can normally be specified in English-type commands, but their construction and syntax is critical.

REPORT PROCEDURES

A report procedure consists of a series of commands, each related to the facilities provided by the report generator. The basic requirements of a report generator are that it should be able to accept instructions concerning:

1. The report heading.
2. The order in which items are to be sorted.
3. The data item values to be printed out.
4. Various ways of editing the output.
5. Simple arithmetic.
6. Translation of codes.

Each of these will be discussed in turn.

HEADINGS

A report may have several headings; three would be typical: a main heading and two subheadings. For example:

PERSONNEL COMPUTER SYSTEMS—SALARY REPORT

MAN NUMBER	SURNAME AND INITIALS	LAST SALARY	% INC	CURRENT SALARY

The heading statement needs to state which heading it is dealing with, what is to be printed, and where it is to be printed. It is useful if the individual words or phrases in each heading line can be specified separately from one another, because it will then be easier to adjust them if a word is out of place.

SORT ORDER

This is simply a matter of specifying which items the system is to sort on, and the order in which it is to sort them. For example, it may be salary within job title within department. In this case the sort order would be: (1) department (2) job title (3) salary. It should be possible to specify whether the sort should be in ascending or descending order. Ascending is the obvious default value.

DATA LINES

All that is required here is a statement of which data items are to be printed and where they are to be printed. In other words, for every entry retrieved by the find procedure it must state which item values are to be printed across the page, and where they are to be positioned.

EDITING

Reports may be edited in a variety of ways. First of all, certain data item values may be clearer if they are broken up in a specified way. A date looks better as 80/06/01 than as 800601. It looks better still as 01/06/80. These are all forms of editing. The edit statement needs to indicate the insertion of slashes ('99/99/99', for example), and must be referenced by all appropriate data statements. Other types of editing would be suppressing zeros or inserting dashes.

Sometimes a body of text that involves substantial repetition can be made clearer by leaving the repeated items blank. For example, if the report is sorting by department and reporting department number, every line will be printing out the same department number. A useful edit feature would be to suppress all repetition, and print out the number only when it changed.

Editing will also be necessary in the sense of skipping lines and pages. It will normally be desirable to skip two lines after the heading, and to skip a page after each major change of sort. It should be possible to add an instruction to this effect on to the end of one of the other statements.

The last type of editing that should be mentioned is entirely concerned with heading lines. It may be useful to build into the report procedure an instruction to print the date, the time, and the page number.

SIMPLE ARITHMETIC

It was mentioned earlier that a simple report generator need not do any more in the way of arithmetic than count the number of entries in a set, total data item values (such as salary), and average them. Therefore, an arithmetical statement must be able to accept instructions on which item it is to act on, and whether it is to count, total, or average. It must also know where to print the answer. This needs to be specified both in terms of the position across the page where it is to print and in terms of the points in the report at which it is to print. For example, if it is counting the number of people in each department, it will need to print out after each department.

How can this be done? It can be done by relating the arithmetic statements to a sort level. If an entry count is required after each department, and department is the first sort, then the arithmetic statement containing the count instruction must contain a reference to sort level 1 (it could be labelled '1', for example). Arithmetic statements will also need an explanation of what they are. It is no good printing a number in the middle of a report without explaining what it is. Therefore, there should be a facility for printing a phrase before the result of an arithmetical statement. The words to be printed and the position in which they are to be printed are all that is required.

TRANSLATION OF CODES

Many of the items on the personnel and recruitment data bases are coded. On some occasions the code may be what is required. But normally the report should show the expansion stored in the dictionary. As the dictionary may be storing information other than the expansion, it is important to indicate which positions in the dictionary are to be referenced. In some systems the report generator might have an automatic means of referencing the subdictionary appropriate to the item in question, but it is more likely that this information will need to be given. The subdictionary to be referenced and the character positions to print must be related to the appropriate data lines.

WRITING A REPORT PROCEDURE

Report generators vary in the way they operate. They are all designed, however, to make report generation as simple as it can be. If the requirements are simple (as they are in a personnel computer system), the mechanism for writing reports should reflect this. The report generating mechanism can be as straightforward as the instructions it needs to execute.

What is the simplest form in which a complete set of instructions for generating a report can be given? Basically the system needs to know what kind of an instruction it is being given, what it is to print, and where it is to print it. Types of instruction have already been identified: headings, sort order, data, arithmetic, and edits (print date, time or page number at the top of the report; suppress repeat items, insert slashes between dates, skip lines, and skip pages). What to print must be either the precise words given or an item value or the result of a calculation, as appropriate to the particular type of instruction. That is, if a word is given after a heading statement, it is clearly a word that is to be printed in the report heading. If a word is given after a data statement, it must be the name of a data item the value of which is to be printed on the report for each entry. Arithmetic and edit instructions are slightly more complicated. Rules must be laid down for the way they are to be used in a given report generator. But an impression of the simplicity of report generation can be gained by studying the report illustrated in Fig. 7.1, and the

123

statements below, which comprise a complete set of instructions for producing it. The numbers in brackets are the print positions for each statement.

1st heading:	Salary report	(32)
2nd heading:	Employee	(9)
	Department	(15)
	Surname and initials	(35)
	Salary	(45)
	Date salary	(59)
3rd heading:	Number	(8)
	Number	(16)
	Awarded	(57)
Sort order:	Department	
	Salary	
Data:	Employee number	(6)
	Department	(14)
	Name	(39)
	Salary	(46)
	Salary date	(58)
Arithmetic:	Sort 1 print 'Total salary' (30) and calculate total salary (46) End of report print 'Grand total' (29) and calculate grand total salary (46) End of report print 'Average' (25) and calculate average salary (46)	
Edits:	Print date on heading 1	(9)
	Print time on heading 1	(15)
	Print page on heading 1	(54)
	Suppress repeats of department	
	Insert slashes in salary date	
	Leave 1 line after heading 1	
	Leave 1 line after heading 2	
	Leave 1 line before totals of sort 1	
	Leave 2 lines after totals of sort 1	
	Leave 1 line after grand total—end of report.	

These are the instructions that would need to be given to the report generator to produce the report. Any particular report generator would have its own shorthand way of conveying these instructions, and this would reduce their length, particularly those concerning arithmetic and edits. Edit instructions can normally be included in the heading or data statement to which they relate. The details of how this is done in any particular case are not important. The point to note is that report

| 0 | 5 | 10 | 15 | 20 | 25 | 30 | 35 | 40 | 45 | 50 | 55 | 60 |

| 19/09/79 | 12:08 | *Salary report* | | *Page* 999 |

Employee number	*Dept number*	*Surname and initials*	*Salary*	*Date salary awarded*
2751	550	HIGGINSBOTTOM A.B.C.	12 000	80/06/01
3231		BROWN A. J.	11 000	80/07/01
1057		BAYSWATER D. P.	10 000	80/04/01
2912		RIGSBY E. E. O.	9 000	80/02/01
7347		JOHNSON M. P.	8 000	79/12/01
2423		FRIMLEY T. W.	7 000	80/03/01
1012		TOWATER N. T.	6 000	80/05/01
		TOTAL SALARY	63 000	
2012	492	ANDERSON P. T.	15 000	80/02/01
7052		JAMES D. V.	13 000	80/09/01
1937		SMITH N. A.	11 000	79/11/01
1214		BENTALL L. D.	9 000	80/01/01
2740		CROWE W. E.	7 000	79/12/01
1902		ELIOT W. H.	5 000	80/06/01
		TOTAL SALARY	60 000	
3250	142	ALLINGTON T. V. R.	25 000	80/07/01
0105		OPUS D. E.	20 000	80/02/01
7109		SEDDON O. P.	15 000	80/04/01
2539		DRINGHAM G. F.	10 000	78/03/01
0004		SARGENT A.	9 000	80/05/01
8215		TURNER D. J.	8 000	80/01/01
9014		HICKS J. B.	6 000	79/09/01
4017		UNDERWOOD M. P.	4 000	80/10/01
6210		MURDOCH V. E.	2 000	80/07/01
		TOTAL SALARY	99 000	
		GRAND TOTAL	222 000	
		AVERAGE		

Figure 7.1 A sample report

generators are designed to provide maximum simplicity, so that an operator can sit down at a terminal and compose a one-off report, perhaps in as little as five minutes. They are powerful tools, and an essential component of the overall flexibility of a personnel computer system.

CREATING AND EDITING REPORT PROCEDURES

Although there may be cases where it is convenient to type in some report commands on the terminal, look at the output, and leave it at that having obtained the desired result, it is more usual to keep report procedures in the system for future use. Many requests for information are of a recurring type, and there is no point in typing in all the commands whenever the request is received. Furthermore, it is easy to make a mistake when typing in a string of report commands, and if they have been kept in the system as a procedure, it will only be necessary to modify the incorrect statements. If, on the other hand, the commands are typed individually, they may all have to be typed in again for the sake of a single mistake.

Report procedures must be easy to create and edit. It was mentioned earlier in Chapter 3 on letter writing that most modern computer systems have software that enables an operator to create and edit files. This can be used for report procedures as well. Alternatively, the report generator may provide independent facilities. The minimum requirement is that it should be possible to type commands and keep them, delete lines, insert or add them, and modify them. A crude form of modifying is to type the line again. More sophisticated packages would include facilities for changing parts of a line, and inserting or deleting phrases.

A personnel computer system will probably contain about 80 standard reports (see Chapter 8) and the report generator will be responsible for the majority of them. Although requests for information which does not fit any of the predesigned formats will be received from time to time, it will be very rare for a report to be requested which bears no relation at all to any of the existing ones. The normal procedure when a new request is received should be to decide which of the existing reports comes closest to meeting the requirement, and to modify it accordingly. This can save a significant amount of time. It saves the retyping, but it also saves the tedious task of calculating print positions. There is nothing difficult about this, but it is easy to make mistakes, especially where the heading is a different length from the item.

Most requests for information will be handled by running a standard report with a nonstandard find. Some will require minor editing of an existing procedure but if a comprehensive suite of standard reports has been written—as it should be—the writing of new reports should be an unusual occurrence. Familiarity with existing reports is at least as important as aptitude for report generation. In a well-designed personnel computer system with a powerful report generator it should never be necessary to refuse a request for information if the data requested is stored on the system.

Statistics

Earlier in the chapter the distinction between enquiries and reports was explained in terms of find procedures and report procedures. A find procedure is a command that instructs the computer to select a specified group of people. The request for information is given in the form 'find everyone who satisfies a given set of criteria', and the answer supplied is the number of people found. A report procedure goes on from there to specify the details that are to be reported and the form in which they are to be reported. Each line of the report prints the details of one of the entries that has been found.

A statistical report differs from this in that it does not normally print the details of any particular entry. It reports how many entries have been found in each of a series of categories. For example, it may report the number of staff in each department, how many of them are permanent and how many temporary, show the split between technical and non-technical, and indicate how many of them are on assignment.

A statistical report is therefore like a series of finds. However, there are two important differences, the first one concerning the format of the output, and the second concerning the manner in which the analysis is performed. To take the first point: when a find procedure is performed in the normal way, the answer will be printed out (or displayed on the screen) on a single line. If another find is performed, it will occupy the next line, and so on. Therefore, a series of figures will be printed down the page without any heading or explanation. A statistical report, however, normally involves presenting information in tabular form with headings across the top and down the side. A series of find procedures will not produce the desired result. It could produce the answers, but they will have to be reformatted with headings to be of any use.

The second point is that a series of find procedures is not an efficient way of tackling a series of related questions. A find procedure is designed essentially as a one-off enquiry; therefore, it will search right through the data base when it is executed. This means that if a statistical report is tackled as a series of find procedures, each figure on the table will involve a search through the entire data base. This will inevitably be a lengthy process. It is also likely to be an unnecessary one. Each position on the table can be defined by a set of criteria, and if these criteria are fed into the computer in advance, a single search through the data base should suffice. Each record will be compared with each set of criteria, and allocated as appropriate, incrementing the count for that category. This approach can result in dramatic savings in time and processing power.

Clearly, a special program is required for handling statistical reports, and the next task must be to consider the facilities it should include to provide the required flexibility. This is difficult, because statistical reports are so varied that there are problems in constructing a general framework into which they can be fitted. The problem can be expressed as follows: construct a series of questions which the computer is to ask the operator, and which will enable all the information necessary for generating a statistical report to be fed in. Another way of putting the problem is simply 'What are the essential features of a statistical report?'

	Statistical enquiry report						
	Head office		Branch office		Total head/branch	Affiliates		Grand total
	M	F	M	F		M	F	
Executives	8	0	1	0	9	2	0	11
Professional	10	0	0	0	10	0	0	10
Technical	25	2	11	0	38	2	0	40
Total	43	2	12	0	57	4	0	61
Sec./clerical	64	20	26	5	115	10	0	125
Manual	100	35	40	2	177	0	0	177
Total	164	55	66	7	292	10	0	302
Grand total	207	57	78	7	349	14	0	363

Figure 7.2 A sample statistical analysis

Perhaps the essential feature of a statistical report is that it tends towards a matrix structure. Fig. 7.2 illustrates this point. In this example, categories have been specified down the side of the report and across the top; some of the ones across the top have been further subdivided into two. Thus three levels of criteria have been included. It is highly unlikely that this could be exceeded since the matrix would become unintelligible. The third level might divide the second one into more than two parts, but it could hardly be further subdivided by a fourth level. Some statistical reports might have no second or third level; there is no compulsion to present the results in matrix form.

The first requirement of a statistical report generator is, therefore, that it should be able to accept up to three levels of criteria for categorizing records, and to use them in conjunction with one another to assess the number of records that qualify under each combination. The second requirement is that it should be possible for the operator to tell it where on the page the answers are to print out. And the third requirement is that it should be possible to specify headings for vertical and horizontal columns, and to indicate where they should be printed.

Within each level there may be any number of groups, provided that they fit on the page. In the example above, level one had five groups:

executives, professional, technical, secretarial/clerical, and manual (total columns will be discussed later). Level two had three groups: head office, branch office, and affiliates. Level three had six groups, which happened to be three identical pairs: male, female, male, female, male, female. If level one is always the categories down the page, and level two is the ones across the top, it will be possible to give the criteria for all the groups in level one, without at this stage making reference to levels two and three.

Levels two and three are more closely connected. Some headings may be split into two parts at level three, some into three, and some not at all For example, a column headed 'permanent technical staff' might be further subdivided into 'home office', 'branch office' and 'site'; alternatively, it might be subdivided into 'home office' and 'assigned', or not subdivided at all. If all the level two criteria are given, followed by all the level three criteria, the system will not know how the level three sets of criteria are to be related to the level two sets of criteria. For example, the system would have no way of distinguishing between the following two statistical formats:

1. Executives   – – – Technical – – – – – – Nontechnical – – –
           H/O Assigned Temp. Perm.   Temp.   Contract

2. Executives   – – – Technical – – – – – – Nontechnical – – –
   H/O Assigned   Temp.   Perm.   Temp.   Contract

The solution to this is to arrange the input to the program such that each level two set of criteria is immediately followed by a level three set. The system should prompt for the input, and carriage return may be taken to mean that no level three is required. Therefore, the system will prompt for all level one sets of criteria, followed by alternate sets of level two and level three criteria. An example of this will be given shortly, but first it is necessary to consider what information the system will need to prompt for.

It is clear that the system must be able to accept three levels of criteria, and any number of groups within them. How are the criteria for each group to be specified? Essentially each group can be specified by a find procedure, as discussed under reports and enquiries. Whether the input is made in exactly the same format is immaterial. The concept is the same: a series of inclusions, exclusions, ranges, and alternatives. For example, the category 'executives' may be specified by reference to a range of job titles, and the number of leavers in a given division by reference to a range of department numbers in conjunction with a range of leave dates (the range for the period in question). The specification of group criteria is therefore analogous to a find procedure.

There is an important diference in the way these group criteria are used as compared with find procedures. A find procedure is self-sufficient; it is executed as it stands. Group criteria have to be combined with one another in accordance with the requirements of the matrix. If the category 'executives' is at level one, and the heading 'leavers' is level two, the system must combine the group criteria for executives with the group criteria for leavers before it can calculate the number of leavers in the category 'executives'. Where level three criteria are in use, this process is still more complicated.

This concludes discussion of what was identified earlier as the first requirement of a statistical report generator, namely 'that it should be able to accept up to three levels of criteria for categorizing records, and to use them in conjunction with one another to assess the number of records that qualify under each combination'. The other two requirements identified earlier were indicating where on the page the answers were to be printed out and giving headings (with print positions) for vertical and horizontal columns.

The procedure outlined above for specifying group criteria can easily be expanded to deal with print positions and headings. Each set of group criteria will be associated with a heading and a print position. Therefore, the system should prompt for this information at the same time. Overall, four items of information are required: the group heading, the print position for the group heading, the group criteria, and the print position for the answer derived in response to the group criteria. The system will derive the precise print position by combining the line number of the level one group with the print position given by the level two or three group. In other words, the print position given by the operator will be the column position across the page, and therefore only relates to levels two and three. There needs to be a facility for leaving blank lines down the side of the matrix, in other words for controlling line positions at level one. The simplest solution is to add a command on to the end of group headings at level one if a line is to be left blank. At level one, therefore, only three items of information are required: group heading, print position for group heading, and group criteria.

The question of totals must now be tackled. There needs to be a means of instructing the system to insert a total line (or column), and to derive the figures by totalling the appropriate lines (or columns). The heading and print position can be dealt with in the same way as for any of the other groups. However, there will be no group criteria. Instead, there will be an instruction to total a given set of line or column numbers. If a total command occurs at level one it will be instructing the computer to total line numbers. If it occurs at level two or three, it will be instructing it to total column numbers. Typing the word 'total' in the place allocated for group criteria should be sufficient to indicate to the system that the numbers that follow are line or column numbers to be totalled, and not group criteria.

This completes discussion of how the system is to be instructed to perform a given statistical analysis. It may now be useful to give an example of the way in which these instructions should prompt for the input. If no entry is made in response to a level one request, it should be interpreted as 'pass to level two'. No entry at the heading for level two would mean 'there is no level two (and therefore no level three)', or if entries had already been made, it would mean that there were no more. No entry at the print position for level two would indicate that there was a level three associated with it, and therefore a level two print position was inappropriate (the print positions would be given at level three). Conversely, if a print position were given at level two, there would be no need for the system to prompt for level three. The example given below is the input that would be required to produce the statistical report illustrated in Fig. 7.2 (see page 128); words in capitals are prompts for the system. The rest is operator input. The system begins by prompting for the overall heading for the report after which it will leave two lines. The date should be added automatically in all cases. In this example, level categories are specified by job title ranges. If job title is a four character code, it is possible to find all those in, say, the D range by 'job title > D & < E'. The lowest in the D range will be DAAA, which is greater than D.

Report heading Statistical enquiry report

LEVEL 1	GROUP 1	HEADING:	Executives, 10
		CRITERIA:	Job title > B
	GROUP 2	HEADING:	Professional, 12
		CRITERIA:	Job title > B & < M
	GROUP 3	HEADING:	Technical, 9
		CRITERIA:	Job title > M & < X
	GROUP 4	HEADING:	Total, 5, 1 blank line
		CRITERIA:	Total 1, 2, 3
	GROUP 5	HEADING:	Sec/clerical, 12
		CRITERIA:	Job title > X & < Y
	GROUP 6	HEADING:	Manual, 6
		CRITERIA:	Job title > Y
	GROUP 7	HEADING:	Total, 5, 1 blank line
		CRITERIA:	Total 5, 6
	GROUP 8	HEADING:	Grand total, 11
		CRITERIA:	Total 4, 7
	GROUP 9	HEADING:	
LEVEL 2	GROUP 1	HEADING:	Head Office, 31
		CRITERIA:	Location is H/O
		POSITION:	
LEVEL 3	GROUP 1	HEADING:	M, 23
		CRITERIA:	Sex is M
		POSITION:	23

		HEADING:	F, 28
	GROUP 2	CRITERIA:	Sex is F
		POSITION:	28
	GROUP 3	HEADING:	
LEVEL 2	GROUP 2	HEADING:	Branch Office, 46
		CRITERIA:	Location is Br/O
		POSITION:	
LEVEL 3	GROUP 3	HEADING:	M, 37
		CRITERIA:	Sex is M
		POSITION:	37
	GROUP 4	HEADING:	F, 43
		CRITERIA:	Sex is F
		POSITION:	43
	GROUP 5	HEADING:	
LEVEL 2	GROUP 3	HEADING:	Total Head/Branch, 65
		CRITERIA:	Total 1, 2, 3, 4
		POSITION:	57
LEVEL 2	GROUP 4	HEADING:	Affiliates, 77
		CRITERIA:	Location is Affil
		POSITION:	
LEVEL 3	GROUP 5	HEADING:	M, 70
		CRITERIA:	Sex is M
		POSITION:	70
	GROUP 6	HEADING:	F, 75
		CRITERIA:	Sex is F
		POSITION:	75
	GROUP 7	HEADING:	
LEVEL 2	GROUP 5	HEADING:	Grand total, 90
		CRITERIA:	Total 5, 6, 7
		POSITION:	86
LEVEL 2	GROUP 6	HEADING:	

This example shows how the first three requirements of a statistical report generator can be met:

1. Performing analyses on groups of criteria at as many as three levels.
2. Specifying where the answers should be printed out.
3. Indicating the headings, and where they should be printed out.

There are two further aspects to consider when designing a statistical report generator, one of them concerning input, and the other concerning output. The point about input will be discussed first. A system has been proposed for preparing statistical analyses. In some cases the analysis may need to be performed on the entire data base. However, it is more likely that it will concern only a limited section of the data base. Even if the only exclusion is 'leavers', this could significantly reduce the number of records to be sorted. Therefore, a question which must be considered is whether the statistical report generator should operate on the data base or on the workfile. If it is to operate on a workfile, a preliminary exercise of defining the records to be included can be performed, prior to specifying the nature of the analysis to be performed. This could be done by means of a find procedure, and it should reduce the time required to prepare the analysis.

The aspect of statistical reports concerning output is less open to debate. When a statistical report is issued, parts of it are liable to be questioned. Alternatively, further elaboration may be requested. What are the qualifications of the people included in a certain category? What are their salaries? Where are they located? To answer these questions it is necessary to know, at the very least, who is included in each category. Failure to come up with a list of names in support of the figures at short notice undermines credibility. It is sensible to provide key information along with names, for example, job title and department.

The only way to meet this requirement is to produce two versions of every statistical report (or at least to provide the option to do so); these would be a full report and a summary report. The summary report should provide the basic statistical details, as already discussed. The detail report should supply names and essential details. The operator should be requested to list the items required and the sort order, as in a normal report generator. Items for which dictionary entries exist should be expanded automatically from the subdictionary.

How is the layout to be arranged? The summary report will print figures across the page, but the detail report will only be able to print one record per line. Consequently, all three levels of criteria will have to print out down the page. A system of indentation should be used to distinguish them from one another. Level two could be indented by four characters, and level three by eight characters. Each group of records should be totalled, and the total should be printed regardless of whether or not there are any records in the group. The detail report will therefore be very lengthy, and the best way to appreciate its relation to the summary report is to take a simple example. The summary report below shows three job title categories and the number of people within each of them who have up to two or up to five years experience, subdivided into male and female.

	---0–2 years' exp. ---			---2–5 years' exp. ---			Total
	Male	Female	Total	Male	Female	Total	
Executives	3	1	4	4	0	4	8
Crane operators	0	0	0	0	0	0	0
Telex operators	2	0	2	2	1	3	5
Total	5	1	6	6	1	7	13

The detail report to back this up would be as follows (items shown are employee number, name, department number, job title, and start date):

Executives

2 years' experience

MALE

1024	Smith P. A.	204	Dir. Personnel	78/01/01
7059	Brown J. E.	531	Proj. Manager	77/06/01
2012	Adders D. V.	127	Eng. Manager	76/12/01

TOTAL MALE = 3

FEMALE

3012	Baxter D. P.	132	Commerce Manager	77/03/01

TOTAL FEMALE = 1

TOTAL 2 years experience = 4

5 years' experience

MALE

5054	Rogers G. A.	307	Dir. Production	71/03/01
6201	Ainsworth W. G.	127	Sales Manager	74/02/01
4000	Worthy E. D.	204	Chief Accountant	73/09/01
3102	Stephens J. D.	149	Proj. Manager	72/07/01

TOTAL MALE = 4

FEMALE

TOTAL FEMALE = 0

TOTAL 5 years' experience = 4

TOTAL EXECUTIVES = 8

Crane operatives

TOTAL CRANE OPERATIVES = 0

Telex operators

2 years' experience

MALE

3734	Thompson A. J.	201	Senior Telex Op.	78/03/01
4912	Brainsley D. W.	503	Telex Op.	77/04/01

TOTAL MALE = 2

FEMALE

TOTAL FEMALE = 0

TOTAL 2 years experience = 2

5 years experience

MALE

1095	Rider A. D.	327	Supv. Telex	71/09/01
2125	Goldsmith T. M.	412	Snr. Telex Op.	74/07/01

TOTAL MALE = 2

FEMALE

3191	Durrell A. E.	412	Snr. Telex Op.	73/09/01

TOTAL FEMALE = 1

TOTAL 5 years' experience = 3

TOTAL TELEX OPERATORS = 5

There is no denying that the production of statistical reports is a complex business. To the difficulties of report generation it adds problems of grouping and summation. The complexity lies not in the system, but in the nature of the problem. The only consolation is that, however complicated it may appear, it will nevertheless be infinitely quicker and more accurate than trying to produce the same results manually. Presenting consistent sets of statistics in different formats is one of the most difficult administrative tasks facing a personnel department. If a solution is not found, the department loses credibility. If a solution is found, it will not result in anything more than grudging approval. The system proposed in this chapter is designed to provide the required solution. One of its strongest features is the option to produce both summary and detail reports so that questions about the figures can always be answered, and further information supplied.

Enquiries, reports, and statistics have a critical place in a personnel computer system. However, they are not the most difficult features of it to get right. It is true that they present the worst problems to a manual system, because performing them manually in any quantity is impossible; and even in small doses, they will never appear consistent. But they need not be given such prominence in the design of a computer system, because software for handling them is fairly readily available. The problems of enquiries, reports, and statistics arise in many functions other than personnel, and this is why software packages exist for dealing with them. Provided that the user has a clear appreciation of the problems, the solutions are attainable. There is far more experience to draw on for the design and implementation of these systems than for, say, a recruitment system. Selecting suitable software for the enquiry system is, however, only the first stage in meeting the requirements of the system. The second stage is to define these requirements, not in terms of the general facilities required, but in terms of specific reports. This is the subject of the next chapter.

8. Reports

Chapter 7 discussed the requirements of an enquiry system, in particular the facilities that it would need in order to generate a wide range of reports. It was mentioned that a personnel computer system might well include about 80 standard reports, and that the majority of these should be produced by the report generating mechanism, the remainder being handled by specially written application programs. If such a high proportion of reports are produced by a means that can easily be understood and manipulated by the user, it might at first appear that the analysis and specification of reports is not an important matter.

This is a misconception. While it is true that errors and oversights in the specification are necessarily less critical when application programs are not required, they can still lead to serious problems. However you look at it, 80 reports is a large number. They all have to be specified, written, tested, and documented. If at the end of this, it turns out that they are not what was really wanted, a great deal of time and effort will have been wasted. The writing of reports is a relatively straightforward process—even those that require application programs will be substantially easier to write than any of the principal update programs—but the analysis of them is not.

The specification of individual reports does not pose any great problem. The difficulty is that there is no straightforward method of identifying the overall requirements. If a personnel computer system is to replace the manual system in its entirety, the reports that emanate from it must be comprehensive. But they should also aim to avoid duplication. Of course, the enquiry system will be available to deal with *ad hoc* requests, but it must be possible to deal with the majority of requests by standard means, or the system will get out of control.

The possibility of the reporting system getting out of control is a serious one. If there are indeed around 80 reports, and the reason for requiring so many will soon become clear, there is a genuine problem about remembering what they all do, and, therefore, about deciding which one is the best to use in a particular case, unless they are clearly defined within an analytical framework. It is for this reason that all reports must be clearly documented, even ones that take a very short time to write. Unless the personnel records officer is able to pick out the required report quickly on every occasion it might as well never have been written.

A clear analytical framework is required, but it is not very easy to come by. The lack of information in personnel departments is such a chronic problem that few people have a clear idea of what is really required. In fact, it is not possible to develop the required framework from first principles. The question 'What reports are required from a personnel computer system?' can only really be answered by monitoring the demands made on a system over a number of years. Once management realizes that the personnel department is at long last capable of supplying information, it will begin to request reports, and as the useful ones are gradually filtered out from the superfluous ones, a framework emerges.

The details of this framework will differ from one company to another, but the main outlines will be the same. This chapter presents a framework that meets the principal requirements and was developed in the way suggested over a number of years. Each of the reports in the framework is discussed in turn, and its purpose explained. If this framework were to be adopted as a starting point, it might save years of wasted effort and frustration in designing and implementing a personnel computer system. Subsequent modifications to meet individual requirements should be easily manageable. There is nothing more frustrating than having a system that meets the production requirements of the department perfectly well, but which is unable to produce the reports requested quickly and efficiently.

The framework proposed consists of two parts: personnel and recruitment, of which personnel is much the larger. For this reason it will be useful to deal with the recruitment reports first, before launching into the labyrinthine complexity of personnel.

Recruitment reports

There are five principal recruitment reports: vacancy, position, source, offer, and an applicant dump. Each of these will be discussed in turn. It is interesting to note that three of them contain features that might be outside the scope of a simple report generator, this being a much higher proportion than in personnel. These three (vacancy, position, and source) involve calculating ratios from the totals at the bottom of the report. Many report generators would handle this with ease, but not all. If the report generator could not handle it, an application program would have to be written. Alternatively, the ratios could be omitted altogether, but this would seem a little drastic, since ratios are of great assistance in analysing the efficiency of a recruitment campaign.

VACANCY REPORT

The purpose of the vacancy report is to give the overall recruitment picture. The status of each vacancy is summarized on one line. The details required are: the vacancy code and description, the number of people required, and the numbers of applications received, regrets before interview, interviews held, regrets after interview, interviews outstanding, offers made, offers accepted, offers declined, offers withdrawn, offers outstanding, offers confirmed, starts, future starts, and total starts. This is basic statistical information that should be reviewed on a monthly basis.

PERSONNEL COMPUTER SYSTEMS

This report is required at two levels of detail: vacancy and group. The significance of this was discussed in Chapter 4 on recruitment (page 66). The essential point is that a recruiter must have a report which summarizes the status of each vacancy individually, but a manager is more likely to be interested in a summary by vacancy groups, for example, what is the overall position on project engineers, rather than what is the position on chief project engineer, principal project engineer, senior project engineer?

Whether the report is run for individual vacancies or for vacancy groups, it should end with a series of ratios: applications sent to application forms returned; applications returned to interviews held; interviews held to offers made; offers made to starts. These ratios give a useful picture of the overall effectiveness of the recruitment operation, and enable the recruiters to estimate how many applicants and interviewees they will have to process to meet outstanding vacancy requirements.

POSITION REPORT

The position report is the most fundamental of all the recruitment reports. It is the one used by a recruiter to monitor the precise status of each vacancy. It shows the detailed progress of every applicant within the vacancy. The name of the vacancy is given at the top of the page, and applicants are listed alphabetically with their details printed across the page:

Applicant number
Applicant name
Source of application
Date application received
Date regret sent
Date of interview
Date of regret after interview
Date offer made
Date offer accepted
Date offer declined or withdrawn
Date offer confirmed
Date of start
Name of person reviewing application
Notes

Effectively there is a date column for each of the nine operation levels (see page 69 for an explanation of operation levels). If each of these dates were printed in full, there would not be enough space for an applicant's details on one line. Fortunately, it is only necessary to print the month and the day. It would be unusual for a report of this detail to be concerned with a period of over three months, and no useful purpose could be served by examining a 12-month period since the applicants would have found other jobs. This is essentially a report for following applicants through the recruitment process. Different reports would be used for extracting old applicants for reconsideration or for summarizing progress over an extended period.

The column 'Notes' is for indicating intermediate operations, that is, operations that do not have individual operation levels assigned to them but are different from the majority of those carried out at the given level. Under the operation levels proposed in Chapter 4 the possible notes would be:

Hold
Nonattendance at interview
Chase offer
Decline offer
Withdrawal (either by applicant or by recruiter)
Re-contact

Some of these would have to be abbreviated slightly to fit on the page. If, as a result of a duplicate operation (see page 69), an applicant were to have more than one operation, the dates of the duplicate operations should be printed on the line below in the appropriate columns.

Finally, a summary should be produced at the end of the report, containing the following numerical information:

Applications sent
Applications returned
Regrets before interview
Interviews held
Future interviews
Regrets after interview
Offers made
Offers accepted
Offers declined/withdrawn
Offers outstanding
Number started
Future starts
Ratio of applications sent to applications returned
Ratio of applications returned to interviews
Ratio of interviews to offers
Ratio of offers to starts.

The ratios are useful as a quick check on the efficiency of the recruitment for the position, and can be compared with the cumulative ratios given on the vacancy report.

SOURCE REPORT

The source report is another detailed document, showing the status of each applicant, but its purpose is different. It is designed to highlight the effectiveness of a particular source of recruitment (an advert or open house, for example). The details given are the same as in the position report, but there are the following differences:

1. The sort order is alphabetical within position within source, instead of just alphabetical within position.
2. The heading at the top of the report is the name of the source instead of the name of the position.
3. The name of the position is printed on the source report in the place where the name of the source is printed on the position report.
4. Instead of summaries after each position within the source, a matrix is printed at the end of the report to provide information on the vacancies within the source:

Code vacancy	A/F recd.	I/V held	Offers made
xxxx xxxxxxxxxxxxx	9999	999	999

5. At the end of the report, the total number of people required for all vacancies within the source should be given, together with the source cost per start as a percentage of starters' salaries.

This last piece of information is a good indication of the cost effectiveness of a source. It can be compared with the percentage charged by an agency. It is also necessary to have a source listing, that is, a list of source codes in numerical order with the source description and cost shown against each one. This is required primarily as a reference document for operators using the system.

OFFER REPORT

The offer report fulfils two functions: run on a regular basis, it provides a useful guide to the recruitment picture on a monthly basis throughout the year, but it is also useful as a working document. In this capacity it should be run whenever the status of offers is being reviewed (probably weekly), and can be used to chase them up, to expedite references, to check that the various clearance procedures are in hand, to highlight forthcoming start dates, and to indicate any general trends in the rejection or withdrawal of offers.

The information required is: applicant number and name, job title, department, salary, salary grade, location, date offer made, date offer accepted, date offer declined or withdrawn, start date, number of references required, number of references cleared, whether medical clearance has been received, whether client approval has been given (if required) and a comment to indicate the reason why an offer has been declined or withdrawn. As on the position report, the year should be omitted from dates across the page, as there is no room for it, although the full date of the period under consideration should be given at the top of the report.

APPLICANT DUMP

It is important that there should be a report which dumps all the processing information held on a given selection of applicants. The principal purpose of this is to report applicants' details before deleting them from the data base. Such a report was discussed in Chapter 4 under housekeeping (pages 77–78). It may also be of use in providing a recruiter with detailed information on a specific group of applicants. The dump report does not decode operation numbers, and so can fit substantially more information across the page. It tells the recruiter, for example, not only the date on which an applicant was sent a regret letter, but also the precise letter which he was sent. In this sense it is a specialist's variation on the position report.

Personnel reports

The reports required in a comprehensive personnel records system can be divided into seven main categories: employee documents, manpower listings, information reports, staff movements, salary control, statistics, and benefits. Each of these will be dealt with in turn, together with a full explanation of the areas they cover, and it will be seen that they further subdivide into detailed report groups, some of which have several individual reports within them.

Throughout discussion of these reports, it should be remembered that a system with the required degree of flexibility will enable the operator to distinguish between the group of people to be reported and the format of the report. This chapter is concerned with the format of the report, and it should not be thought that the term 'standard report' is intended to refer to a standard selection of people as well. Some reports will normally be run for a standard selection of people. For example, reports on addresses and relations will generally include everyone. Reports on such things as staff movements, on the other hand, will need to have the period of time under consideration updated each time they are run. And some reports, for example, people who have worked at a specified location, will need to use a specific selection statement every time they are run. Varying the find procedure should be a totally separate process from varying the report procedure, and this chapter is concerned with report procedures.

The majority of reports to be discussed should be produced by a report generator, and are standard, therefore, not in the sense that they require the writing of application programs, but in the sense that they will be used regularly, and so should be stored as permanent procedures within the system. Reports that might require the writing of application programs if only a simple report generator were available will be identified when they are discussed.

Employee documents

The term 'employee document' is used here to signify output from the system which is concerned with a single individual. Most reports concern a limited amount of information on a wide range of people. An employee document contains a large amount of information on one person only. It may occupy a whole A4 sheet, or even an entire print-out. There are three basic documents in this category, and each of them could well be beyond the scope of a simple report generator, and so require the writing of an application program. The reason for this is simply that some report generators are designed only to produce ordinary reports, that is, listings with headings across the top of the page and with the details of specified individuals shown below. They may not be able to cope with placing a large number of items on a single individual at specified points on a sheet of paper. The reports in question are: the payroll document, personal details forms, and a print-out of someone's full details.

PAYROLL DOCUMENT

The payroll document contains all the information about a new member of staff which the personnel department needs to pass to payroll. It can also conveniently double as an initial information document for the employee's manager, and this should be borne in mind when deciding what to include on the form. Since each sheet will relate to a single individual, the form should be designed to fit on A4 paper, so that it can be put straight into an individual's personal file. The items that should be included are:

Staff category
Employee number
Surname and initials
Address and postcode
Telephone number
Department
Salary
Uplifts
Job title
Location
Hours worked
Eligibility for overtime
National Insurance number
Bank name
Bank address
Bank sort code number
Bank account number
Date of start
Date of birth

Sex
Marital status
Pay period
Type of contract
Pay code
Cost code
Qualifications
Institute membership
Languages and fluency
Next of kin name
Next of kin relationship
Next of kin address
Next of kin telephone number.

Space should be provided at the bottom for the form to be dated, signed, and approved.

This is a substantial list of current details, and it assumes that the payroll system is totally separate from personnel. This assumption has been made because the two often are separate, and because this book is concerned with personnel systems, not with payroll ones. If personnel and payroll were to operate on the same data base, or if information were passed automatically from one to the other, the payroll document would be superfluous.

PERSONAL DETAILS FORM

The majority of information stored in a personnel records system is put to practical use on a regular basis since it affects the amount people are paid, when they are paid, and such things as their job titles and locations on reports. If any of this information is incorrect, the error should be spotted quickly, and with integrated letter production the incidence of errors on critical items should always be very low. However, there is one specific area of weakness: personal details. Procedures can be laid down for employees to notify personnel department when they marry, give birth to children, move house, lose their next of kin, or acquire additional skills and qualifications. But there is no means of knowing whether these procedures are being followed.

The only way to be sure that the information on the system is up-to-date is to provide members of staff with a printed sheet from time to time showing their personal details as stored in the computer, and to ask them to sign and return it, after making any necessary corrections. Therefore, the system must have the facility to produce these forms. The output is best designed to fit on an A4 sheet of paper, and should consist of:

Surname and initials
Name known by
Employee number

Department
Marital status
Nationality
Date of birth
Name of spouse
Nationality of spouse
Permanent address and telephone number
Temporary address and telephone number
Next of kin name
Next of kin telephone number
Name of each child
Sex of each child
Date of birth of each child
Institute membership and grade
Qualifications
Languages spoken and fluency

The headings can be preprinted on the form to save time, with the exception of the heading for 'qualifications, institutes, and languages'. This must be printed by the system because it needs to appear underneath the details of children, and the amount of space required will vary considerably from one person to another.

FULL DETAILS
The need for a facility to print out the full details of an employee, that is, everything about them that is stored on the system, including all their employment history, has already been discussed in Chapter 5 in the section on housekeeping within the personnel records system (pages 99–100). It was mentioned there that a print-out of a person's full details was clearly required prior to deleting them from the data base. But such a print-out is useful whenever it may be necessary to refer quickly to an employee's details at a location which is some way removed from a terminal. The most obvious use for such a print-out is as a document for managers. The information should be printed out in the same form as the one in which it appears on the formatted screens in the personnel records program. This will make it easy to read and interpret.

Manpower listings

Manpower listings are reports giving basic employee details arranged in different ways so as to indicate the distribution of such things as jobs, locations, and ages through the company. One of their functions is to highlight features of the distribution that require investigation: Why have we got so few process engineers? Do we really have half our technical workforce working in Saudi Arabia? Who is due to retire in the next three years? Another purpose is to enable demands such as 'Give me a list of all

144

our cost engineers' or 'Find out whom we have in Peru' to be met immediately. Information on what people do and where they are is fundamental to a personnel records system, and it must be possible to issue reports containing this information on request.

The most accurate way to describe the general nature of these reports is to say that they deal with the distribution of basic employee characteristics. This may sound a little alarming, and conjure up visions of complex graphs and diagrams. Nothing of the kind is required. The questions referred to above can all be answered by means of straightforward listings. The same basic employee details are required in each case. The only thing that needs to change is the sort order. A report sorted in job title order will show the distribution of job titles, and everyone doing a given job; a report sorted in location order will show the distribution of locations and where people are.

Nearly all reports in the category of manpower listings can contain the same details: number, name, department, job title, location, date assignment starts (if any) and approximate length, sex, marital status, start date, birth date, number of children under 21, and staff status. The first seven of these are the critical items, but the others are often useful. The subsections below consider the uses to which this information is likely to be put on a regular basis, and the sort order needed to meet these requirements.

PERSONAL

One of the most mundane but also one of the most fundamental requirements of a personnel records system is that it should be able to tell you who the company employs, and some of their basic details. This information should be available in a report that can be referred to immediately by anyone involved in answering queries about past or current staff. The details listed above should be printed out alphabetically to provide a basic employee reference document. It may also be useful to produce a separate report sorting them by employee number. Both of these should be run on a monthly basis. Finally, it is useful to have the same information sorted by date of birth. This only needs to be run once a year, and can be used both to identify staff due to retire over a given period and to examine the company's age distribution.

LOCATION

A report on the locations at which a company is working, how many people are at each of them, and who they are, is another basic requirement. The same details are required, but the sort order needs some thought. Clearly, it is useful to have a departmental sort, so that it is apparent at a glance how many people at each location belong to each department. The third sort should be alphabetical. The report should be run monthly.

Current locations is not the only subject of interest for reporting purposes. The question of who has worked at a given location is frequently raised. This information is available within the system, because the history data-set stores location as one of its items (see page 85). The information required in this case is simply number and name, historical location, current department, current location and current job title. This report would only be produced on request, and would be used solely for identifying people who were suitable for a particular job that had become vacant.

JOB TITLE

This is the same information again sorted first by job title code and then alphabetically. It is important that the sort should be on job title code and not on job title itself. The coding structure will be designed to sort job titles in a logical sequence, whereas an alphabetical list of job titles will have no logic to it at all. This report can be used for reviewing the distribution of jobs throughout the company, for answering the question 'Who do we have who could do the job of . . . ?' and for dealing with statistical enquiries concerning job function. There is no need to run it on a regular basis, but it should be available to be run when required.

DEPARTMENT

So far attention has been directed towards the need to sort some basic employee details in a variety of orders. The principal sorts discussed are straight alphabetical, location, and job title. Number and date of birth are less critical, and the historical location report is a special case. If attention is directed to the principal three sorts, however, it is immediately apparent that a large number of variations on the same theme are possible. Once department is taken into account as a principal sort, over 60 possible sort orders can be derived by juggling the four elements around, and it is possible to imagine a use for all of them.

Part of the difficulty in specifying standard reports is to distinguish between sort orders that could be of use and those that will be of use on a regular basis. This is where monitoring the requirements becomes important. The number of combinations retained as standard reports must be kept down, or the system will become unmanageable. If fact, it is not normally productive to have too elaborate a sort order since the result can be confusing. Most of the complications that can be imagined can also be avoided. The one that cannot be avoided is the departmental sort.

It is frequently necessary to review manpower on a departmental basis, and therefore each of the other principal sorts—alphabetical, location, and job title—may be required within an initial departmental sort. This produces the additional sort orders: alphabetical within department, job title within department, and location within department. These reports will answer the same questions as their counterparts without a departmental sort: 'Who is Mr . . . .? How many process engineers do we have? Where are people?' But it will answer them on a departmental basis instead of a companywide one. It will often be useful to distribute the relevant parts of these reports to departmental managers on a regular basis.

Information reports

Manpower reports are concerned with critical items of information which have to be sorted in different orders depending on the use to which the information is to be put. Information reports provide additional information which may be required for a specific purpose. Generally speaking, information reports come into their own when specific questions are asked about a particular individual—questions concerning addresses, relations, training, employment history, and medical details. The majority of reports which are run will be concerned with permanent staff. In most cases it is best to exclude agency staff altogether. For example, the company will not wish to know the address or relations of an agency employee. Substantially less information is stored about them (see page 95). Thus information about agency employees forms a special class of its own, which is best dealt with separately, and which may conveniently be included under information reports.

ADDRESSES

The requirements in this area are straightforward: address and telephone number. Most employees will have a permanent address, some will have a temporary address, and some (those whose next of kin lives at a different address) will have a next of kin address. These addresses should be printed out one after another, and the report must indicate which is which. Two versions of the report are required: one in strict alphabetical order for use by the personnel department, and the other sorted alphabetically within department for distribution to departmental managers.

RELATIONS

It is important to have a next of kin report which can be distributed to departmental managers since they may need this information quickly in an emergency. There is no need to report other relations (sons and daughters). They can be extracted direct from the system if necessary. The need to identify someone's next of kin rapidly will not arise very often. Therefore, it is not necessary to produce two versions of this report, as it was for addresses. Queries about addresses arise with sufficient frequency for a straight alphabetical list for the personnel department to be justified. Queries about next of kin do not. The report should be sorted alphabetically within department, so that it can be distributed to departmental managers. A copy of this report should be sufficient for the needs of the personnel department.

TRAINING

Four training reports are required: institutes, qualifications, courses, and languages. These should all be sorted alphabetically within department, so that they can be distributed to departmental managers. The reports on institutes and qualifications should contain employee number and name, job title, and qualification or institute. The report on courses should also include the date on which the course was attended (month and year) and the course organizer. The language report will need to be sorted by language prior to the sorts by department and name, since the principal purpose of it will be to identify individuals who speak a specified language. Fluency (written and spoken) must be included, and there is a case for including location as well, since it is no consolation to know that Mr Smith speaks Urdu if he has been assigned to Saudi Arabia for 12 months.

HISTORY

One of the most fundamental information reports is full employment history. Whenever the details of specific individuals are under examination to review their suitability for a particular job, this information will be of paramount importance. Again, departmental managers will be among the principal beneficiaries, so the report should be sorted alphabetically within department. The first line on any individual should include some current details: number and name, department, sex and marital status, continuous service date, and total number of years with the company. This should be followed by the individual's employment history, printed out line by line, and consisting of: date of change, department, location, job title, salary, and reasons. The principal information recorded here will be transfers, assignments, promotions, and salary increases. A long service employee might easily have 50 lines of history, so this will certainly be the longest report of all. It should be sufficient to run it annually.

MEDICAL

The question of what medical information should be stored has already been dealt with (page 88). It is limited to the date on which a medical was given, and the dates of immunizations and vaccinations. Therefore, the only reports required are those concerning the dates on which individuals should have medicals and when their immunizations are due for updating. These reports should be issued on a monthly basis for the next month.

AGENCY

The reason for including agency reports under the general heading of information reports has already been explained. The information required about agency employees is who they are, starters and leavers, changes, and hourly rates. It will be sufficient to produce listings of who they are on a monthly basis. The basic alphabetical listing is best combined with the one for permanent staff, otherwise it will be necesary to refer to two reports whenever anyone asks the question 'Do you employ a Mr W. Green?'. A separate listing of agency staff by employee number may be of use, since the accounting procedures for agency staff will be unconnected with those for the permanent payroll (agency employees are paid via invoices from the agent).

The basic agency information document will, however, be a listing sorted alphabetically within order number within agent. This report will relate directly to the invoices received, and will indicate the importance of each agency to the company. It should be run on a monthly basis, and should include: number and name, job title, order number, location, agency, rate per hour, the date this rate was agreed, conditions, and start date. Conditions can be represented by a numeric code indicating the set of conditions under which the individual in question is working.

A report on agency starters and leavers should be run weekly. The majority of the information can be the same as on the basic agency staff listing, but department number, eligibility for overtime, and leave date (where applicable) should be included. To make room for this additional information, it will be necessary to dispense with something, and the date on which the rate was agreed is the obvious candidate. In the case of starters it will be the start date; in the case of leavers it is of no interest. The report should be sorted alphabetically within order number.

The report on changes will be required on a weekly basis. It should report changes to job title, order number, location, agency, and rate. These are, therefore, the items which the report should include, together with the date of change, a comment highlighting the nature of the change, and, of course, the individual's number and name. This report too should be alphabetical within order number.

Finally, it will be necessary to produce a report for reviewing agency rates. This will not be required so frequently—quarterly should be sufficient—and the only essential items are job title, average rate, and the individual rates that make up the average. The report should be sorted by job title code. It will be the basic document used for monitoring rate movements, and ascertaining whether the targets set in terms of rate boundaries have been achieved.

Staff movements

An organization must know, firstly, what it has got in terms of manpower, and secondly, how the picture is changing. The first requirement is met by manpower reports, the second requires information on staff movements. The movements critical to an organization's development are: starters, leavers, transfers, promotions, and assignments. Until regular reports are produced for each of these areas, very few organizations have a clear conception of their rate of change. Some organizations are remarkably static. This in itself is of interest but what is much more interesting is the speed with which the shape of an organization can change without its directors being aware of what is going on. Each director should be aware of developments in his own area, but the effect of pooling this information is often not appreciated. Each of the staff movement reports should be run on a monthly basis.

STARTERS

Information about starters is required in two separate forms. First, there is the management report. This should consist of number and name, start date, department, job title and salary, and should be sorted alphabetically within department. Secondly, there is a need for a weekly starters list. This is a basic company information document, and should be issued to any group within the company which needs to know about new employees, for example, reception, the switchboard, the post room, and telex. It should be similar to the management report, but will not include salary.

LEAVERS

The immediate requirement with regard to leavers is similar to that for starters: a monthly management report sorted by leave date, and a weekly list for general distribution. The weekly leavers' list should follow the same format as the weekly starters' list, except that start date will be replaced by leave date. The management report should consist of: number and name, department, job title, salary, date of birth, date of start, continuous service date, date of leaving, reasons for leaving, and whether the company would re-employ the individual.

Two further variations on the management report should be available, the first sorted alphabetically, and the second sorted by job title code with date of leaving and department as subsidiary sorts. The purpose of the former is simply to provide a list of all leavers on the system in strict alphabetical order; this is essential information, and should be provided monthly. The purpose of the latter is to review leavers on specific job titles either with a view to re-employing them or with a view to examining the rate at which people are leaving in particular areas. This report will not be required on a regular basis. It will always be run for a special selection of people, and it will come into its own when specific problems of recruitment or wastage arise.

TRANSFERS

The transfer report should include number and name, old department, new department, and the effective date of change, sorted alphabetically within old department. The same list can be used for management and general distribution, as it does not include confidential information.

150

PROMOTIONS

The promotions reports should include all changes of job title, even if they are not strictly speaking promotions. The items required are number and name, department, previous job title, new job title, and effective date. The sort order should be alphabetical within department.

ASSIGNMENTS

The assignments report should include everyone whose location has changed during the month in question. It should give number and name, department, old location, new location, and effective date, sorted alphabetically within department.

Salary control

Salary reports are one of the most basic requirements of a personnel records system. They may be required in five distinct areas of salary administration: reporting the current status, monitoring increases, performing reviews, carrying out surveys, and maintaining a grading system. Each of these areas has a number of specific requirements within it.

SALARY STATUS

There are three salary status reports: the first two are similar and may be referred to as the departmental and the consolidated salary reports. Most companies recognize the need for two such reports and often they are produced from the payroll system, if the personnel records are not computerized.

The departmental salary report lists one line of detail on each member of staff, sorting firstly by department, secondly by job title, thirdly by salary, and fourthly by name. It should give number and name, job title, age, staff status, start date, and salary details. The salary details should include current salary, date of last increase with percentage increase, and date of last but one increase with percentage increase. If an increase has been awarded within the last three months, a flag should be printed on the right-hand side of the report. Space should be left on the right-hand side for salary proposals to be written, so that the report may be used as a working document.

The consolidated salary report is designed for comparing salaries across the company. Therefore, it omits the departmental sort, and groups together all employees on the same job title. After each job title, it reports on the number in the group, minimum, maximum and average salaries, upper and lower quartiles, and median. It must also report the department in which each individual works. Apart from these differences it resembles the departmental salary report.

The third report is a summary of total and average salaries for permanent employees by department within division. This is best run immediately after the departmental salary report, for use in conjunction with it.

151

Comparing these reports over a number of months gives a useful picture of salary movements within departments and divisions.

SALARY INCREASES

A monthly salary increase report is essential, sorting increases by job title code within department. The information required is number and name, department, job title, previous salary, new salary, effective date, and reasons for the change. Two versions of the report should be issued, one for scheduled increases, and one for nonscheduled ones. Scheduled increases are those occurring as a result of individuals' annual reviews; of course, these will only be a monthly occurrence in companies operating a rolling review system. Nonscheduled increases are those relating to such things as promotions and increased responsibilities.

REVIEW SYSTEM

The requirements of a salary review system were discussed in detail in Chapter 6, and the various ways in which salary proposals should be printed out or displayed were dealt with in the section on displaying the workfile (page 106). Once the proposals have been approved, payroll will need to be notified by means of a report giving number and name, department, new salary, and effective date, unless there is an automatic link between personnel and payroll. The sort order of this report will depend on the way payroll keep their records. It may be possible to use the salary proposals document for this purpose, but there is likely to be a confidentiality problem over the performance and promotability indicators shown there. It may also be useful to have a six-month review report, to prompt managers about new employees who were offered a review after six months service with the company when they joined. This should be sorted alphabetically within department, and should include number and name, job title, salary, start date, and department. Managers should also be sent a similar report showing employees due for appraisal, and the date when the appraisal is due.

SURVEYS

A computer can bring about great savings in time when the input for a salary survey is compiled, and it enables compensating adjustments to be made relatively easily, where necessary, when the results are analysed. The means of dealing with surveys is provided through the enquiry system. Each group to be examined can be defined by means of a find procedure, and the details required can be specified through a report procedure. The details of this were discussed in Chapter 7. Any survey in which a company participates regularly should be set up as a permanent file within the system containing the relevant series of find and report procedures. When the input to the survey is due, the file is simply run with no manual effort, and absolute accuracy. A file is set up for each specific salary survey.

How are general salary surveys to be handled, that is, those in which the company only participates once? It is not worth setting up files for all these. Specifying the find and report procedures is a long business, which can only be justified if the resultant files are to be used a number of times. The answer is to have a general file which is run, say, quarterly, and which counts the number of people on each individual job title within the company and totals their salaries. If the totals are performed at job title level, salary averages for specified functional groups can be derived simply by combining the appropriate totals. This may not sound very sophisticated, but it can save a great deal of time.

GRADING SYSTEM

Companies operating a salary grading system will no doubt wish to produce reports to ensure that the system is meeting its objectives. The most obvious requirement is for a report on the average for each grade. In addition to this, it may be useful to have reports showing basic salary details sorted in different orders to enable the system to be examined from several angles. The details required would be number and name, salary grade, department, job title, salary, and annual review date (this last item is only of interest where a rolling review is in operation). A report on these details sorted by salary within grade will show the range and distribution of salaries in each grade. One sorted by department within grade would show the distribution of departments through the grading system. And one sorted by grade within department would show the distribution of the grading system within each department. Finally, a sort by salary within department would show the salary distribution within each department. These reports can be of use, but they are not as critical as most of the other reports discussed so far. It should not be necessary to run them very often.

Statistics

The way in which statistical reports can be generated was discussed at length in Chapter 7. This section, therefore, avoids this aspect of the subject altogether, and concentrates on what is required.

STANDARD SUMMARIES

Standard summaries are statistical reports which every company is likely to need in order to keep track of its shape and development. First of all, a monthly summary of overall status is required, relating recruitment activity to current strength, outstanding vacancies, and labour turnover. The figures required on recruitment can be taken from the vacancy report (see page 137): applications received, interviews held, offers made, offers outstanding, and future starts. The personnel records system should

153

supply figures for starters, leavers, and current strength. The number of outstanding vacancies should then be shown both as a total and as a percentage of current strength, and finally the quarterly and annual labour turnover. All these figures should be shown for technical and nontechnical staff (or whatever the most relevant division of staff into categories may be within a given company), in addition to being shown as an overall total.

The summary of overall status should be supplemented by a departmental breakdown of staff strengths and movements. This too should be run monthly, and should go into more detail than the overall summary. It should differentiate between divisions within the company, showing them on separate pages with totals at the bottom. The departments in each division should be listed with their staff strengths alongside. Totals should be shown for technical and nontechnical staff, with further subdivisions to differentiate between permanent and agency staff, and to pick out the number of people on assignment. The number of starters and leavers in each department during the month should be shown, and it may be useful to have a breakdown by sex. All this information can be fitted on a single line, alongside department number, so that the state of each division is shown clearly.

It is important to have a functional breakdown as well as a departmental one. This need not have as much detail as the departmental breakdown since the only essential piece of information is how many employees there are in each category, but it is needed to display the shape of the company from a different point of view. To some extent, specific job titles are associated with specific departments. If this is invariably so, a functional breakdown is superfluous. Normally, however, many job titles will be in use in a number of departments other than the one to which they normally belong. In this case, the size of the technical staff in the cost and planning department, for example, will not be a true indication of the number of cost and planning engineers in the company. This can be very misleading. Job titles should be grouped together into functions, and a report on the number of people in each function should be run quarterly both for comparison with previous ones and as a cross-check on the departmental breakdown.

The last type of standard summary which should be mentioned is a breakdown of years experience with the company. How many people in the company have: 0–2 years experience, 2–5, 5–10, 10–15, 15–25, or over 25? The answers should be supplied by job function, as in the functional breakdown above, although it is neither practical nor necessary to go into quite as much detail because the number of parameters involved in a statistical summary must always be kept within manageable limits.

GENERALIZED TOOLS

When dealing with statistical enquiries, certain facilities are required over and over again in different circumstances. Therefore, it is worth writing report procedures which can be used as required to handle them. Once a group of people has been selected, it is frequently necessary to split them into departments, and to say how many there are in each one. Therefore, a procedure that simply totals the number of staff in each department is most useful. Equally useful, is a facility for totalling the number of staff in a given group and calculating their average salary. Finally, a procedure for reporting some basic details about the people in a given group is often useful: number and name, department, job title, and salary. The best sort order may well be job title, department, and then salary, because statistics normally relate to job function, and so to job title. These are three simple facilities, and they could be written each time they were required, but it saves time to store them away in the system.

SPECIFIC TASKS

These are the statistical reports that are not common to all companies. Most companies have to produce specific statistical reports on a regular basis for internal consumption, for a parent company, for a client, or for a government body. Such reports can be a nightmare. The Industry Training Boards, for example, complain that no one seems able to complete their returns without immense effort, and consequently a high risk of inaccuracy. Any such statistical report should be set up as a standard report, as described in Chapter 7.

Benefits

Some companies get involved in elaborate schemes of benefits. This section is only concerned with the most common ones: staff status, medical insurance, holidays, service awards, and company cars.

STAFF STATUS

Some employees may be awarded a special status for benefits, probably based on a combination of length of service and job seniority. Since this special status affects the benefits for which they are eligible, it is important to know who they are. Therefore, an alphabetical list should be produced on a monthly basis showing number, name, department, and any other details relevant for the benefits in question. A variation of this, alphabetical within department, should also be available for distribution to departmental managers.

MEDICAL INSURANCE

All the private medical insurance firms operating large-scale company schemes use basically the same system for billing clients: the client is billed at the beginning of the year on the basis of the total number of single, married, and family members, and the scale they are on. It is usual now to offer two scales appropriate to the area in which the company is situated. At the end of the year, figures are again submitted, the subscription is again calculated, and the company's payment is adjusted to the average of the two subscriptions (beginning and end of year).

The basis for billing is simple enough, but problems arise when the company tries to allocate the cost between departments. It is then necessary to work out the number of eligible staff in each category in each department, and to calculate the portion of the subscription to be allocated to each one. This is a tedious operation to perform manually, but to a computer it is straightforward. The subscriptions appropriate to each category can be stored as dictionary entries. The system can then produce a report showing the number of eligible people in each category in each department, and the subscription due. Eligible people can be defined by reference to the data base item staff status; the scale indicator is stored as a separate item. This report would require a specially written application program. It is not the kind of thing which a report generator would normally handle.

HOLIDAYS

Two requirements can be identified with respect to holidays. Firstly, it is necessary to have an alphabetical list within department showing number and name, department, and holiday entitlement. Managers need to have this, so that they know how much holiday their staff are entitled to. Secondly, it is important for purposes of budgeting and overall control to know how many people in each department fall into each entitlement category (20, 22, or 25 days, for example).

SERVICE AWARDS

A report on service awards is important both to identify staff who will fall due for an award during a given year and to pick out people who are eligible for a special service related benefit. The different circumstances will necessitate different find procedures, but the information required is the same: number and name, name known by (as a prompt at the presentation), department, and continuous service date. It should be sorted by continuous service date, and then alphabetically within department, and run when required.

COMPANY CARS

All that is required here is an alphabetical list of people with company cars, giving their number, name, and department. How frequently it is run will depend on how frequently employees are offered company cars.

This concludes the review of reports that should be available in a personnel computer system. It should be clear by now that the requirements are more extensive than at first appears. Unless this aspect of the system is tackled thoroughly at the outset, it will lead to confusion and

156

frustration at a later stage. However good the enquiry system may be, a great deal of effort is required to create a complete body of reports that will be internally consistent, replace the manual system, and provide all the additional information that management expect.

The last six chapters have been concerned with the detailed design of a personnel computer system, that is, the design features that need to be taken into account if the system is to meet the objectives outlined in Chapter 1. When the objectives were first stated, they sounded relatively straightforward, but the complexities which arise in the course of trying to implement them are considerable. This is why the design of a personnel computer system is such a perilous undertaking. Tiny oversights can have a catastrophic effect; they can make the difference between scrapping the manual system entirely and having to keep it going solely to make good the deficiencies of the computer system. A system that results in this kind of duplication has failed.

It was because of the difficulty of dealing satisfactorily with all the design factors that Chapter 2 concluded with the statement that the most important single piece of advice offered in this book is: buy a package. The user's energies should be directed towards implementing a system, not designing one. Implementation is itself a major undertaking, but it is considerably less hazardous than design. To select a package it is important to have a clear idea of exactly what it should do. The last six chapters have covered this. However, it is necessary to put the information into a more succinct form in order to evaluate packages effectively. The next chapter itemizes the points to look for when screening packages, and then goes on to show how a system can be tested, prior to purchase, to ensure that it has all the features referred to in this book.

9. Screening and testing a system

Buying a package saves time. Nevertheless, selecting the right one to buy can be a lengthy business. It is also possible to make serious mistakes. Many systems which look impressive at a presentation lack the detailed design facilities required in a live environment. A personnel manager who selects one of these may well be making the most expensive mistake of his career. However, there is no need to feel paralysed by the difficulty of the decision. Making the right decision depends firstly upon asking the right questions, and secondly upon carrying out a thorough test to see whether the system really does what it is supposed to do. These two activities may be referred to as:

1. Screening a system.
2. Testing a system.

This chapter deals with each in turn, but first it will be useful to consider the stages through which it is necessary to pass in selecting a system.

The first stage is the initial enquiry. Most people waste too much time over this. Salesmen are always anxious to invite potential customers to lavish presentations, but this does not mean that they have anything substantial to offer. It is important to make a list of key questions, that is, questions that are central to the definition of a personnel computer system, and to elicit the answers to them over the telephone. If a negative picture emerges, there is no point in continuing the investigation.

When an enquiry produces a positive result, it is time to move on to the second stage. This involves meeting with representatives of the organization offering the package to ask more detailed questions about each aspect of the system, to attend a demonstration or presentation if possible, and to discuss the basis on which the system would be sold. The purpose of this discussion is to gain an impression, necessarily at this stage a very approximate one, of the probable cost of the system, the implementation schedule, and the support the organization would provide on such things as training, procedural definition, and program maintenance. It is also the right time to get a feel for whether it is a proven package, and whether the people selling it have the experience necessary to provide the support they are offering. These matters are covered in depth in Chapter 10. This chapter is concerned with the questions to ask and the tests to carry out in order to ascertain whether the system will meet its objectives.

Stage three follows only if the questions asked at stage two have been answered satisfactorily, and the discussion has produced a favourable impression. It involves carrying out a comprehensive test of the system, and this is necessarily time-consuming. Drawing up a system test is a laborious business, and it will probably take at least one complete and very intensive day to carry it out. It is also bound to involve the assistance of people who are familiar with the system.

At stage four the organization selling the package will need to carry out a survey on location of the precise requirements, and to put together a formal proposal. This will involve finding out exactly how various matters are handled, and the numbers concerned. Even if the survey is carried out in a highly organized fashion and the proposal is a straightforward one, it is unlikely to be completed in less than a fortnight, including about three days of intensive interviewing in the company where the system is to be installed. Stage five is the negotiation of the contract, which involves tying up all the loose ends. These last two stages are dealt with in Chapter 10. This chapter covers stages one and two (screening), and stage three (testing).

Screening a system

The first question to ask when making an initial enquiry about a package is 'Will it replace all the existing manual systems?' If the answer is 'No', there is no point in pursuing the enquiry any further. A system which is not sufficiently fast and comprehensive to replace the manual systems is duplicating work, and so will make the situation worse rather than better.

The second point to establish is broadly what kind of computer system is being offered. Chapter 2 explained the need to exploit modern developments in hardware and software. What is needed is a real time data base management system running on a stand-alone mini computer. Input and output should be handled through VDUs and printers by members of the personnel department. The system should make use of select screens, formatted screens and cursor positioning to facilitate rapid interaction with the operator in the user department. There are so many permutations of computer systems (and they are developing so fast) that it is impossible to lay down rigid requirements. Nevertheless, these are the features to look for. Any mention of batch processing should bring the enquiries to an end immediately. It has no place in a personnel computer system. And terms such as 'mainframe' and 'bureau' should be regarded as major red lights. They involve shifting control away from the user, and generally result in costs which are both high and unpredictable. They belong to an era which has passed.

The third area to ask about is the basic facilities provided. There are two things the system must include: integrated letter writing and a dictionary. Unless the act of updating a record through a VDU, whether for recruitment, personnel records, salary reviews, or anything else, automatically causes the appropriate letter or document to the individual to be produced, two of the major advantages of a computerized system are lost: the certainty that what is stored on the records accurately reflects what the person was told, and the total elimination of letter writing as a separate (and normally sizeable) operation within the personnel department. Dictionary facilities are essential because they are the only means of ensuring that the system has the required degree of flexibility and that it is immediately comprehensible to the people who use it. Baffling codes are one of the most common drawbacks of computer systems.

The final point to check is the scope of the system. Does it cover recruitment as well as personnel records? Apart from the fact that the major tangible cost benefits normally occur in the area of recruitment, it is absurd to go to great expense purchasing a computer system for personnel records if it cannot also be used for recruitment. The way recruitment can be handled, and the degree of control over it, are transformed by a computer system. It is also important to ask whether the system has special streamlined facilities for dealing with bulk updates, such as salary reviews and redundancies. Finally, does it have an enquiry system, that is, a method of producing reports and statistics that will be powerful enough to handle 80 per cent of the output and simple enough to be operated by users with a minimum of training? A system without such facilities is useless since report generation is central to information management.

These are the points to check up on when making an initial enquiry. They are all fundamental prerequisites of a satisfactory system, and unless a positive response is received on all counts, there is no point in proceeding any further. It should be possible to cover them all over the telephone. If the answers are evasive (for example, 'You really need to see the system for yourself before I can answer that question'), it means that the package offered does not meet the basic requirements, and no further time should be wasted on it.

In summary, the questions to ask are:

1. Will the package replace all the existing manual systems?
2. Is it a real time data base management system on a stand-alone mini computer with VDUs and printers located in the user department?
3. Does it make use of such facilities as select screens, formatted screens, and cursor positioning?
4. Is the system designed around integrated letter writing and a dictionary?
5. Does it include recruitment, personnel records, bulk salary reviews, redundancy calculations, and a powerful user-orientated enquiry system for reports and statistics?

There is always room for misunderstanding as to what precisely the questions imply, but this will be clarified during the second stage, when more detailed questions are asked.

Once the nonstarters have been eliminated, the second stage can begin. Although some general discussion takes place at this stage, the most important point is to establish exactly what the system does and how it operates. Questions about training and support will always be open to negotiation. What the system can do is a question of fact. Although a package can be tailored, it is unwise to tamper with any of its salient features. To do so is to drift into a development project, and this should always be avoided. .

During stage two detailed questions must be asked about every aspect of the system: letter writing, the dictionary, recruitment, personnel records, salary reviews, redundancies, and the enquiry system. It is advisable to work from a checklist, marking each point with a tick, a cross or a note. If a presentation of the system is given, answers to most of the questions should become clear. Nevertheless, it is still worth running through the checklist openly with the organization selling the package both to remove misunderstandings, where possible, and to make it clear what is expected from the system. A systematic approach strengthens a company's negotiating position from the start and frightens off organizations which are overselling their systems.

Each of the areas of enquiry will therefore be dealt with in turn. The questions will be numbered, so that they can be used as a checklist when screening packages. The significance of these questions, and the kind of answers that may be considered to be satisfactory, can be found in the appropriate chapters of the earlier part of the book.

LETTER WRITING
(See Chapter 3.)

1. Does the letter writing system provide an automatic link between updating a person's record and generating the appropriate letter to them?
2. Does it enable a standard text to be combined with entries from the data base, the dictionary, and the operator, and is it capable of performing calculations?
3. Can letters be generated out of recruitment, personnel records, the salary review program, the redundancy program, and the enquiry system?
4. Are the signatory and the company name controlled by the operator?
5. Is the process of running letters off separate from the means by which they are generated through programs?
6. Is the appearance of the letters acceptable?
7. Are they printed fast enough?
8. Does the system have the range and flexibility to produce 99 per cent of the letters which the department will need to send out?
9. Is a comprehensive suite of standard letters provided with the system, so that a company new to the system does not have to start from scratch?
10. Is there a clause handling mechanism to enable highly variable documents, such as contracts of employment and assignment letters, to be constructed from standard building blocks?

161

11. Is the maximum use made of automatic additions to the letter (for example, name, address, reference, extension number, date, name of signatory, job title and company)?
12. Is it easy to generate new standard letters? Is there a simple means of creating and editing standard text and is there a program for generating instructions to the system on the way each standard letter or clause is to be treated: number of copies, which data base, type of salutation, data base items to insert, editing to perform, free entries from the operator, dictionary insertions, and arithmetic?

DICTIONARY FACILITIES

(See Chapter 3.)
1. What subdictionaries are available?
2. Is it simple for the operator to create, update, and delete dictionary entries?
3. Is the entry format under the control of the operator?
4. Can all subdictionaries be listed?
5. Are all coded items that appear on formatted screens translated, and is this done by the system without any significant delay being apparent to the operator?
6. Is special provision made for dealing with the upheaval involved in major revisions of the coding structure? Can it be handled from a file created by the operator? Does this file update both the dictionary and the data base? Does it list what it has done and report errors?

RECRUITMENT

(See Chapter 4.)
1. Does the system store everything that is required for it to replace the manual system?
2. Is it fast enough? (It should be possible for the operator to put on 100 new applicants in an hour, and the simplest form of update should take between seven and eight seconds.)
3. Is the vacancy structure capable of handling both a broad and a narrow definition of vacancy? Can several job titles be regarded either as one vacancy or as individual ones for reporting purposes?
4. Has the recruitment process been successfully reduced to a series of operation levels? Do they correspond to logical report groups? Are they simple from the operator's point of view?
5. Does the structure of the operation levels allow for duplicate operations?
6. Does it allow for going back down the operation ladder? Can it distinguish between genuine cases and mistakes?
7. Is the means of updating items on the formatted screen rapid and straightforward, and does the cursor pass only to those items which need to be updated?

8. Are there facilities for chaining through applicants and chaining through vacancies? Is there a means of skipping records in the chain which do not need to be updated?
9. Are there facilities for holding and terminating vacancies? Is the system capable of examining each applicant in the vacancy concerned and determining which letter, if any, to send?
10. Is there a facility to store and update vacancy requirements?
11. Can applicants be accessed by partical name as well as by full name or applicant number?
12. Can applicants be removed by reference to how long they have been on the system? Is it possible to override the deletion criteria in respect of some applicants? Is there a means of identifying permanently unresolved applicants for deletion? Does the system report adequately on the applicants deleted?

PERSONNEL RECORDS
(See Chapter 5.)
1. Does the system store everything that is required for it to replace the manual system?
2. Does it manage both to conserve space and to cater for the fact that far more information will need to be stored about some people, particularly in areas such as employment history, than about others?
3. Is there a partial names facility?
4. Are the commands used with the program displayed clearly and intelligibly on the screens?
5. Are there rapid update facilities for dealing with the following things: salary increases, assignments, changes in staff status, agency updates, and leavers?
6. Do changes in critical items of current information (job title, department, salary and location) create automatic entries in employment history?
7. Can all the information stored be accessed and updated quickly and easily? Are the screens logically constructed and clearly laid out, and is there a rapid means of passing from one to another?
8. Can new employees be transferred across automatically from the recruitment system?
9. Can leavers be transferred to another data base and retained for manpower planning purposes when required? Are their details printed out clearly and in full when this occurs?

BULK SALARY REVIEWS
(See Chapter 6.)
1. Does the system provide a means of experimenting with different kinds of adjustments and examining the results without affecting the data base?

2. Does it produce letters to individuals, update the personnel records, and generate reports for payroll and pensions on a given command as an automatic extension of the process of experimentation?
3. Is there complete flexibility about the people included for experimentation and updating at any time?
4. Can it perform both bulk updates and individual ones?
5. Is there a chaining option for use when everyone is being reviewed on an individual basis?
6. Can the bulk update mechanism handle amounts, percentages, ranges, and limits?
7. Can it apply the parameters specified either to everyone or to a department (or range of departments) within the selection, or to a job title or job title range?
8. Can the system distinguish between a modification to what has already been proposed and a completely new set of parameters?
9. Can the results be displayed on either a VDU or a printer in both full and summary form?
10. Is it capable of updating proposed salary on the data base instead of current salary for budgetary purposes in a rolling review set-up, and can it recall a selection of people from the data base with proposed salaries at a later stage?

REDUNDANCY CALCULATIONS
(See Chapter 6.)

1. Is the program capable of experimenting with alternative redundancy policies and displaying the results without implementing anything?
2. Can it produce letters to individuals and update the personnel records when requested as an automatic extension of this process?
3. Is there complete flexibility about the way people are selected?
4. Does the program produce a report with all the information required for carrying out a redundancy?
5. Does it have the requisite rules built into it for calculating statutory redundancy payments?
6. Is it able to calculate pay in lieu of notice?
7. Are there facilities for calculating optional redundancy payments? Do they cater for a percentage over the statutory entitlement, a lump sum, a lump sum per year of service, a specified number of weeks salary for each year of service, or a combination of these?

THE ENQUIRY SYSTEM
(See Chapter 7.)

1. Is it simple for a layman to learn and use?
2. Is there complete flexibility to select the people required by reference to a large number of items and parameters at once?

3. Will it accept instructions concerning headings, sort order, data items, editing, and arithmetic?
4. Can it translate codes?
5. Can the commands involved be used either interactively or from stored procedure files?
6. Is there a straightforward mechanism for creating and editing procedures?
7. Can the system cope satisfactorily with statistics?
8. Are the statistical facilities able to accept up to three levels of criteria for categorizing records, and use them in conjunction with one another to determine the number of records that qualify under each combination?
9. Are the vertical and horizontal headings (and their print positions) under operator control?
10. Can the system cope with a number of separate groups within each level of criteria?
11. Are there facilities for inserting vertical and horizontal totals as required?
12. Can the system provide both full and summary output for statistical analyses?
13. What reports are provided already written with the system to save a company which is new to it from having to embark on the laborious task of creating them all from first principles? (The whole of Chapter 8 was devoted to detailing reports that might be provided as standard within a system.)

This completes the inventory of questions that should be explored during stage two of selecting a package. Although there are a formidable number of points to be assimilated, most of them can be covered rapidly by a person who has absorbed their full significance. There is no short cut to acquiring the information. The only consolation is that far more time will be wasted at a later stage if these points are not properly investigated at the outset. All of them are, however, secondary to the questions that need to be dealt with at stage one. Once stage two has been successfully accomplished, it is time to move on to a considerably more demanding activity: testing the system.

Testing a system
A system test fulfils two objectives. Firstly, it is a definitive test of the functions within a system, exploring every path that exists through the programs that comprise it. Secondly, it is the most detailed specification in nontechnical terms of what a system should do. All other types of specification are open to some degree of interpretation; however detailed they may be, they are by their nature making general statements about the functions a system should provide. A system test is specific. It

specifies precisely what should be fed into the system and what should come out. The operator follows a set of instructions concerning input, and compares the output with a prepared listing of the expected results.

Carrying out a system test is of critical importance when selecting a package, partly because it is essential to be sure that the system is free from errors, and partly because it is the only way that is not open to misinterpretation and omission of finding out what a system can really do. However, system testing as part of package selection is fraught with difficulties. First of all, systems may differ considerably as to how they operate, even though they are designed to meet the same basic objectives. The update mechanisms will be different, and a system test will have to reflect this. There are bound to be differences in the facilities offered, and some problems may be capable of several different but equally satisfactory solutions. It follows that there is no such thing as an ideal system test which may be applied to any prospective personnel computer system. The test must be tailored to suit the system; naturally, without compromising on any of the functions for which it is testing.

The first problem with system testing is that it will never be the same for two systems. The second problem is that system tests take a long time to devise, and require an intimate knowledge of the system to which they are to be applied. If every path through every program is to be tested, it is first necessary to know what these paths are, and there is no short cut to acquiring this information. For these reasons it is never really practical for an outsider who is trying to select a package to carry out a satisfactory system test without assistance.

The solution to these difficulties is to ask the organization offering the package to supply the materials for the system test, and assistance in carrying it out. This is a perfectly reasonable request. Any competent organization offering a package will have devised a system test for their own purposes during the development phase, and should have retained it for testing future modifications. Furthermore, it is only reasonable that such a service should be provided since a company cannot be expected to purchase a complex package without witnessing a system test, and equally well they are clearly not in a position to handle it entirely themselves.

It might at first appear that for an organization to provide assistance with system testing as a service is self-defeating. Is it not supposed to be something devised by the prospective purchaser to find out whether the system really meets the requirements? This idea is a little muddled. The system test is supposed to give a comprehensive and unambiguous display of what the system can do. But this is something which it will do by its nature. It does not matter who writes it. If it is properly designed, it will fulfil its objectives regardless of who has written it.

The important point is that the company examining the package should know two things:

1. What a properly constructed system test looks like.
2. What facilities they expect to see demonstrated.

Questions will already have been asked at stage two about the facilities provided, but it is not until they have been demonstrated during the system test that they can be considered to have been resolved satisfactorily. For example, one of the questions asked at stage two was 'Is it easy to generate new standard letters?' Clearly, if the answer is 'No', it is pointless to investigate the package any further. However, even if the answer is satisfactory, some doubt will still remain as to what precisely is involved, until the facility has been demonstrated. A system test demonstrates every facility.

The question of what a properly designed system test looks like must now be examined. When this has been covered, it will be appropriate to consider the specific points that should be included in a system test for a personnel computer system. By then it should be clear that it is possible to assess the worth of a system test and benefit from participating in its execution without actually designing it.

A system test consists of a series of transactions, and every document relating to the test should be marked with transaction numbers so that they can be related to one another. The first document required is a set of input instructions. These should cover every command which the operator is to enter on the terminal during performance of the test. Normally, the input instructions would be processed through a VDU, since many of the programs will make use of formatted screens. The instructions must be unambiguous. Everything which the operator has to type on the screen must be listed in sequence in the input documents. Sometimes it will be necessary to indicate where an entry is to be made either by providing an item name or by giving the layout of the formatted screen. The operator instructions should also include notes on messages to look for, and deliberate mistakes to make, to ensure that the system rejects them.

In the case of error messages and deliberate mistakes that are rejected by the system, there is nothing to check apart from the appearance of a message or the rejection of an action. No data is modified or processed. The majority of operations, however, will modify or process data, and it is therefore essential to check the results. For this purpose it is necessary to have output documents. When data is modified by an interactive program, it should be printed out afterwards to check that it has been updated correctly. Thus each input operation will normally have an output operation corresponding to it. If the input consists of a command to generate a report, no data will be modified. The output will be the report.

Reports will produce output without any prompting other than the initiating command. Interactive programs, on the other hand, will update data, but will not of themselves print out the results. Since it is essential to examine the results, a further set of instructions must be provided with the system test comprising the commands to type in to generate the required output. A sensible procedure is to use the enquiry system for this purpose. An interactive program updates the data base, and the enquiry system prints out the results. In this way a check is kept on the results of an update which is entirely independent of the program that generated it.

One final check should be kept during a system test in addition to the ones mentioned so far: a check on the integrity of the data base. It was explained in Chapter 2 (pages 29–30) that a data base management system differs from conventional file structures in that it maintains an index of the information stored, and so enables records with specified data item values to be retrieved more quickly than would normally be possible. When the data base has been updated, the output produced through the enquiry program will show whether the data has been correctly updated. However, an independent check should be kept on the state of the index. A program should be available within the system (it might be part of the enquiry program) for printing out the state of the index. The information required is the number of records which the index believes to exist in each data-set. These figures should never be incorrect, but it is foolish not to check them. If they are ever wrong, data base corruption has occurred, and this is the worst thing that can happen. Any suggestion of data base corruption must immediately put an end to any thoughts of purchasing a package. It means that the system is losing track of the information which it is storing, and this cannot be tolerated in a live environment.

In summary, a system test consists of three basic documents: input instructions, output instructions, and output. The input instructions include all the operator commands that need to be entered, and any notes on deliberate mistakes to make or error messages to look for; they are normally put in through a VDU. Output instructions are only required to print out the effect on the data base of modifications made through one of the interactive programs; they may be typed on the printer (assuming it has a keyboard). The output itself will appear on the printer, and will consist of information just updated on the data base, reports, and information on the state of the data base index.

These documents will be cross referenced by transaction number. Although every transaction must be checked, it is not really necessary to print the result of an individual update immediately it has been performed. It should normally be adequate to perform a series of related transactions (say six), before printing out the results. Therefore, the normal sequence throughout the system test will be:

1. Perform several transactions on a VDU from the operator commands in the input documents.

2. Enter any output instructions on the printer keyboard.
3. Print off the results of the update or report, followed by the check on the data base index.
4. Check the output.

The output which comes off the printer should be identical to the output listing provided with the test. Any departure from the anticipated output must be investigated immediately.

This completes discussion of the documents comprising a system test. It is now necessary to consider the specific facilities for which it should test. The operation of letter writing facilities will be adequately tested by the printing off of letters relating to recruitment, personnel records, salary reviews, and redundances. Facilities for creating new standard letters should be tested as well, and this is best done by means of a complicated example, such as an assignment letter. The letter should be so designed as to test all the features with which a letter parameter generating program, as defined in Chapter 3, should be able to cope: number of copies, recruitment or personnel data bases, type of salutation, data base items, edit forms, free entry questions, dictionary inserts, and arithmetical operations. Facilities for dictionary handling can be tested by creating, updating and deleting dictionary entries, and by carrying out a minor coding reorganization.

To test the recruitment system it will be necessary to create at least 30 applicants and three vacancies. It will then be necessary to test all the operations that can be performed within the system, any special combinations of events, all the options on the select screen, the ability of all items on the screen to accept data, validation routines, procedures for correcting errors, and error messages. Finally, letters generated during these operations should be run off, and all recruitment reports tested. Achieving this requires a considerable degree of coordination. When all the operations have been performed, the progress of applicants must be distributed in such a way as to provide sensible output on reports. As far as possible, the other points that need to be tested should be covered as the standard operations are performed. For example, deliberate mistakes can be made to test error messages and validation. Testing the select screen options should involve creating applicants, updating them, displaying them, chaining through them, chaining through a vacancy, holding and terminating a vacancy, and updating vacancy requirements.

Special combinations of events that may occur are of two types. First of all, any updates that involve changes to the index in the data base management system must be tested, as they will necessarily involve a more complex mechanism, and it is essential for the system to be able to perform them satisfactorily. Items contained in the index will vary from system to system, but they are likely to be the items that are most frequently used for identifying applicants or groups of applicants, that is,

169

name, applicant number, vacancy number, and source number. Applicant number should never be updated by the operator since it is the primary means of identification within the system, and should be allocated and changed by the system itself. Consequently, changes to critical items involve only the other three, either individually or in combination with one another:

Change name
Change source
Change vacancy
Change name and source
Change name and vacancy
Change source and vacancy
Change name, source and vacancy.

The other type of special circumstance that must be rigorously tested is the creation of a second record. This situation was discussed in Chapter 4, and can arise either from a duplicate operation (second interview or second offer, for example) or from an applicant's going back down the operation ladder. These possibilities should be tested in the following ways:

1. On their own.
2. In combination with the critical updates listed above.
3. In combination with one another.
4. In combination with one another and the critical updates.

This results in a total of 31 key operations to be tested. Finally, a selection of applicants should be deleted by the housekeeping program.

In summary, then, the recruitment test must satisfy the following requirements.

1. Involve the creation of at least 30 applicants.
2. End up with a logical distribution of applicants and operations.
3. Test all options on the select screens and the formatted screens.
4. Test all standard operations.
5. Test all key operations.
6. Test the ability of all items to accept data.
7. Check validation.
8. Check correction mechanisms.
9. Check error messages.
10. Test all recruitment reports both to check their formats and functions and to check that the final recorded state of each applicant is correct.
11. Run off the letters.
12. Use the housekeeping program to delete a selection of applicants.

The test should be entirely contained in three carefully prepared documents: input instructions, output instructions, and a listing of anticipated output. It would be likely to run to about two hundred transactions.

170

Many of these points apply with equal force to the test to be performed on the personnel records system. Once again it will be necessary to have about 30 people in the test. However, it is not practical for all of these to be put on by the operator during the system test, as it was in the case of recruitment. The personnel records system stores considerably more data than the recruitment one, especially for individuals with a long employment history. Several people should be transferred across automatically from recruitment, and one or two should be put on direct without being transferred. The rest should already be there at the beginning of the test. Obviously, this means that someone must put them on at some point. The sensible solution is for a dummy data base to be created for testing purposes, and for it to be stored on tape for use when required. Therefore, the first step in performing the personnel system test will be to copy the dummy data base from the tape on which it is stored. The second step will be to transfer some applicants from recruitment and the third step will be to put some new employees on direct through the personnel update program.

The select screen options must all be tested, that is, putting on a new permanent employee, putting on a new agency employee, selecting employees by number, name, and partial name, and altering the values for signatory and operator when letters are written. All these options can be tested in the course of carrying out updates which check some other feature of the system, for example, updating salary or assignment details. Similarly, every option on each of the other screens must be tested. The main screen will need to be tested for all the short update options (salary, assignments, staff status, agency, and leavers), as well as for the full update, the letter writing command, and the means of passing to other screens. The other screens are: history, addresses, relations, training, and immunizations. On each of these it will be necessary to test adding, inserting, updating, deleting, and displaying records; it will also be necessary to test facilities for generating a letter, and passing to one of the other screens. These facilities should work in the same way on each screen, but all cases must be tested.

As with recruitment, default values and validation must be checked. Error messages too must be tested, particularly such things as what happens if the operator attempts to put on a new employee with a name or number identical to an existing one, or asks the system to call up someone who does not exist. Special facilities in the update mechanism must also be tested; updates to the main screen that produce automatic histories or cause the question 'Do you wish to send a letter?' to be asked, for example. Finally, a wide range of reports will need to be produced both to check employee details and to ensure that the reports work, and a selection of employees should be removed from the live data base and transferred by the housekeeping program to the one for manpower planning purposes. It is also sensible to use the housekeeping program to

171

dump the complete details of everyone on the data base. Although each transaction is checked as it is performed, there is always a possibility of an update upsetting something other than the data printed out. This is much more likely—and much more difficult to spot—in the personnel records system than in the recruitment system, because of the volume of data and the complex way in which records are linked together. To carry out all these tests on the personnel data base will probably require about 100 transactions.

Testing the recruitment and personnel records update programs is the most complex part of the system test. The programs for salary reviews and redundancies must be tested as well. The principles illustrated above should be used throughout, and there is no reason to spell out the steps to be followed in this chapter. The options required in each program were discussed fully in Chapter 6, and the system test should work systematically through each of these options in turn.

For example, in the case of the salary review program, a workfile should be set up and then modified by means of individual changes, chained updates, and bulk updates involving various selections of departments and job title groups, and various ranges and limits of salaries. Facilities for setting letter signatory and comment should be tested, and updates should be made to the data base to involve both current and budgeted salary. The state of the workfile should be printed off after each change, testing the various print options, and the updates to the data base should be checked. Similarly, the test for the redundancy program should first of all check the calculation of statutory entitlements under various sets of circumstances, and should then test the facilities for calculating optional payments by the various methods provided within the program. It will also be necessary to check facilities for setting up the workfile, generating letters, and updating the data base.

The enquiry system is tested by the running of all the reports and statistical analyses it is supposed to produce. Since these should comprise at least 80 per cent of all reports in the system (see Chapter 8), this is a lengthy task. However, it is shortened by the fact that a test data base with only a few people on it is being used. Running these reports is, unfortunately, the only way to make sure that they work, and that the enquiry system provides the required facilities. It is tedious but unavoidable.

The tests mentioned so far are all directed towards testing the facilities of individual programs. Two things should be tested which are concerned not with individual facilities but with the environment in which the programs operate. These are multi-terminal tests and tests for response times. It is essential that it should be possible to operate critical programs, notably, recruitment, personnel records, and the enquiry system, from more than one terminal at once. A system that is designed in such a way as to enable a data base to be updated from several terminals at once is said to have multi-update facilities. This is a complicated subject, and there is no need to go into the technicalities of it. The important point is that someone purchasing a package should be aware of the problems involved in multi-terminal update, and know how to test whether they have been dealt with satisfactorily. The first point to check is that it is possible to run the update programs on two terminals at once. Then the difficult cases should be tested, for example, to see what happens if an attempt is made to update the same record from two terminals simultaneously? The system should assign priority to one of the updates, and return a message to the terminal from which the other has been requested, indicating that this operation cannot be processed yet. However, there should be no problem about updating different records simultaneously, or about displaying a record on one terminal while updating it on another. Each of these conditions should be investigated in the multi-terminal tests.

Testing response times means checking that the system operates fast enough to enable the anticipated workload to be handled satisfactorily. It is essential to determine the criteria of acceptability in this respect. Response times vary considerably between systems, and it is possible for a system to provide all the facilities specified and yet to be too slow for operating in a live environment. Something that appears acceptable at a demonstration may well be infuriating when it is in constant use every day. As a general guideline, an operator should never have to sit and wait when using one of the standard interactive programs. The system should almost always be ahead of the operator. To check this point it is advisable to choose some clearly defined operations, and to use them as a yardstick for measuring system performance. For example, it should be possible to put 100 new applicants on to the recruitment system within an hour.

This chapter has been concerned with establishing whether a package meets the requirements of a personnel computer system. The decision that is made is critical. It may pave the way for transforming the role of the personnel department or it may lead to an expensive mistake. The importance of the decision justifies the thoroughness advocated in this chapter, even though it is difficult to achieve. The first essential is to subject all prospective systems to a rigorous and ruthless initial screening. Do they satisfy the five key requirements identified on page 160? If not, eliminate them immediately. Those that pass the initial test must be subjected to more detailed screening. And any packages that survive this investigation as well should be given a comprehensive system test. An organization offering to supply such a package should be prepared to submit a system test for approval by the client and to supply assistance in running it. This test should consist of input instructions, output instructions, and an output listing, all cross-referenced by transaction number, and should follow the principles expounded in this chapter. To embark upon implementation without following this procedure is suicidal. Screening and testing a system is difficult but it is nothing like as difficult as trying to achieve results from a system that is not designed to supply them.

$10.$ Implementation

Selecting the right package is critical. If the wrong one is chosen, the project has no chance of success. This is why so much attention has been directed in this book towards clarifying what is required of a personnel computer system: the problems it should address, the type of computing techniques it should utilize, the facilities it should provide, and the stages to go through when screening and testing a package. However, even if the right package is selected, there is still plenty of scope for disaster during implementation. To implement a package successfully it is necessary to be aware of all the activities involved in implementation, the problems associated with them, and the way that these problems should be tackled. Each activity needs to be carefully planned and controlled. The principal activities from the time that a suitable package is identified are as follows:

1. Survey and proposal
2. Contract negotiation
3. Installation of the computer
4. Training
5. Coding
6. Standard letters
7. Reports
8. System development
9. Testing
10. Data preparation and entry
11. Procedures
12. Project control
13. Project managment

Each of these activities will be discussed in turn in this chapter. It will become clear during this exposition of the problems of implementation that it is impossible for a company to tackle such a project without a considerable amount of assistance. It is important, however, to know enough about the problems at the outset to make a realistic assessment of the realism and competence of the organization offering the package. This assessment should be made primarily on the basis of the proposal they present, and the steps they go through in preparing it.

Survey and proposal

Just as there is no short cut to selecting the right package, so there is no short cut to assessing the problems and the cost of implementing it in a given environment. Before an organization can prepare a proposal for installing their package, they must carry out a detailed survey of the personnel department in which it is to be used. This cannot be done in a brief meeting. Matters which appear as points of detail to the personnel manager may be of critical importance in the context of the proposed system. The most common reason for failure in computer projects is that insufficient attention is paid to points of detail in the early stages.

Some of this work will already have been covered. The fact that the user has performed a system test successfully, albeit with the aid of the organization offering the package, shows that the facilities provided meet the personnel manager's requirements. There is very little scope for misunderstanding what the system does. But a system test is performed in the abstract. There may be procedural details in the company purchasing the package which create difficulties during implementation. Such problems should never be insuperable. An acceptable package must provide a considerable degree of flexibility if it is to survive for any length of time. Nevertheless, the fact that a package has the flexibility to accommodate a wide range of circumstances does not mean that it can be adapted in a negligible amount of time. The classic examples of this problem are coding, standard letters, and reports. Each of these areas should provide almost limitless flexibility, but a package should be supplied with a working set of codes, letters, and reports, and the amount of time it takes to install will depend to a large extent on the degree to which these have to be modified.

The dictionary will comprise about 30 subdictionaries, some of them containing several hundred entries. There may well be several hundred standard letters and a hundred reports in the system. Drawing up a coding structure, devising a standard letter, or writing a report are time-consuming activities. It is important to establish how much revision will be required. Almost certainly, some of the coding structures will need revision; such things as job titling structures are rarely the same from one company to another. It is also unlikely that two companies will ever be content with an identical set of standard letters. Reports are more likely to be compatible, but there will normally be a few special requirements in any particular case.

It is one thing to establish that a system is capable of meeting a company's requirements, and quite another to determine how long it will take to implement those requirements. The survey needs to establish which coding structures will have to be revised, which standard letters are required, and which reports need to be written. To do this it is necessary to examine every procedure within the personnel department in turn. There may be some cases where the existing procedure cannot reasonably be accommodated by the package. However, it should be possible to design a different procedure which meets the same objectives, and can be accommodated by the package. Any such changes in procedure should be identified and agreed in advance, to avoid friction during the project.

The survey will also need to identify any program modifications that are required, and these together with the amount of work required on

175

coding, standard letters, and reports, will determine the amount of planning and the time required for testing. The size of computer needed will depend on the number of people employed and the rate at which changes are processed. These factors affect the amount of time required for data preparation and entry, but this also depends on the state of the manual records at the present time, and the ease with which they can be accessed and analysed.

A survey of this kind will probably take about two man weeks to perform, assuming that it is carried out by competent people who are fully familiar both with the vagaries of their own package and with the practical problems facing a personnel manager. Anything up to half this time might be spent in detailed discussion with the personnel manager himself or with the specialists in a particular area. At the end of these discussions, a document should be prepared by the organization carrying out the survey, detailing the points covered and agreements reached. This should be signed by both parties.

A formal proposal can then be prepared. This should be based on the document signed at the end of the survey, but it must go a long way beyond that document. It must identify not only what needs to be done, but also who should do it, how much help will be provided, how much it will cost, and how long it is likely to take. It must identify the hardware and software required, and specify their cost. It should make recommendations on project control. Above all, it must identify the training required to run the system successfully, and should propose a training plan for achieving this.

In other words, the survey and proposal should cover most of the points dealt with in the rest of this chapter, as they relate to a specific case. Inevitably, an organization will wish to charge for such a survey and proposal, and it is only right that they should do so. Effectively, the survey is itself the first stage of implementation. It does not commit the prospective purchaser to buying the package, but it identifies what needs to be done to install it. If the project goes ahead, the work performed at this stage will become the foundation of all that follows, that is, the basis for project control. There is no way of assessing the size and difficulty of a project accurately until this work has been performed.

Negotiating the contract

A contract may be said to consist of three parts: financial, legal, and practical. This is to some extent an artificial distinction, because in one sense the entire contract is a legal document, but it serves to direct attention to the separate areas requiring consideration. Financial considerations may be dealt with first. Is the entire project to be tackled on a fixed price basis or do some parts of the proposal consist of services that will be supplied on demand for a stated hourly or daily charge? Hardware should be supplied on a fixed price basis, as should the basic software.

However, program modifications could be carried out on a time and materials basis against an agreed estimate. Training and implementation may be carried out on this basis as well, especially if the degree of assistance which the company may require is in doubt.

There are clear advantages for an uninitiated user in signing a fixed price contract since it provides some measure of protection against unscrupulousness and incompetence. However, its value should not be overestimated. If the organization selling the package shows signs of running over budget, it will start to cut corners, and it will be difficult for the uninitiated user to be sure when this is happening. For example, were the program modifications carried out in a professional manner and were they properly documented? A nonspecialist will have difficulty in answering such questions. Furthermore, the fact that a fixed price contract has been signed does not prevent the organization selling the package from coming back and asking for more money. Taking legal action is a lengthy business, and does not really achieve anything. It is not within the power of the courts to make a personnel computer system work, and when a board of directors makes a capital appropriation for a computer system, they do so in the expectation of a working system, not a successful lawsuit. The most effective weapon a personnel manager can have for upholding the contract is his influence over the reputation of the organization selling the package, and he has this influence regardless of whether or not the contract is for a fixed price.

These points have been made to guard against the view that the signing of a fixed price contract protects a project from financial difficulties. They do not detract from the fact that a fixed price adds a welcome degree of clarity to the situation. But there are some disadvantages with fixed prices for services which by their nature, are a little uncertain. The classic example is program development. A competent programmer can make a reasonably accurate estimate of the amount of time required to make a particular modification, but there must always be some degree of uncertainty. If the client insists on a fixed price, the supplier must build in a sizeable contingency to cover the worst possible combination of problems, including inflexibility on the part of the client. This inevitably means that the price will be high. If the work were performed on a time and materials basis, no contingency would be built in, and there would probably be scope for modifying the specification in the event of unexpected problems without undermining the basic objectives. The best solution may be for hardware, basic software, training, and essential assistance with implementation to be handled on a fixed price basis, and for program development and additional support during implementation to be charged for on the basis of time and materials.

The legal side of the contract should be dealt with by a solicitor. It consists of ensuring that all the points covered are expressed unambiguously, and that clauses are included to cover eventualities which, however unlikely, represent a risk that needs to be taken into account at the outset.

The practical side of the contract is the specification of the precise scope of the work to be undertaken. The facilities to be provided by the package must be clearly specified. This is best achieved by means of referring to the system test. The scope of the services to be provided must also be specified, in particular, formal training and assistance with implementation. The kind of thing that should be included is indicated in the sections that follow. A system specification should be referred to for any program development that is to be carried out. Finally, it is essential that the contract should include a detailed project schedule, which can be used for monitoring progress at a later stage.

Installation of the computer

The impression given by many manufacturers of mini computers is that their equipment can be plugged in and left to run in a normal office environment without any difficulties. It is true that modern computers do not require the construction of a special room, as earlier models did, but it is unrealistic to think of installing a computer without any disruption. Computers have two main problems associated with them: heat and noise. Most computers hum distractingly when they are switched on (mainly as a result of internal air conditioning to keep them cool), and a marked chuntering noise occurs whenever the disc is accessed, that is, whenever anyone is doing anything. Fast printers vary in the noise they make from continuous squeaking to intolerable screeching, and high quality printers of the type suitable for letter writing sound like a slightly magnified typewriter going at about ten times its normal speed.

The purpose of these observations is to point out that, even if a mini computer is capable of operating in a normal office environment, it is not practical to think of installing it in the middle of an open plan office. The obvious solution is to put it in a small room of its own, but this gives rise to the second problem: heat. A mini computer in a small room will generate an excessive amount of heat with the result that the temperature will rise, the disc may be affected (temperature is critical for disc performance), and the maintenance contract may be invalidated. Therefore, the room will need to be equipped with additional fans for extracting air to maintain a reasonably constant temperature.

A room must be set aside for the computer with additional ventilator fans, and preferably a tiled floor to reduce dust. This room should contain the fast printer and high quality printer in addition to the computer itself. VDUs, the normal means of communicating with the computer, should be positioned wherever they are required around the main office. They do not make a noise or generate a significant amount of heat. They will be connected to the computer by cables, which will require the soldering of plugs on each end. This soldering is an intricate business. It should only

178

be undertaken by someone who is experienced at using a very small soldering iron and who has a clear specification from the manufacturer of the correct points to connect up. This may sound like an obvious point, but poor workmanship can cause immense problems. It is not always easy to distinguish between software errors, problems to do with line lengths, and bad soldering. Therefore, every effort must be made to avoid the last of these, and an expert investigating a problem in this area would almost certainly insist on the job being redone if he saw any sign of poor workmanship.

A computer is generally supplied with its own cabinet. Printers are normally supplied with pedestals, but when they are not, thought must be given to what to stand them on, a trolley, for example. VDUs can be positioned on ordinary desks around the office, although if they are to be moved around frequently, there should be no problem about this and it may be worth purchasing a purpose-built VDU trolley on castors.

Thought must also be given to the ancillaries of the system. Stocks of one-part, two-part, three-part, four-part, and perhaps five-part station-ery will be required in varying quantities, and a significant amount of shelf space must be set aside for this purpose. Print-out covers will be needed for the reports produced from the system, together with a cup-board in which they can be hung. Since many of the reports will be confidential the cupboard should be capable of being locked securely. Letter stationery will be required for the high quality printer, together with a device for feeding it through and collecting it. Stocks must also be maintained of such things as ribbons for both the fast printer and the high quality printer, print heads and print wheels. Finally, a supply of mag-netic tapes will be required for back-up purposes, and preferably a fireproof safe for keeping them in.

There is nothing complicated about installing a computer system, but it has to be carefully planned. Most of the ancillary items required have a lead-time on delivery, and unless these points are thought out in advance, there is a genuine danger of the entire project falling behind schedule for some such absurd reason as the right paper being unavail-able or the lines to the VDUs not functioning properly. All these points should be mapped out on the implementation schedule.

Training

Training staff to run the system is perhaps the most difficult and the most critical task that has to be undertaken during implementation. All the other tasks depend upon it. Few personnel specialists have any under-standing of computers. By the time the project is completed they must be capable of running a complex modern system entirely on their own, diagnosing problems, and taking recovery action as required. The success with which such tasks as designing coding structures, agreeing standard letters, and handling data preparation and entry is carried out will depend in large measure on how far members of the personnel department have grasped the principles behind the system.

The organization supplying the package must provide training to meet these requirements; training which, in short, will ensure the successful running of the system when no further support is available on a regular basis. The difficulty is that the personnel manager has to decide when negotiating the contract, that is, before undergoing training, whether the training provided is adequate. The purpose of this section is to indicate the type of training that will be necessary to provide a person with the skills required to run a system of the scope and complexity proposed in this book.

The essential point to recognize is that, if an organization selling a package simply states that training will be provided as required, or that training will be provided in the course of implementation, they have not given sufficient thought to the matter. Running a personnel computer system is a complex business, and although it is undoubtedly true that the requisite degree of familiarity with operational principles can only be acquired by reiterating them during implementation, it is also important to have the whole system fully explained at the outset, so that, even if the details are not absorbed, the outline becomes clear. Learning by doing is much quicker if it has a frame of reference.

It is essential that a formal training scheme should be provided with the package. Formal training schemes should be provided at two levels. The project should begin with a basic training scheme covering the things which it is necessary to know to run all the programs in the system. Practice of the skills acquired will then be gained during implementation, when the training staff should be on hand—at least some of the time—to reinforce the principles adumbrated during the formal scheme. When the process of implementation is reasonably well advanced, a further training scheme should take place with the objective of bringing anyone who participates in it up to the standard required to take full responsibility for a system: sorting out problems when things go wrong, as well as understanding the basic operation of the programs.

The basic and advanced training schemes each need to be of about a fortnight's duration. Each should consist of a series of lectures on aspects of the system, followed by practical exercises on the computer. The subjects to be covered in the basic course should follow the pattern of the chapters in the earlier part of this book: letter writing, dictionary facilities, recruitment, personnel records, salary reviews, redundancies, enquiries, and reports. The advanced course should be more concerned with such things as: recognizing data base corruption and taking the appropriate action; dealing with system failures; maintaining the files in the account; diagnosing errors; writing complex reports, and introducing new letters into the system.

The provision of two formal courses—a basic one and an advanced one—at approximately the beginning and the end of the implementation period is as important as the package itself. An organization selling a package should have a detailed schedule ready for each of these courses, and people trained in running them should be available. Any prevarication on these points, or attempts to suggest that formal training is not really suitable, should be treated as a serious danger sign. Formal training is at least as important as support during implementation. In some cases a fortnight will not be sufficient for basic training; the time required depends on the scope of the system. If points requiring special attention have been identified during the survey, there may be a need for additional basic training of up to one week's duration. This is a peripheral matter, however. The key point is that running a computer system requires specialized training of a sustained sort. It is one thing to design an adequate software package, and quite another to develop the training schemes and implementation support services necessary to enable an uninitiated user to run it effectively. The latter task requires a much greater degree of professionalism and an understanding of the operating environment.

Coding

Chapter 3 identified 25 items that could reasonably be stored in the dictionary (see pages 53–54). The precise number will vary with the requirements of individual systems, but it is clear that the amount of work involved in drawing up coding structures for every subdictionary, let alone compiling a complete catalogue of codes, is considerable. For this reason work on designing coding structures should begin as soon as computerization becomes a serious possibility. Even if the project never goes ahead, the work will be of benefit. A systematic catalogue of company job titles, for example, is of use whether or not a personnel department has a computer system. It is normally only the discipline of computerization, however, that brings about a rigorous approach to such matters. A manual system accommodates exceptions without difficulty, for example, a note is written on a record card. In a computer system, everyone has to be fitted into an existing structure. It should be possible to modify the structures, but not to make exceptions to them.

This is sometimes thought by people who are instinctively antagonistic to computers to show that a computerized system lacks the flexibility of a manual one. This is not correct. Computer systems can, and should, be flexible, but they will not accommodate sloppy thinking. The supposed flexibility of manual systems is in reality an excuse for sloppy thinking, and this is part of the reason why they are unsatisfactory. A computer system forces the operator to ensure that any data entered conforms to agreed criteria.

The first decision to make when embarking on the design of coding structures is which items should be coded. A suggested list was given on pages 53–54, but it is worth considering the principles on which such a decision should be made. Why should an item be coded? The first reason is that it may need to be sorted in a particular order which can only be achieved by coding. For example, if the following job titles were stored in an uncoded form, they could only be sorted alphabetically:

Accounts clerk
Chief accountant
Senior accountant

This is clearly not a logical order. If codes were assigned to them, the same alphabetical sort by the computer would produce a more satisfactory result:

GAAA Chief accountant
GBAA Senior accountant
GCAA Accounts clerk

The first reason, then, for coding an item, is to enable item values to be sorted in a logical order. This will normally involve grouping job functions together and deciding on the seniority of individual titles within them. The question to be asked when designing the coding structure is 'In what order should the job titles appear on reports?' Resolving this question is not simple. The requirements of different reports may conflict. For example, a report which sorts the entire company by job title code will make most sense if the structure progresses through job functions, working from the most senior level to the most junior within each one, and grouping related functions together. However, this same structure could produce odd results on a report which sorted first by department and then by job title. If the department crosses several functions but only employs junior members from some of them, a junior job title from a function that occurs early in the structure will come before a senior job title occurring later in the structure. Similarly, different statistical analyses may require job functions to be grouped in different ways. Sorting out these problems is part of the job of designing a coding structure, and this is why it is difficult.

The second reason for coding items is that it saves space on the data base. Space is a serious problem in a personnel computer system, because so much has to be stored on each individual. A job title may be over 40 characters long. It should be possible to abbreviate it intelligibly to eighteen characters, but if this occurs in every line of employment history, it will soon absorb an unacceptable amount of space. A four character code is much more satisfactory and if a dictionary is available, as it must be, to expand the code on formatted screens and reports, there is no loss of accessibility.

A third reason for using codes is that the item to be stored only exists as a code, or exists primarily as one. The first case, which might be represented by National Insurance number, for example, does not require an expansion because none exists. An example of the second case might be department number. Many companies make a habit of referring to departments by numbers. These numbers have a meaning, which should be stored in the dictionary and printed out or displayed when required, but in general there will be no problem about storing the information as a number, and referring to it by this.

The fourth reason for using a code, which will normally be combined with one or more of the other reasons, is to enable a series of common details or operational instructions to be related to a given item. Examples of this would be the location dictionary or the dictionary of recruitment operation levels. In the case of the former, there are a number of employment conditions that relate to everyone at a particular location, and instead of storing them on every individual's record, thereby wasting a great deal of time and space, they are stored in the location dictionary. Every employee to whom they are relevant is linked to them by means of location code, and they can be accessed by the system when generating assignment letters. In the case of recruitment operation levels, the system needs to know how to behave when an applicant is given a particular operation: what to do about cursor positioning on the applicant screen; which letters to send; what to do in the event of a vacancy being held or terminated; what note to print on reports; and when to generate an additional record. Only by storing this information in the dictionary can the operation level structure be given sufficient flexibility.

Before any work can begin on coding, it is necessary to decide what should be coded and why, the information that should be stored against each coded item in the subdictionary assigned to it, and the structure of each of these subdictionaries. When this has been done, an attempt may be made to draw up a coding manual. Until this has been done, it is impossible to begin coding data in preparation for the transfer from a manual to a computerized system. Since coding, data preparation, and data entry are all lengthy tasks, and each one depends on the prior completion of the one before, they constitute a critical path through the project, and it is essential that work on coding should begin at the earliest opportunity. This should explain the contention with which this section began that work on coding should start as soon as computerization becomes a serious possibility.

Standard letters

The extent to which standard letters and clauses are central to a personnel computer system was explained in Chapter 3. A considerable degree of flexibility is required, but it must never be forgotten that standardization is at the heart of the matter. The administrative processes of a personnel department can be reduced to a series of standard operations, however complex. The kind of standardization proposed reflects consistent policy decisions, not a denial of individuality. It is important to recognize the difference between a flexible administrative process and a nonexistent one.

Administrative procedures must be standardized partly to save time and partly to ensure that policy is applied consistently. But how flexible can they be? There is a straightforward practical answer to this question; they may be as flexible as it is possible for them to be without their complexity becoming too great for the people who have to operate them. The practical limitation on the number of standard letters and clauses is the ability of the people using them to select the right one quickly and confidently in a given set of circumstances. Each letter or clause should have a description which is readily comprehensible to a person familiar with the workings of the department. When the operators become uncertain which letters or clauses to use, the system has become too complex, and is falling apart. There may well need to be several hundred letters and several hundred clauses to cope with all the ramifications of the administrative process. Clauses should be arranged into standard combinations (see pages 45–46). They will normally be accessed by means of a combination number, but it should also be possible to access them individually, when required.

In the personnel records system letters will be required to cover such things as salary increases, promotions, changes in employment conditions, service awards, redundancy, and retirement. It is clear that there could be a considerable number of letters in each of these categories. There are many possible reasons for a salary increase, each of which needs to have a standard letter corresponding to it. The same applies to a lesser extent to promotions. With regard to employment conditions, provision must be made for all the conditions that are likely to change, for example, changing from weekly to monthly pay, or the provision of a company car. Service awards provide an example of a case in which different wording will be required, depending on how well the person presenting the award (and signing the letter) knows the person receiving it. If they have been working together for 25 years, it will be inappropriate to begin 'Dear Mr Smith'. On the other hand, if, as is likely in a large company, they are unknown to one another, 'Dear Bob' will seem artificial and insincere. Again, letters concerning termination of employment will need to reflect the variety of circumstances in which people leave their jobs. The number of circumstances for which standard letters may be required in a personnel records system is considerable, and the possibility of these circumstances occurring either on their own or in combination with one another serves to increase it still further.

The requirements of a recruitment system are no less extensive. The main categories into which recruitment letters fall are: sending application forms, regretting that application will not be taken any further, inviting for interview, making offers, withdrawing offers, confirming offers, and apologizing for delays in reaching a decision. Each of these can have many variations within it. A letter to someone who has applied to an advertisement in the normal way will need to be different from one to an undergraduate whose university the company will be visiting later in the year, or a school leaver who will not be available until the summer. Regret letters need to reflect both whether the applicant has been in for interview, and the extent to which the company may be interested in discussing the possibility of employment again at a later date. Interview letters may need to refer to a university visit or an open house. Offer letters need to accommodate a great variety of circumstances. Is it a permanent offer or a fixed term contract? Is there a probationary period? Is there a salary review at the end of the probationary period? What is the continuous service date? Are there any special benefits included? Will any assistance be given with relocation? Is the offer subject to client approval? The list is not endless, but it is certainly extensive.

The complexity apparent in connection with offers of employment is even more intimidating in the case of assignment letters. However boldly the principle of standardization is applied, there are almost certain to be structural differences between a letter for an assignment in Saudi Arabia and one for the United Kingdom (obvious differences like the location, for example, would be handled by the location dictionary and would not affect the basic structure). Again, there will be substantial structural differences between a letter to someone going on a single status assignment and one to a person going with their family. The problem of assignment letters affects both the personnel records system and the recruitment system.

The reason for highlighting these difficulties is that it is essential not to underestimate the size of the problem. It is possible to develop a system of standard letters and clauses to deal with these situations, provided that the policy decisions affecting them are reasonably consistent. However, it involves a great deal of work. The problem may be tackled from two angles. Firstly, an attempt should be made to analyse all the situations with which the company in question has to deal, and the way in which they are combined with one another. This is the analytical approach. Secondly, an inventory should be compiled of all the letters the personnel department has produced over a substantial period of time—six months is a minimum—and an attempt made to reduce these to a standard set of letters and clauses. This is the empirical approach. A combination of the two approaches is desirable. An even better approach is to attempt to take over a set of standard letters and clauses from a company with similar personnel problems which has already developed one. This may be possible if the package to be purchased has been developed or used in a similar environment.

Ideally, standard letters and clauses should be finalized well before a computer project begins, so that they can be tested out on the manual system to see whether they meet all the requirements that arise. However, it is unlikely that sufficient time will be available for this. If it is possible, care must be taken to ensure that adequate account has been taken of any restrictions that will be imposed by the computerized letter writing system, for example, the necessity to print job titles at the end of a paragraph, because of their variable length. If it is not possible to experiment with a standard manual system, efforts must be made to involve all members of the department in agreeing the standard texts. Using standard letters requires a change of attitude; it requires a disciplined approach to administration, and an appreciation of the fact that people do not feel that they have lost their individuality simply because they receive a standard letter.

Reports

The subject of reports was covered fully in Chapter 8. It is included here because it is of central importance during implementation. The amount of time required for implementation will be affected to a considerable extent by the number of reports that have to be modified or written. Since the majority of reports in a personnel computer system should be produced by means of the enquiry system, no single report should require an undue amount of time. However, it is not uncommon for minor procedural differences in the way a company works to involve modifications to a large number of reports. The entire operation, including testing and documentation, may require a substantial amount of time. A package should be provided with a standard set of reports. The layout of each one of these should be discussed with the client, and any modifications agreed. New reports must be specified at this stage. Estimates for making the changes must then be made, and fitted into the project schedule.

System development

When buying a package, the objective must always be to make as few program modifications as possible. If too many modifications are made, the project becomes increasingly dominated by system development, together with the accompanying uncertanties and traumas. It is always preferable to modify company procedures, if at all possible, rather than to modify the software, but some program modifications are almost certain to be necessary.

System development, however, may mean far more than the making of a few program modifications. It may include writing totally new programs, or even extending the scope of the system to deal with a different type of environment, for example, linking up systems at different locations. It should be possible to limit the number of program modifications to a good package, because essentially it is providing the facilities required. But the writing of new programs or the extension of the scope of a system are not avoidable. If the package is basically satisfactory, but lacks certain facilities for manpower planning which are essential for the company purchasing it, then it clearly makes more sense to develop the package than to start again from the beginning. Again, if the company operates from a number of locations, and the package is designed for head office use only, it is clear that a great deal of work will have to be done to adapt it, but this will still be preferable to designing an entirely new package.

It should be clear by now that there are three basic types of system development: system changes that are fundamental, but not specifically related to any single program (extending the scope of a system to cope with communication between locations, for example); the writing of new programs to cover specific areas, such as manpower planning; and modifications to existing programs to accommodate differences over points of detail. The first of these may be regarded as principally of a technical nature. The basic facilities required are no different, but someone has to devise a means of fragmenting the system without losing overall coordination, and then experiment with the technical matters involved in implementing it. Such work would have to be undertaken on a time and materials basis; if anyone offered to do it for a fixed price, it would probably mean that they had insufficient experience of the difficulties involved in this kind of work. The problems should be tackled in logical stages, starting with a feasibility study, so that progress could be reviewed regularly and a decision made on whether or not to continue. The normal work of implementation should not begin until the system problems have been fully resolved. It is at this later stage that the major expenditure will be incurred, and, therefore, it is potentially disastrous to embark on this until the system problems have been resolved.

The writing of new programs is altogether less hazardous. Costs are still difficult to estimate, because the user has a major contribution to make in defining the requirements. For this reason it is not really practical to operate on a fixed price basis. If problems arise, it will merely result in the people providing the software sticking rigidly to a specification that is now known to be unsatisfactory, and so providing a useless product. Reasonable estimates can normally be made, and this is all that can really be expected.

The cost of program modifications should be relatively easy to estimate, provided they are small ones. However, they must be kept to a minimum. Programmers prefer writing new programs to modifying old ones. It is tedious work, and the burden of specifying every detail of it in advance, and documenting it afterwards, rarely seems justified by the importance of the resultant change.

The message emerging from these notes is plain: avoid system development. If it cannot be avoided, the following points should be borne in mind.

187

1. Overall system changes are very risky, and must be completed before the rest of the project goes ahead.
2. The writing of new programs should be tackled as a separate project, going on concurrently with the main one as they are modular additions to a system that is already complete in itself.
3. Program modifications must be kept to a minimum since nobody likes working on them, and they generally cause more problems than they are worth.

Testing

The way to test a personnel computer system that is offered as a package was discussed in detail in the last chapter. This type of testing needs to be carried out before the package is purchased. However, there are other types of testing that need to be carried out during implementation. Any system change, as already mentioned, must be completed and tested before the main phase of the project begins. New programs will require testing, as will modifications to existing ones. Finally, all adjustments to standard letters and reports must be tested before they are released for live running.

In total there may be a substantial amount of testing to be performed, and this must be accurately estimated in advance, and carefully scheduled. The worst mistake it is possible to make is to begin live running before a system is fully developed and tested. Live running creates its own pressures, and if these are added to the necessarily severe problems of implementation and development, the result is intolerable. The conflict between the erratic demands of live running and the exigencies of the project schedule leads to the making of counter-productive decisions. People working on the project become frustrated and depressed, and those who have been led to expect something from the system adopt a 'jaundiced' view of it at an early stage.

The strict answer to these problems is that testing must be completed before live running begins. However, this is not entirely practical. A system cannot suddenly be converted to live running. Putting in the data requires a substantial amount of time, and while this is in progress a live running situation will necessarily exist in respect of updating information, otherwise the system will be out of date by the time the data entry is completed. But then, updating is not entirely separate from letter writing (one of the main features of a satisfactory package would be a link between the two), and in some cases updating is connected with reporting, as in the salary review program.

These are problems that have to be worked out when the project schedule is drawn up. How they are resolved will depend on the scope of the changes planned in each of the areas indicated. Two things, however, are certain:

1. It is not practical to draw a rigid line where development and implementation end and live running begins because live running will always be phased.
2. If the project manager yields to the temptation to commence live running of something that has not been fully tested, the project will be heading for disaster.

Data preparation and entry

The type of computer system described in this book is not normally associated with such terms as 'data preparation' and 'data entry'. They belong with the old batch processing systems, where large quantities of data were gathered together on specially designed forms and key punched at a given time. Modern computer systems enable data to be updated the whole time through VDUs without the need for any special forms. However, there is one time when these old techniques may be of use on a modern system and that is when it is first set up.

One of the most tedious tasks that has to be performed during implementation is the feeding of information into the system. A personnel records system stores a considerable amount of information, and there is no simple way of converting it suddenly into electronic form. To undertake such a conversion successfully it is necessary to have a data preparation plan, which should identify the tasks to be performed, estimate how long they will take, specify the data entry methods that will be used, and calculate the number of people required.

The person who draws up the data preparation plan must be clear about the objective of the exercise. The objective is to get the current information up and running in the shortest possible time. This formulation of the objective requires explanation. The principal difficulty with data preparation is that it takes a long time, and that while it is going on the situation is changing. By the time the data is ready for live running, it is already out of date. Two solutions may seem to suggest themselves.

1. Process the updates concurrently with putting the information on.
2. Stockpile the updates and process them all at the end.

Neither of these apparent solutions is satisfactory. Attempting to do updating concurrently with basic data entry is impossibly confusing, especially since the manual system must be kept going as well at this stage. Very often the person to be updated will not yet be on the system, and so cannot be updated. Alternatively, some of the items requiring updating may have been entered, but not others. The potential for error in sorting this out is high, and the complexity of it has a serious effect on the speed at which the main exercise proceeds because attention is directed too much away from the principal objective.

The second alternative—stockpiling the updates and processing them all at the end—is equally unworkable. Collecting all the data and putting it on is a task that is bound to extend over many months, and the amount of updating which goes through the personnel department during this time will undoubtedly be considerable. Tackling the updates can be a formidable task in itself, leading to further delays, and so to further stockpiled updating forms.

The root cause of the problem with both these alternatives is that the current situation is changing so fast. There is no absolute solution to this problem since the changes cannot be stopped, but it can be reduced to manageable proportions by shortening the elapsed time required before live running can begin. How can this be done?

The first step is to make a distinction between current information and historical information. Only the current information is required for live running. Historical information will not be affected by updates, by virtue of the fact that it is history and, therefore, not susceptible to further change. This may sound a rather trivial point, but a large part of the information stored in a personnel records system is employment history. This is also the area that causes most difficulty at the data collection stage. Historical records may be incomplete or confusing, whereas current information should be readily available. In a data preparation and entry exercise extending over six months about five months would probably be taken up with employment history, and one month with current information.

The second step is to distinguish between current information that is personal and that which is not. Personal information includes such things as addresses, relations, and next of kin. There are two problems with this information:

1. It is often not up to date.
2. It is not normally very accessible.

It may be necessary to go through the personal files to get some of the information, and this takes too long. The quickest and most accurate way of collecting the information is to ask people to supply it themselves. The design of a personal details form was discussed on pages 143–144. Normally such a form would be used to notify people of the personal details the system is storing about them, but there is no reason why a blank form of a similar type should not be used for collecting the information in the first place. It is essential that management pressure should be applied to get the forms returned quickly.

The third step for speeding up the data preparation and entry exercise is to make use of key punching. The personal details forms should certainly be key punched since it would take too long to put them on through VDUs. If this cannot be done in-house, it could be handled by a bureau. In either case the design of the form should be discussed in advance with the people who are going to punch it.

The fourth step is to identify the sources for the rest of the current information. If the information is all available in one place (the personnel records) and there is sufficient machine time available—this will depend largely on the amount of development work in progress—it is worth considering direct input through VDUs. A sample portion should be timed, and an estimate made of how long the exercise will take. However, it is most unlikely that all this information will exist in one place. It will, therefore, normally be necessary to collect it together from a number of sources into a single form. If such forms are prepared, it is best for them to be key punched.

In summary, the objective of the data preparation and entry exercise is to input all current information in the shortest possible time. One month is a reasonable target. Anything over six weeks is too long. Employment history can be dealt with at a later date. Personal information is best supplied by individuals themselves, and should be key punched. Other current information may be input direct from the records through VDUs, if this is feasible, but it is perhaps better dealt with by the key punching of specially prepared forms. On rare occasions it may be possible to use direct input from another computer system (payroll for example). Any items of information that are inessential but may be difficult to collect should be left until later. It is not generally worth putting on leavers' records. These will accumulate over time, and may be used in manpower planning, but the effort required to put them on outweighs the use to which they can be put. Similarly, there is no point in putting past applicants on to the recruitment system. The first applicants to go on should be the ones who apply on the day the system goes live and, therefore, there is no problem of data preparation and entry in a recruitment system.

Procedures

A distinction must be drawn between the operational instructions for using a system, and the procedures for running it. It is one thing, for example, to know how to call up the main personnel records screen and update the items on it, and another to know what they should be updated to and when. The first question should be covered by an operations manual, which should be supplied with the package when it is purchased. The second one should be covered by a procedure manual, which will have to be written by members of the department in question, although the suppliers of the package may provide guidelines on some of the points that should be covered, and may even supply certain sections themselves, particularly those dealing with overall system procedures.

System procedures are such things as checks that should be made to ensure that the system is functioning correctly: how to spot data base corruption, how to deal with it, how to maintain the efficiency of the data base, and what to do in the event of a system crash. Some procedural points are partly a matter of the particular application, for example, conventions for naming and documenting files, the layout of the subdictionaries, looking after the hardware, creating new reports and letters, and dealing with errors. Other procedures are entirely the responsibility of the company that will be operating them: how to go about updating the personnel records, processing recruitment applicants, transferring data from recruitment to personnel records, generating assignment letters, processing agency records, carrying out a salary review, or issuing service awards.

Although responsibility for writing the procedure manual is mixed, it must rest finally with the user department. The important point, however, is not who writes it, but that it should be written. A system without a procedure manual will fall into disarray, and will never fully achieve its objectives. Control procedures ensure the security of the system, and the production of consistent reports depends on an agreed procedure for updating and reporting.

Project control

The need for project control must surely be apparent by this stage. A large number of related activities have to be undertaken during implementation, some of them depending on the prior completion of an earlier one. Each of them consists of a series of small activities, similarly related. The first requirement for project control is that all these activities should be identified and allocated to specified individuals, and that an estimate should be made of how long each one will take. The major activities will be the ones dealt with as section headings in this chapter. Every activity, however small, should be listed and given an activity number. The activities should then be plotted on a bar chart, so that it is immediately apparent which things should occur concurrently.

A progress meeting should be held every week, at which progress against schedule can be reviewed. In general, the only point of interest is whether or not an activity has been completed, not what percentage of it is complete. Activities should be broken down into sufficiently small units to make this practicable. There may be some activities for which this is not possible. In this case percentage completion reporting may be used, but evidence should be sought of the percentage claimed, otherwise there is a danger of the project slipping behind schedule through the back door—all the items which need to be underway are indeed underway, but the amount of work required to complete them is underestimated. On a cumulative basis this can be disastrous. There is no point in holding progress meetings unless progress is correctly reported. Action to be taken depends on the circumstances. The objective of project control is to determine where you are, not what to do about it. This is an essential activity, and much more difficult than it sounds.

Project management

The difficulties of managing a project of the type described in this book cannot be overemphasized. In the first place, there is no consensus of opinion as to precisely what a personnel department should do and, therefore, it is difficult to define what a personnel computer system should do. Analysing the problems and agreeing the objectives of the project are inseparable from much wider issues about the role of the personnel department. Secondly, translating the objectives into a detailed specification is subject to the overriding problem of all computer projects because tiny oversights of detail can undermine the entire system and render it useless. Thirdly, the potential for development work based on individual circumstances is immense, and although the project will undoubtedly be regarded by outsiders as a purely practical exercise, it has many of the hazards and uncertainties normally associated with research and development. Fourthly, the principal participants in the project—the users—normally have no prior knowledge or experience of computers. Therefore, not only must they undertake exceptionally demanding work, but also undergo specialized training to equip them for these tasks.

It is for these reasons that the project manager cannot normally be a member of the user department. The job requires someone with prior knowledge and experience of developing and implementing personnel computer systems, and this person should be made available from the organization that supplies the package. It will be their job to ensure that the problems inherent in a project of this sort are kept within manageable limits. The last chapter summarized the requirements of a personnel computer system, describing the points to look for in a package. This chapter has been concerned with the problems that the project manager will have to deal with during implementation. The personnel manager must decide, on the basis of the proposal and of discussions with the people who prepared it, whether the prospective project manager is capable of doing this job.

Conclusion

Personnel computer systems have been talked about for a long time, but there are not many of them in evidence. The reason for this should now be clear: they involve a great deal of work. This book has attempted to show how the amount of work involved can be minimized, and the chances of a successful outcome improved. Basically, the answer is to buy a package and to ensure that the organization selling it can provide the support and training required. A personnel manager cannot realistically take on the responsibility of designing a system, but he should be able to evaluate the available packages. Even this is a difficult task, however, and without the most thorough preparation it can easily end in disaster.

There is no easy solution, and any suggestion that there is one indicates an inadequate grasp of the problems. Many of the packages on the market at the present time are clearly based on an inadequate analysis of the problems. They are expensive but useless. A personnel manager who

193

wants to succeed will need to adopt an aggressive approach, particularly towards computer specialists who advise him to leave all the problems to them. It is not possible for a person who is unfamiliar with the detailed operation of a personnel department to oversee a project of this kind, and at the end of the day the personnel manager will be left with the problems. An inescapable part of the wider application of computers is the increased involvement of the people who want to use them, and this shift of emphasis fits in well with recent technological advances, that is, the developments associated with mini computers.

Is it worth it? The answer must be 'Yes'. If personnel departments are to improve their credibility, they must sort out the problems of basic administration. Until this is done, the principal role of the personnel department can only be to provide everyone else with something to complain about, and the higher tasks to which every personnel manager aspires will remain an idle dream.

Index